Brenda Shaffer
Iran is More Than Persia

Brenda Shaffer

Iran is More Than Persia

Ethnic Politics in Iran

DE GRUYTER

ISBN 978-3-11-162752-6
e-ISBN (PDF) 978-3-11-079633-9
e-ISBN (EPUB) 978-3-11-079638-4

Library of Congress Control Number: 2022944814

Bibliographic information published by the Deutsche Nationalbibliothek
The Deutsche Nationalbibliothek lists this publication in the Deutsche Nationalbibliografie;
detailed bibliographic data are available on the Internet at http://dnb.dnb.de.

© 2024 Walter de Gruyter GmbH, Berlin/Boston
This volume is text- and page-identical with the hardback published in 2023.
Cover image: DZarzycka/iStock/Getty Images Plus

www.degruyter.com

Acknowledgements

While widely known in the West as Persia and its people as Persians, Iran is a multiethnic country, where over half of the population of Iran is non-Persian. Mainstream Iranian and Middle East studies have claimed for decades that Iran is an outlier, and that unlike many other multiethnic empires, Iran's ethnic minorities do not seek language and cultural rights or self-rule. In contrast, the research reflected in *Iran is More Than Persia* shows that Iran's ethnic minorities are an important factor affecting both Iran's domestic and foreign politics and posing a challenge to the rule of the Islamic Republic. I appreciate that De Gruyter Press has given me the opportunity to present new research on ethnic politics in Iran. I would especially like to thank Faye Leerink, acquisitions editor at De Gruyter, Maximilian Gessl, content editor at De Gruyter, and Antonia Mittelbach, production editor at De Gruyter. I would like to thank the Foundation for Defense of Democracies (FDD) in Washington, DC for hosting me and this research project while I was researching the book. Several people made outstanding contributions to this research. From the FDD team, I would like to especially thank Reuel Marc Gerecht, Jonathan Schanzer, Erin Blumenthal, and Daniel Ackerman. Lively discussions with Prof. S. Fred Starr contributed to the analysis. Special thanks to Prof. Bernard Hourcade for data, maps, and sharing insights and assessments over decades. Several researchers contributed information and analysis: Jalal Roshani Areshtanab, Karim Asghari, Behzad Jeddi Balabaygloo, Mohammmadhassan Gholami Hamed, Vahoura Kasiri, and Maghsoud Varmazyar. I would especially like to thank Ahmad Obali and Mohammad Rahmanifar, who provided invaluable information on the activities of Azerbaijanis in Iran. Ramin Jabbarli contributed research to this book and I appreciate his insights. Ahmad Hashemi contributed research to this book, especially on the Iranshahr ideology. Rahim Hamid and Kamil Alboshoka provided important research on the demographics and history of the Ahwazi in Iran. Rahim Rashidi and Salah Bayaziddi shared information on the Kurds in Iran. Avdygafur Satash ("Charyar Turkmen") shared information on the Turkmen in Iran. Thank you to Miles Pomper for comments on this manuscript.

This book has benefitted from access to primary documents and information from Iran. Dozens of people living under the Islamic Republic that cannot be named provided important information, at risk to their lives and freedom and that of their families. I am indebted to these people.

Brenda Shaffer

Contents

1 Introduction —— 1

2 **Demography and Geography** —— 11
Iran's Ethnic Groups —— 13
    Persians —— 13
    Azerbaijanis —— 13
    Gilaks and Mazanis —— 15
    Kurds —— 15
    Lurs —— 16
    Ahwazi Arabs —— 16
    Baluch —— 17
    Turkmen —— 17
    Qashqai Turks —— 18
    Talesh —— 19
Iran—Numbers of Ethnic Groups —— 19
    Official Statements —— 21
    The Iranian Government's Values and Attitudes Survey —— 22
    Council of Public Culture Study —— 27
    Iranian Military Survey —— 28
    Estimated Numbers of Iran's Ethnic Minorities in 2020 —— 30
Socioeconomic Indicators for Ethnic Groups —— 31
Different Levels of Services, Infrastructure, Health Services, and Environmental Protection —— 34

3 **The Islamic Republic's Policies Toward Ethnic Minorities** —— 37
Ethnic Nationalism—A Twentieth-Century Issue —— 37
Ethnic Minorities During the Islamic Revolution —— 38
    Khomeini Tricks the Ethnic Minorities by Appealing to Ethnic Sentiments —— 42
    Rebellions: Tehran Imposes its Rule on the Provinces —— 43
Approach of the Islamic Republic Post-Revolution to Iran's Ethnic Minorities —— 48
Tehran Knows —— 53
Use of Ethnic Minority Languages in Schools and Official Settings —— 54
Criminalizing Use of Minority Languages and Government Promotion of Persian —— 58
Incarceration and Execution Rates —— 59

Suppression of Protests and Other Political Activity —— 61
Assassinations of Leaders of Ethnic Movements Abroad —— 62
Province Gerrymandering, Settler Programs, and Place Names —— 64
Gubernatorial Appointments and Their Language Policies —— 65
Electoral Appeals to Ethnic Minorities —— 68
Ethnic Minority Activity in Iran's Parliament —— 69
Portrayal of Ethnic Minorities by Iranian State Media —— 74
Instigation of Conflict Between Ethnic Groups —— 81

4 Ethnic Activity —— 83
Sports —— 85
Environmental Activity —— 89
　　Ahwazis —— 90
　　Caspian Groups' Activities —— 91
　　Kurdish Activities —— 92
　　Azerbaijani Environmental Activity: Focus on Lake Urmia —— 93
Militias and Violent Ethnic Organizations —— 95
Threat to Iranian Oil and Natural Gas Production —— 97
Local Council Elections —— 98
University Student Groups —— 98
Iran's Ethnic Minorities Prefer Foreign Television —— 100
Cultural Activity —— 102

5 The Mainstream Opposition's View on Ethnic Minority Rights —— 107
Increased Persian Nationalism Increases Minority Distinct Identification —— 114

6 Iran's Foreign Policy: The Domestic Ethnic Factor —— 118
Case Study: Iran's Relations with the Republic of Azerbaijan and Policy Toward the Armenia-Azerbaijan Conflict —— 120
　　Iran's Direct Involvement in the Armenia-Azerbaijan Wars —— 125
　　Iranian-Azerbaijani Mobilization in the Armenia-Azerbaijan Conflict —— 129
Case Study: The Kurds and Iran, Turkey, and Iraq —— 136
Case Study: The Baluch in Iran and Pakistan —— 139

7 The Future: Impact on Regime Stability —— 143

Appendix: Notes on Transliteration and Terms —— 152

1 Introduction

When Mikhail Gorbachev first came to power as leader of the USSR, one of his first major decisions was to appoint Gennady Kolbin, an ethnic Russian, as First Secretary of the Communist Party of the Kazakhstan Soviet Socialist Republic (SSR). With this appointment, Gorbachev replaced Dinukhamed Kunayev, a Kazakh and longtime leader of the Soviet republic. Gorbachev aimed to root out the extensive corruption in the USSR and he tasked Kolbin, a trusted technocrat, with the job in Kazakhstan. The appointment in December 1986 of an ethnic Russian breached the long-standing practice in the USSR that each Soviet republic would be headed formally by a member of a republic's nominal ethnic group, while his deputy, the second secretary of the republic's communist party, would usually be a Russian or Ukrainian, loyal to Moscow. However, defying this custom did not seem risky at all. The Soviet leadership viewed Kazakhstan as one of the republics most integrated into the Soviet system. Moscow's trust was so deep that Kazakhstan was one of only four Soviet republics to house parts of the Soviet strategic nuclear arsenal, and it was the only non-Slav republic among the four. Kazakhstan had one of the highest levels of Russification among the non-Slavic Soviet republics, and during the Soviet period few university-educated Kazakhs were even fluent in the Kazakh language. Thus, Gorbachev did not hesitate to replace Kunayev with an ethnic Russian.

Yet contrary to expectations, massive demonstrations and riots broke out in December 1986 in Alma-Ata, the capital of Soviet Kazakhstan, in response to Kolbin's appointment. It took Soviet forces two weeks to quell the violent protests. In the process, it is estimated that 100 people were killed and up to a thousand injured. Many of the slogans voiced by the demonstrators were ethnic-based. For example, "The Kazakh Nation Deserves a Kazakh Leader," and "Kazakhstan Belongs To Kazakhs."[1] The Soviet news agency *TASS* reported at the time that the riots were "incited by nationalistic elements."[2]

The 1986 protests in Kazakhstan were a shock to Moscow and to most researchers observing the USSR. Few researchers had thought that Kazakhstan

---

[1] "Kazakhstan: Zheltoqsan Protest Marked 20 Years Later," *Radio Free Europe/Radio Liberty*, December 16, 2006 (https://www.rferl.org/a/1073453.html); "Riot in Soviet Republic Protests Leadership," *Chicago Tribune*, December 19, 1986 (https://www.chicagotribune.com/news/ct-xpm-1986-12-19-8604040861-story.html).
[2] Soviet news agency *TASS* quoted by "Soviet Reports Rioting in City in Central Asia," *New York Times*, December 19, 1986.

https://doi.org/10.1515/9783110796339-002

could be a hotbed of ethnic nationalism.[3] Even among those that tracked ethnic politics in the USSR, the focus was on the Baltic states and the South Caucasus.

The Kazakh outrage after Kolbin's appointment manifested ethnic sentiments that were lying under the surface in the USSR, feelings strong enough to lead to spontaneous demonstrations. The protests in Kazakhstan became known as the Zheltoqsan (December in Kazakh) Protests. Retrospectively, historians would view the protests as the beginning of the collapse of the USSR, which occurred five years later.

But it was not just Kazakhstan. In fact, many underestimated the potential potency of ethnic-based sentiments throughout the USSR. For most of the Soviet period, the West tended to refer to Soviet citizens as the "Russians" and assumed that the regime's efforts to Russify non-Russian citizens across the Soviet Union were successful. Not until the mid-1980s, when Moscow removed some limitations during Gorbachev's reforms, did it become clear that ethno-nationalism was a politically potent force in the Soviet Union. When the Soviet Union collapsed in 1991 and fifteen new countries emerged, there was no denying that the Russification of the Soviet ethnic minorities had been a myth.

The case of the USSR is not alone. Several times in recent decades, policymakers have had to play catch-up when central governments have weakened, and ethnic and other communal cleavages took center stage. This was true in the Yugoslav Wars and the Syrian civil war. There may be a similar blind spot regarding Iran's multiethnic composition's potential impact on regime stability.

Could Iran be the next Kazakhstan or USSR, where the potency of ethnic-based identity and sentiments is underestimated by the academic mainstream and many policymakers? Iran is a multiethnic country; Persians comprise less than half of Iran's population. Overwhelming majorities of non-Persian groups inhabit most of Iran's border provinces, in contrast to Iran's Persian-dominated center. Moreover, more than 40 percent of the population of Iran lacks fluency in the Persian language. Iran's ethnic minorities undergo more severe hardships—economic, environmental, public health, water shortages—than the Persian-populated center, likely reinforcing their sense of ethnic-based discrimination and depravation.

---

[3] An exception was Harvard University Professor Richard Pipes, who had visited Kazakhstan during the Soviet period. In many of his writings, Pipes assessed that Central Asia, including Kazakhstan, could be a source of significant anti-Soviet activity. He led the analysis in several U.S. government policy documents, which called for the U.S. to support the USSR's ethnic minorities as part of efforts to bring to the Soviet demise. See, for instance: the declassified document *NSDD 75 on "U.S. Relations with the USSR"* January 17, 1983 (https://irp.fas.org/offdocs/nsdd/nsdd-75.pdf).

Iran has been largely immune to the waves of democracy that swept over most of the world during the twentieth century and has sustained control over vast territories and minority populations that do not enjoy the same rights as the Persian core. The twentieth century was not kind to multiethnic empires. During that time, more than half of the states in the world transitioned from subjects to citizens. And, in most of the empires where a minority group ruled over other ethnic groups, the second-tier ethnic groups seceded from central control. One of the few outliers is Iran. Any major challenge to the rule of the Islamic Republic in Iran, would create a new opportunity for Iran's ethnic minorities to attempt self-rule.

Mainstream academia and policy communities claim that Iran is an exception and that significant ethnic-based politics and challenges are absent in Iran. They assert that most of Iran's minority groups have lived within the borders of the Iranian state for many centuries, and thus view themselves consequently primarily as Iranian. However, it is a myth that Iranians have been bound together over centuries as one big happy unified group. Over the last century, each time that central rule was weakened, Iran's ethnic minorities have taken advantage of the opportunity to go their own way. For instance, during the 1920s, as Qajar rule waned, Iran's Turkmen, Northern/Caspian peoples, and Azerbaijanis tried to establish self-rule. At the end of World War II, both the Kurds and the Azerbaijanis attempted to establish independent entities, and during their short-lived periods of self-rule, established schools in their native languages. During the Islamic Revolution, all of Iran's major non-Persian ethnic groups rebelled against Tehran. So, common identity as Iranians is likely not the real glue between Persians and the ethnic minorities in Iran, but central government repression is a critical factor. All of Iran's ethnic minorities have a modern history of independence movements.

Proponents of the idea that Iranian identity is strong and supreme among ethnic minorities claim that Iran's ethnic minorities have been speaking Persian and united by Persian culture and language for centuries. However, this claim is also false. First, political struggles over ethnicity and language policy only emerged globally in the mid-to-late nineteenth century. Prior to this, technology did not allow state institutions to touch the lives of most subjects and citizens in a meaningful way. There was no public debate over language choice of government documents, media or schools, given widespread illiteracy, lack of government schools and no large access to media and government documents. Only with the extension of modern infrastructure, such as the telegraph and trains in the mid- and late nineteenth century, did the public have regular contact with state institutions. It is not by chance that the "national question" became prominent in Europe and beyond in the late nineteenth century and early twentieth century. As they did, questions of ethnic identity and language policy took center stage in the world, contributing to the breakup of several multiethnic empires, such as the Austro-Hungarian and Ottoman Empires, and the anti-colonial struggles that led to the end of European colonial rule across several continents. It was an ideological response to the technological changes that enabled government institutions to affect citizens and subjects over long distances in states and empires. Minority groups' interest in self-rule and use of their own language in state institutions emerged after they were exposed to government institutions that often functioned in foreign languages.

Iran was a latecomer to the nationwide extension of state institutions. Only in the 1960s did state schools spread widely to Iran's ethnic dominated provinces. Until then, most of Iran's minority populations living outside the Persian center were not exposed routinely to the Persian language and a large share of provincial minority populations did not speak Persian. Since many were illiterate, most did not read Persian.

In addition, up until the twentieth century, Persian was not in exclusive use in the successive Iranian dynasties. As stated by the premier geographer of Iran, Bernard Hourcade, "Persia was in fact ruled without interruption from the eleventh to the beginning of the twentieth century, by non-Persian-speaking rulers, mostly Turkish, which defended their Iranian empire, but sometimes were unable to speak Persian correctly."[4] According to Hourcade, "Unlike French in France, Persian was not the mother tongue of most Iranian rulers."[5] In this period, Persian and Turkish held prominence in different fields in Iran, such as Turkish in the military and in the royal court and Persian in poetry and literature. Arabic was important in religious literature and some scientific literature. With the establishment of the Pahlavi dynasty in 1925, Persian language and culture was designated exclusive state language status in Iran and the imposition of Persian language and culture was a central feature of the Pahlavi dynasty state-building project. It was forbidden to use languages other than Persian in schools and other public institutions. The Pahlavis constructed a version of Iranian history that claimed that the peoples inhabiting Iran had always been united by the Persian language for hundreds of centuries, ignoring the fact that efforts to impose a common language were fully modern phenomena. Only in 1962 when the

---

[4] Bernard Hourcade, "La recomposition des identités et des territoires en Iran islamique," *Annales de Géographie*, 3, 2004," p. 516.
[5] Bernard Hourcade, "La recomposition des identités et des territoires en Iran islamique," *Annales de Géographie*, 3, 2004," p. 516.

Shah's White Revolution established large numbers of schools in Iran, did Persian become widely used throughout the country.[6]

Most important, as will be presented in this study, Iranian government data indicates that 40 percent of Iran's population is not fluent in Persian. This is true even though the Iranian government is active in promoting use of Persian and suppressing the use of the minority languages. If Persian was so happily embraced by all people in Iran, the government would not have to suppress minority languages.

Furthermore, collective identity trends are dynamic and what may have been true about the attitudes of the ethnic groups decades ago, may not be true today. The advent of modern technologies enabled Iran's ethnic minority members to connect more intensively with co-ethnics at home and abroad as well as more broadly learn about the rights enjoyed by ethnic groups in other countries.

The identity changes have accelerated since the 1990s. Technological changes, such as widespread access to foreign television and social media in minority languages, have strengthened distinct ethnic identities in Iran. Most members of Iran's ethnic minorities primarily watch foreign television broadcasts in their native languages instead of Iranian television. In recent years, ethnic groups in Iran have also been exposed via social media to the wave of identity politics in the United States and Europe. This, too, likely contributes to strengthened ethnic identity and increased opposition to Tehran's control, particularly among Iran's youth.

Some scholars point to various ethnic groups' histories of defending Iran as evidence that the Iranian polity is unified. They point to the fact that Tabriz, an almost exclusively Azerbaijani-populated city, has been the center of Iran's main revolutionary political movements in the twentieth century, and that these efforts are aimed at changing the central government in Iran, not seceding from Tehran. These same voices point out that the Arabs of Khuzestan did not support Iraq's invasion of Iran during the Iran-Iraq War and fought to defend their homes from the Iraqi onslaught.[7] However, again, these historical episodes do not teach us much about the attitudes of these same groups in the 2010s and 2020s. Identities can shift in an instant, even triggered by a single historical event. Moreover,

---

[6] Bernard Hourcade, "La recomposition des identités et des territoires en Iran islamique," *Annales de Géographie*, 3, 2004, p. 516.
[7] Some researchers challenge the Iranian widely held contention that the Ahwazi Arabs fully fought on the side of Iran during the Iraqi invasions. See, for instance: John R. Bradley, "Iran's Ethnic Tinderbox," *Washington Quarterly* (Winter 2006–7), p. 184. Bradley spent time in the Ahwazi-populated areas of Iran conducting field research.

the same Azerbaijanis that led the fight to bring down the Shah also anticipated receiving language and cultural rights under a new regime.

The Soviet breakup and subsequent establishment of the independent states were monumental events that significantly affected identity trends in Iran. When the Berlin Wall fell between East and West Germany, a different wall also fell between the Muslims of the Caucasus and Central Asia and the peoples of Iran and the Middle East. Reestablishment of ties between Azerbaijanis and Turkmen in Iran and the newly independent states, and the fact that these groups in Iran now resided next to ethno-national states which promoted their culture, increased ethnic self-identification of these groups in Iran.

Mainstream scholarship on Iran claims that their common Shia Muslim faith unites most of Iran's ethnic minorities with the Persians. Due to this factor, most scholars have dismissed Azerbaijani ethnic-based aspirations and even that of Iran's Arabs in Khuzestan, who are predominately Shia.[8] By this logic, Russians should share a political orientation with Ukrainians and Georgians because of their common Orthodox Christian faith. Moreover, after over 40 years of a regime ruling in the name of Shia Islam, many in Iran have distanced themselves from religious identity.

Ethnic identity in Iran is strengthened by the fact that members of minority groups face disproportionate economic, environmental, and health challenges. Iran's ethnic minorities inhabit the state's poorest provinces and receive the lowest level of government services and infrastructure. The country's growing environmental challenges, including widening water shortages, hit the ethnic minority provinces harder than the Persian center. The overlay of separate ethnic identities with environmental inequality amplifies the grievances of those groups toward the Islamic Republic. In addition, many members of ethnic minority groups view the gap in services, access to resources and levels of income between the Persian-populated center of the country and the ethnically populated provinces as a deliberate result of Tehran's policies to favor Persians. Ethnic cleavages linked with general dissatisfaction pose a growing challenge to the Iranian regime.

Iran's Persian community's actions may also be spurring minorities' ethnic identification. In recent years, many Persians dissatisfied with the emphasis on religion in the Islamic Republic, and also influenced by global identity trends, have embraced Persian nationalism. This further alienates Iran's ethnic

---

[8] See for instance: Farhad Kazemi, "Ethnicity and the Iranian Peasantry," in Milton J. Esman and Itamar Rabinovich, *Ethnicity, Pluralism, and the State in the Middle East* (Ithaca and London: Cornell University Press, 1988), p. 206.

minorities, demonstrating the myth of "Iranian" identity as a supra-ethnic identity that embraces all of Iran's residents. In fact, a popular ideology that in recent years has gained traction among Iranian intellectuals and the Iranian diaspora promotes the idea of special ties between Iran and speakers of Iranian languages (such as Tajiks, Dari speakers in Afghanistan, Ossetians, and Kurds), which of course, isolates the non-Persian speakers in Iran.

Moreover, Tehran does not offer a model of inclusion to ethnic minorities other than assimilation into Persian culture and language. The Islamic Republic, like the Pahlavi dynasty before it, does not allow ethnic minorities language rights and permits only limited ethnic cultural activity. There are no schools in languages other than Persian and government services are conducted exclusively in Persian. In fact, Iranian media, films and TV programs, regularly mock ethnic minorities and portray them in a poor light according to ethnic stereotypes. The government and Persian cultural elites in Iran and abroad make no effort to listen to or address the grievances of Iran's ethnic minorities and to offer inclusive policies. Ethnic minority appeals for language and cultural rights are met with accusations of separatism, even when most of these activists are not striving to break away from Iran, but rather to win rights within Iran. Tehran frequently claims calls for language rights are the result of foreign government plots to break up Iran, usually blaming the United States and Britain, but sometimes Saudi Arabia and Israel.[9] Tehran also regularly accuses Turkey and Azerbaijan of supporting separatism among Iran's Azerbaijani Turks. Iran's policy of accusing foreigners of influencing ethnic minorities in Iran further delegitimizes the quest for language and cultural rights within Iran.

While rarely formally acknowledging the existence of ethnically based opposition in Iran, the regime goes to great lengths to repress its ethnic minorities. Iran's ethnic minorities are subject to disproportionately high rates of incarceration and execution. Tehran has ordered and carried out the assassinations of leaders and representatives of Iran's ethnic minorities that reside outside Iran, especially in Europe. Evidently not wanting to test the loyalty of local origin troops, Tehran often brings in security units from different provinces to suppress anti-regime activity in the provinces. At times, Tehran even brings in militias from abroad, as it did from Iraq and Lebanon to suppress Ahwaz Arabs in the summer of 2018.

---

[9] See, for example, the Iranian Ministry of Foreign Affairs response to a Twitter hashtag documenting instances of discrimination and racism in Iran: https://twitter.com/Behzad_Jeddi2/status/1490712415427829761?s=20&t=2982dm8ixoXzT4fTtd6I2g; https://twitter.com/endofmonoling/status/1490665050990080000?s=20&t=1oae0mdBlCcQ1QJwnFbUJg.

To prevent the emergence of local power sources, Tehran mostly appoints non-native governors to its ethnic minority provinces. More than 60 percent of the governors appointed in Iran between 2010–2020 were of Persian or Lur origin. In most cases these officials do not speak the local language of the people they govern. Even when a non-Persian is appointed to govern a province, he almost always governs a province inhabited by a different ethnic group than his own.

Despite government repression, Iran's ethnic minorities have shown formidable organizational ability since the 1990s. Activists have carried out sustained political campaigns and waves of protests, despite frequent arrests and imprisonment. The growing importance of the border provinces in anti-regime activity was evident during protests in Iran in 2017–2019. The demonstrations started in the country's provincial cities and were more intense in the minority-heavy provinces than in the Persian heartland. In an all-out regime crisis, revolts in several minority provinces in Iran could pose a significant challenge to the central government.

A new and significant development is that Iran's ethnic minorities have begun to band together against Tehran. In the summer of 2021, a critical development occurred linking Iran's Azerbaijanis and Ahwaz minorities. After several days of demonstrations in the Khuzestan Province by Ahwazis, which resulted in several deaths and mass arrests of Ahwazi activists, Azerbaijanis held solidarity demonstrations in several Azerbaijani-populated cities. These demonstrations took place despite the arrest of more than two hundred organizers and planned participants in the demonstrations held in Azerbaijani-populated cities. This show of solidarity cemented a new strategic bond between Iran's Azerbaijanis and Ahwazis. The alliance between Ahwaz and Azerbaijanis has created a new and potentially formidable challenge to Tehran's rule.

Iran's ethnic minority groups do not limit their anti-regime efforts to non-violent activities. Several of Iran's minorities—the Kurds, Ahwaz, and Baluch— have active paramilitary groups. Most of the violent anti-regime activity in Iran takes place in regions inhabited by the minorities: Sistan-Baluchistan, Khuzestan, Kurdistan, Kermanshah, and the border areas of West Azerbaijan. The armed attacks perpetrated by the ethnic militias focus on the Iranian army, Islamic Revolutionary Guard Corps (IRGC), and government installations. Iranian border areas populated by Kurds and the Baluch are subject to regular attacks on the regime's forces. Ahwazi groups periodically conduct anti-regime attacks in Khuzestan but do not run an ongoing insurgency like the Kurds and Baluch.

A critical variable in assessing the potential ethnic threat to the regime is the attitude of Iran's Azerbaijanis, because of their large numbers, wealth, and perceived status as a mainstay of the regime. A major turning point for this group took place in the fall of 2020 in response to Iran's support for Yerevan during Armenia's war with the Republic of Azerbaijan. Iranian Azerbaijanis witnessed Tehran's concrete support for Armenia in real time during the war, including Iranian trucks transporting Russian arms and supplies to Armenia. Tehran's activities incensed many Iranian Azerbaijanis. During the war, the Iranian government arrested dozens of Azerbaijanis for protesting this support.

The fact that ethnic minorities form a majority in several strategic locations in Iran also poses a threat to the regime. For instance, Khuzestan Province, which is the center of Iran's oil production and home to several important ports and a major road juncture, has a majority Ahwaz Arab population. Sustained anti-regime activity there could affect Iran's ability to produce, export, and transit oil and natural gas. Bandar Abbas, which occupies a strategic location on the Strait of Hormuz and is one of Iran's major ports, is inhabited by sizeable numbers of Arabs. There is also a considerable Baluch presence in the Hormozgan Province, in which Bandar Abbas is located. In addition, Iran's strategic Chabahar Port is located in Sistan-Baluchistan, a perennially unstable province populated almost entirely by Baluch.

Moreover, it is hard to imagine how the Islamic Republic of Iran might solve the ethnic problem. Tehran faces the conundrum of other autocratic multiethnic empires, where democratization poses more of a risk than a solution. While a non-democratic regime rules, violent repression deters and inhibits ethnic groups from seeking self-rule. With reform and democratization processes, and thus the removal of the threat of death, imprisonment, and torture, groups that have been dominated by others often seek independence. Civil war during a regime change or regime collapse also creates opportunity to attain self-rule, with the ruling elite weakened by internal battles, and even groups that did not have strong independence movements often seize the moment and break away from the ruling center. Thus, the trends of democratization and loss of empire are connected.

The ethnic factor not only affects Iran's domestic political arena, but Tehran's foreign policy. The shared non-Persian ethnic groups who straddle much of Iran's borders, especially Baluch, Kurds, and Azerbaijanis, strongly impact Iran's foreign policy with most neighboring states. These ethnic groups are a major challenge in the volatile security situation on Iran's borders with Iraq, Turkey, and Pakistan.

In the academic mainstream on Iran and the Middle East, the presumption that the citizens of Iran are strongly united in Iranian identity and love for the Persian language is a cornerstone that is repeated in multiple academic publications and taught in university courses. Rarely is this presumption challenged. However, once examined, there is substantial evidence of strong self-identity among many of Iran's ethnic minorities, low levels of proficiency in the Persian language, and a history of the drive for language and cultural rights (and for some groups even for self-rule) during the life of the Islamic Republic. Throughout this period, the regime has used force, arrests, executions, and assassinations to suppress ethnic minority activity. If Iran's ethnic groups were so united under Iranian identity and the Persian language, the regime would not need force to impose that identity and language.

Iran is More Than Persia: Ethnic Politics in Iran examines ethnic politics in Iran under the Islamic Republic. The book looks at the population of Iran's ethnic groups, Tehran's policies toward ethnic minorities, ethnically based political activity, and the impact of the ethnic factor on Iran's foreign policy, since all of its neighbors share ethnic group populations. The book also assesses the impact of ethnic political activity in Iran on the stability of the Islamic Republic.

2 Demography and Geography

This chapter will discuss the geography of Iran's ethnic minorities, examine trends in Persian proficiency among the citizens of Iran, and assess the populations of the various groups and their shares of Iran's total population.

There is a strong geographic element to the identities and lifestyles of Iran's ethnic minorities. Persians dominate the center of the country, which is relatively flat and covered in part by deserts. Azerbaijanis inhabit the northwest of the country, which includes many high mountains, with continuous settlement toward the center of the country, reaching Tehran. Kurds dominate the Zagros Mountains. The Mazanis and Gilaks live on the coast of the Caspian Sea. Ahwazi Arabs inhabit Iran's main oil and natural gas producing region, Khuzestan in Iran's southwest, and are a large part of the population in Bandar Abbas on the Persian Gulf and Iran's Gulf islands. The Turkmen live primarily in Iran's northeast, especially in towns and villages on the Caspian Sea coast. Iran's Baluch are concentrated in the southeast. Despite significant migration of people within in Iran, the majority of the ethnic minorities are still based in their traditionally inhabited territories, where they form the majorities and many of these regions bear the name of the primary ethnic group inhabiting the territories— Azerbaijanis in northwest Iran, part of which is called East Azerbaijan Province and West Azerbaijan Province, Kurds in Kurdistan, and Baluch in Sistan-Baluchistan Province. Iran's tribal groups—Qashqai, Lur, and Bakhtiari—also continue to inhabit traditional pasture lands, some of which bear their name.

Most of Iran's frontier provinces have non-Persian majorities. Ethnic self-identity is much higher in the provinces than in the Persian-dominated center, especially Tehran. Several of Iran's ethnic groups—the Kurds, Turkmen, Ahwazis, and Baluch—not only have a separate ethnic identity and language, but also are among Iran's poorest inhabitants. Most of Iran's frontier provinces receive a much lower level of government services and infrastructure investment than the center.

The sense of identity among many of Iran's ethnic groups is affected by ties with co-ethnics in bordering states: Azerbaijan, Turkmenistan, Iraq, Turkey, Pakistan, and Afghanistan. Members of Iran's ethnic minority communities interact directly with co-ethnics in neighboring states on a regular basis, engaging in commerce, cultural exchanges, and extended family meetings. Sociologist Ramin Jabbarli contends that those groups that are Shia and do not share ties with a co-ethnic state in neighboring countries are more likely to be assimilated into Persian identity than the Sunni or those sharing co-ethnic ties. Among the former groups are the Lurs, Mazanis, and Gilaks.

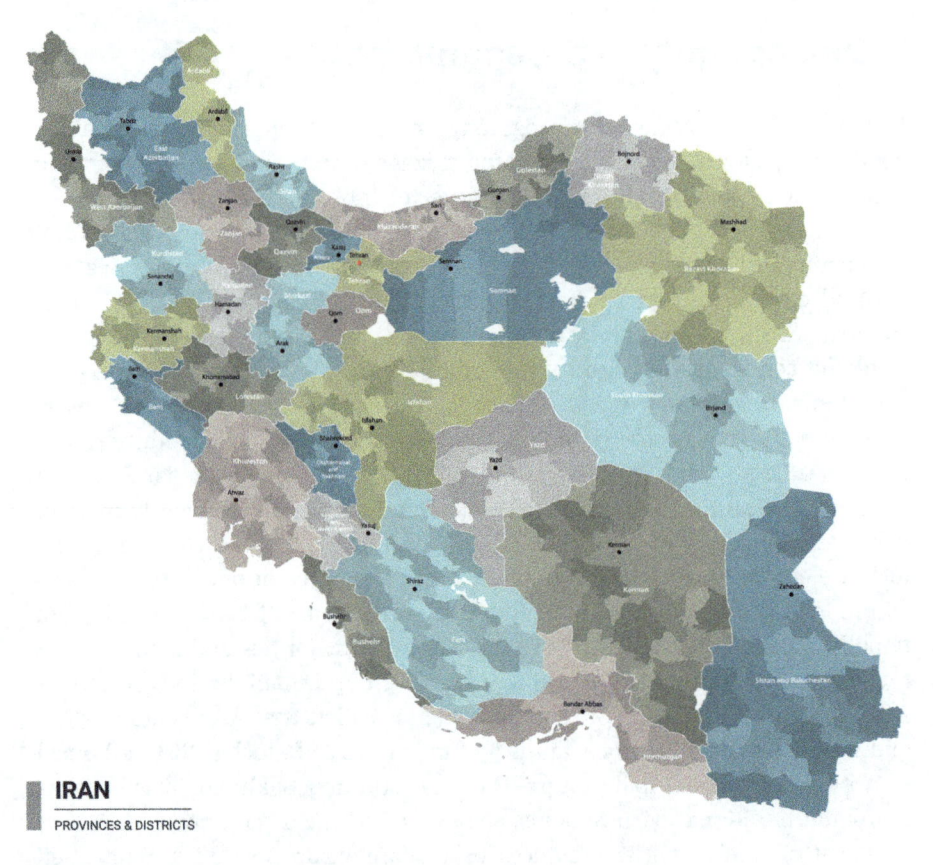

Figure 1: Iran – Provinces and Districts

In Iran's governing system, most of Iran's ethnic groups are spread over 31 provinces (*ostan*). In addition, provinces that bear the name of an ethnic group do not encompass all the main areas where the nominal group is located, such as East and West Azerbaijan, Baluchistan, and Kurdistan. This is most likely intentional government policy.

The urban/rural divide is also a factor in ethnic identity and language use in Iran. Iran's rural communities more commonly use ethnic languages, and as will be seen in data presented in this chapter, have significantly lower levels of proficiency in Persian.

Tehran itself is a multiethnic city; at least half of its residents are non-Persians. Tehran is much more of a melting pot of ethnic groups than most of the rest of Iran. Azerbaijanis are the largest group after the Persians in Tehran, forming approximately 35 percent of the residents of the capital. Many of Tehran's neighboring satellite towns, such as Islamshahr, Shariyar, and Varamin, as well as nearby cities, such as Karaj, the capital of the neighboring province Alborz, have an even higher ethnic minority composition, and minority-language use is stronger in these towns and cities than in Tehran proper. Kurdish groups claim that between a half a million to a million Kurds live in Greater Tehran and its satellite towns.

In several provinces, many towns and cities that grew out of rural areas are populated almost completely by non-Persians. Such is the case for Sanandaj in Kurdistan and Zahedan in Sistan-Baluchistan."[10]

Iran's Ethnic Groups

Persians

Persians are Iran's largest ethnic group. However, they make up less than half of Iran's population. Central Iran has an overwhelming Persian majority. According to a study published by the Iranian government's Council of Public Culture, Persians comprise at least 50 percent of the population in 12 provinces: Isfahan, Busher, Tehran, North Khorasan, Razavi Khorasan, Semnan, Fars, Qom, Central Kerman, Hormozgan, and Yazd. Moreover, in the provinces of Alborz, North Khorasan, Khuzestan, and Golestan, Persians do not form the majority but have a strong presence.[11]

The Persians in Iran are almost all Shia. The Persians tend to consider the groups in Iran which speak Iranian languages—the Kurds, Lurs, Baluch, and Caspianites—as close to them in contrast to the Turks and Arabs. The Persians share language ties with speakers of Dari in Afghanistan and Tajik in Tajikistan and Uzbekistan.

Azerbaijanis

The Azerbaijanis are Iran's second-largest ethnic group. The Azerbaijanis form between over a quarter and one third of the population of Iran. In Iran, Azerbaijanis are often referred to and self-refer as Turks and some of them refer to their

---

10 Bernard Hourcade, "La recomposition des identités et des territoires en Iran islamique," *Annales de Géographie*, 3, 2004.
11 Secretary of the Council of Public Culture Mansour Va'ezi, بررسی و سنجش شاخص‌های فرهنگ عمومی کشور [Study and evaluation of the indicators of the general culture of the country], 2010.

language as Turki. In Persian, the group is referred to as Azeri or Torki. Turkish media refer to the Azerbaijanis in Iran as Turks, Azerbaijani Turks, or Azeri Turks. Some Iranian Azerbaijanis, diaspora members, and in the Republic of Azerbaijan refer to Azerbaijanis in Iran as southern Azerbaijanis and to the provinces they inhabit as South Azerbaijan. The Azerbaijanis in Iran are predominately Shiite.

The Azerbaijanis are concentrated in Iran's northwest provinces, forming a clear majority in the region between the Caspian Sea and the border with Turkey and between Tehran and Iran's border with the Republic of Azerbaijan. Azerbaijani Turks comprise more than half of the population in six provinces: East Azerbaijan, West Azerbaijan, Ardabil, Zanjan, Qazvin, and Hamadan. There are considerable numbers of Azerbaijanis in the Caspian Sea bordering provinces, especially in the cities of Anzali, Rasht, and Astara. Azerbaijanis form the majority of the population in Astara in Gilan Province, which is a border city with the city of Astara in the Republic of Azerbaijan.

The Azerbaijani Turkish language spoken among Iran's Azerbaijanis is similar to the language spoken in the neighboring Republic of Azerbaijan. Azerbaijani Turkish is a part of the Oghuz group of Turkic languages together with Anatolian Turkish (the language spoken in the Republic of Turkey), Turkmen (spoken in Turkmenistan and Iran), and the Turkic language spoken by several Turkic communities in countries in the Middle East, such as Iraq.

Approximately 3.5–4 million Azerbaijanis live in Tehran. This group has a much higher proficiency in the Persian language than those that live in the provinces where Azerbaijanis are the majority of the inhabitants. The Azerbaijanis that dwell in the capital and other Persian majority cities are more assimilated into Iranian identity and use of the Persian language than their co-ethnics in the provinces. These urbanized Azerbaijanis, especially in Tehran, have also intermarried with Persians over several generations creating many ethnically mixed families.

Azerbaijanis make up a high percentage of Iran's merchant class. Relative to other ethnic minorities in Iran, the Azerbaijanis have higher income levels, including in the Azerbaijani-populated provinces.

The Azerbaijanis in Iran number 26–29 million and thus are approximately three times the size of their co-ethnics in the neighboring Republic of Azerbaijan, where close to nine million ethnic Azerbaijanis reside.[12] In Eastern Turkey, adja-

---

[12] The total population of the Republic of Azerbaijan is slightly over 10 million, but about a tenth of the population is non-ethnic Azerbaijanis, including Lezgins, Talysh, Avars, Russians, and others.

cent to the border with Iran and the Azerbaijani exclave, Nakhchevan, live close to a million ethnic Azerbaijani citizens of the Republic of Turkey. Most of the ethnic Azerbaijanis in Turkey are Shia.

Gilaks and Mazanis

The Gilaks and Mazanis together form eight to nine percent of the population of Iran. They often self-refer as "Caspianites." Iranian government sources often refer to Gilaks and Mazanis as "Northerners." They comprise the majority in two provinces: Gilan and Mazandaran, which border the Caspian Sea. The Gilaks and Mazanis are primarily Shia.

In contrast to most of the ethnically populated border provinces, the residents of Gilan and Mazandaran enjoy one of the highest living standards in Iran.

The unique geography of regions these groups inhabit seems to instill in the Gilaks and Mazanis which live in their home provinces a strong distinct identity. They live adjacent to the Caspian Sea, enjoy a very green landscape due to the large rainfall and humidity, and a degree of isolation due to the Alborz mountains.

As the Mazanis and Gilaks live in regions bordering the Caspian Sea, these groups are involved in much direct trade and interchanges with foreign states around the Caspian. Gilan Province is home to Iran's major Caspian Sea port in Anzali.

Due to the comfortable climate of Gilan and Mazandaran and access to the Caspian Sea as well as proximity to Tehran, many urban dwellers from Tehran and other major cities own summer homes in these regions. In recent years, some locals voiced opposition to the increasing numbers of non-locals who have acquired property in the region,[13] viewing it as an onslaught that threatens their local lifestyle and the local nature.

Kurds

Kurds form approximately eight percent of the population of Iran. They inhabit the country's Zagros Mountains bordering Turkey and Iraq and comprise a majority in three provinces: Ilam, Kurdistan, and Kermanshah. There are major

---

13 @CaspianShahram, Twitter, March 6, 2022 (https://twitter.com/CaspianShahram/status/1500390934994984963?s=20&t=P73kLyfFpufCqS5yy_Eicw).

Kurdish populations present in several other provinces. Kurds represent the second-largest group in West Azerbaijan Province, and there is a large Kurdish community in North Khorasan Province. Approximately half a million Kurds reportedly live in Greater Tehran.

Kurds share ties with co-ethnics in Iraq, Turkey, and Syria. Iran's Kurds belong to both the Sunni and Shiite Muslim denominations. The Kurds in Ilam and Kermanshah are mostly Shia. Some Kurds belong to the Yaresan sect. Some of the Kurds in Iran are non-Muslims and adhere to religions, such as the Yezidi faith. Reportedly, 5–10 percent of the Kurds living in Kermanshah are non-Muslims. Kurds speak several different dialects of the Kurdish language, such as Sorani, Kurmanji, and Southern Kurdish.

Many of Iran's major mines for precious metals are located in Kurdistan Province, including several of the country's large gold mines.

Lurs

The Lurs, who form approximately seven percent of the population of Iran, reside mostly in the central and southern parts of the Zagros Mountains and comprise a majority in Lurestan, Chaharmahal va Bakhtiari, and Kohgiluyeh va Boyer-Ahmad Provinces. They are Shiite. The Bakhtiars are one of the major tribal groupings of the Lurs and inhabit the Chahar Mahall va Bakhtiari Province. The Lur language is an Iranian language.

Lurs are relatively integrated in the regime institutions and trusted by the Persians as a loyal group. Accordingly, Lurs make up a disproportionate share of provincial governors.

Ahwazi Arabs

The Ahwazis mainly live in two areas: Khuzestan Province and the Persian Gulf coastal region between Bushehr and Bandar-e Abbas. Ahwazis also inhabit regions in Hormozgan, Ilam, Boyer-Ahmad, and Fars provinces as well as Iran's Gulf islands. Iran's Arabs refer to the greater Khuzestan region as al-Ahwaz, encompassing Khuzestan, Bushehr, Hormozgan, and some parts of the Ilam, Boyer-Ahmad, and Fars provinces.

These people refer to themselves as Ahwaz, while Persians refer to them mostly as Arabs. The Arabic dialects spoken by Ahwazis vary: In the Khuzestan region, the Ahwazis speak a dialect close to Iraqi Arabic, while those in the south, in Busher and Hormozgan, speak the Gulf Arabic dialect. Northern Ahwazis are both Shia and Sunni, while those in the south are predominately Sunni. Tribal affiliations and identity are strong among the Ahwazi.

In 2016, the population of Khuzestan Province stood at 4.7 million. Ahwazi Arabs comprise over half of the province's population. The bulk of Iran's oil production is located in Khuzestan.[14]

The oil and natural gas sector employs a large share of Iran's Ahwazis. However, the province's Persian and other non-Arab residents hold the higher-paying jobs in the oil and petrochemical industry, while Ahwazis hold mostly blue-collar jobs. Khuzestan, overall, has a very high rate of unemployment, compared to other parts of Iran.[15]

Khuzestan suffers from extreme water shortages as well as from health threats created by the oil and petrochemical industry.

Baluch

Iran's Baluch live primarily in Sistan-Baluchistan, which is Iran's poorest province and has Iran's highest unemployment rate and lowest literacy rate. The population of Sistan-Baluchistan is close to 2.8 million, and the majority of the inhabitants of the province are Baluch. Most Baluch are Sunni. Tribal affiliations are strong among the Baluch.

Baluch share ties with co-ethnics in Pakistan and Afghanistan. In Pakistan, Baluch enjoy regional autonomy rights. Interaction with this autonomous region of Pakistan impacts the Baluch in Iran.

Turkmen

The Turkmen are located across several provinces, however they are concentrated in North Khorasan, Mazandaran, and Golestan Provinces. Many Turkmen refer to the Turkmen-populated provinces in Iran as Turkmen-Sahra (Turkmen plane) or South Turkmenistan. Some Iranian Turkmen self-refer as South and

---

14 Khuzestan contains approximately eighty percent of Iran's oil reserves and the bulk of its natural gas production. U.S. Department of Energy, Energy Information Agency, "Background Reference: Iran," January 7, 2019 (https://www.eia.gov/international/content/analysis/countries_long/Iran/background.htm); see also: U.S. Central Intelligence Agency, National Foreign Assessment Center, "Khuzestan: Iran's Achilles Tendon," August 26, 2013 (https://www.cia.gov/readingroom/document/cia-rdp09-00438r000100380001-7).
15 *Bartarinha*, October 2, 2021 (https://www.bartarinha.ir/fa/news/1158103/).

Southern Turkmen, calling those living in the neighboring state of Turkmenistan as North Turkmen. Cities and towns in Iran with major Turkmen concentrations include Gonbad-Kavus, Gorgan, Aqqala, Gomishan (Kumushdepe), and Bandar Torkaman (Bandar). Many of the Turkmen dwell close to the Caspian Sea, and engage in fishing for livelihood.

Like the Azerbaijanis, the main groups of Turkmen have been split from each other for several centuries between the Russian and Iranian empires. With the fall of the USSR, ties were renewed between the Turkmen in Iran and the newly independent Republic of Turkmenistan. The Republic of Turkmenistan is contingent to the main Turkmen populations in Iran.

Most of Iran's Turkmen are Sunni. Tribal groupings are strong among the Turkmen, and several of the tribes stretch into neighboring Turkmenistan. The Turkmen language is Oghuz Turkic, like that spoken by the Azerbaijanis and the Turks of Anatolia Turkey.

Qashqai Turks

The Qashqai Turks are located in multiple locations in Iran and were nomadic up until the twentieth century. Most of the Qashqai are located in Fars Province. There are populations of Qashqai also near Isfahan and in Chaharmahal va Bakhtiari Province. The Qashqai are Shia.

Determining the precise number of the Qashqai Turks in Iran is difficult, especially since the Iranian government studies lump all Turks together (Azerbaijanis, Qashqai and Turkmen). In addition, since the Qashqai are located in multiple locations in Iran and many Qashqai are nomadic, their numbers are not discernible from the Iranian government data on province size. Western academic studies assess that close to a million Qashqai Turks live in Iran. This number is highly disputed by Qashqai researchers and activists that claim their group numbers 3–4 million, based on calculations of the numbers of members of clans and tribes. Iranian studies likely count the Qashqai as Persians, since most live in Persian-majority areas.

The Qashqai speak a dialect of the Azerbaijani language that is understandable to Azerbaijani speakers and vice-versa. Many of the Qashqai are still nomads. Both the Pahlavi regime and the Islamic Republic have engaged in forced settlement programs of the Qashqai.

The Qashqai have strongly preserved their tribal structure and most are aware of their tribal and clan belongings. The Qashqai are much less assimilated into general Iranian culture and the Persian language than the highly urban Azerbaijani Turks.

Distinct ethno-nationalism among the Qashqai has grown in the 2000s. In the 2020s, the regime has increased pressure on this group and limited their presence in their traditional pastoral lands, creating increased conflict between the central government and the Qashqai.

Talesh

There are several hundred thousand Talesh in Iran. The Talesh live mostly in northern Iran, near the Caspian Sea in Gilan Province, bordering the Republic of Azerbaijan. The Talesh share cross-border ties with Talesh that inhabit the south of the Republic of Azerbaijan. The Talesh speak an Iranian language.

Iran—Numbers of Ethnic Groups

The population of Iran's ethnic groups is a highly contested question among researchers. The issue is also very politicized, as ethnic activists tend to inflate the numbers, and Persian nationalists and the Iranian government lower their numbers. Many prominent academic and policy studies on Iran published in English in recent years rely on questionable data in assessing the size of Iran's ethnic groups. Most refer to the CIA's *World Factbook* as their key source,[16] even though the CIA stopped reporting the ethnic breakdown in Iran in 2016 (in contrast to its reporting on most other countries). This cessation likely signaled a lack of confidence in the data.[17] Most likely, the assessments prior to 2015 also were not reliable. From 2000 to January 2011, the *Factbook* claimed the Persian population comprised 51 percent of the population and the next-largest group, the Azerbaijanis, comprised 24 percent. Within less than a year, in November 2011, the *Factbook* published, with no explanation, a significant change in its assessment: the Persian population was increased to 61 percent, and the Azerbaijani share was shrunk to 16 percent (see Table 1). The percentages of the Lurs increased (from

---

[16] Most U.S. think tank publications base reports on Iran's ethnic composition on older versions of the CIA's *World Factbook*. See, for instance: Bijan DaBell, "Iran Minorities 2: Ethnic Diversity," *United States Institute of Peace*, September 3, 2013 (https://iranprimer.usip.org/blog/2013/sep/03/iran-minorities-2-ethnic-diversity).

[17] One of the eye-catching elements of the CIA *Factbook* data is that prior to 2011 it reported that Persians comprise 51 percent of the population, and not 50 percent. It is hard to imagine collection of such precise data that would allow the *Factbook* researchers to distinguish identity trends to the level of resolution of one percent difference.

two percent to six percent) and Kurds (from seven percent to 10 percent) in this new assessment, while Turkmen and Baluch remained the same. The Arabs lost a percentage point and the Gilaks and Mazanis disappeared as separate ethnic groups in the new entry.

Table 1: Ethnic Groups in Iran – CIA *World Factbook*

	2010	January 2011	November 2011	January 2013
Persian	51%	51%	61%	61%
Azerbaijani	24%	24%	16%	16%
Gilaki and Mazani	8%	8%	–	–
Kurd	7%	7%	10%	10%
Arab	3%	3%	2%	2%
Lur	2%	2%	6%	6%
Baluch	2%	2%	2%	2%
Turkmen	2%	2%	2%	2%
Other	1%	1%	1%	1%

Source: CIA World Factbook[18]

The 2010 and 2011 group percentages were reported until 2015. From 2016, the CIA *Factbook* stopped reporting numbers and just listed major groups. Note that Gilaks and Mazanis are missing as a separate category and that Azerbaijanis are referred to as Azeris, though they do not self-reference with this term. The CIA *Factbook* also no longer maintains on its site the data on Iran's ethnic groups that it published before halting its publication of numbers.[19]

The academic and think tank trend of reference to the CIA *Factbook* in academic publications is puzzling, not only because the Agency abandoned its own data, but also because it is not customary in serious academic work to base assessments on a work like the CIA *Factbook*, where there is no ability to access the raw data that forms the basis of the assessment, nor the methodology used by the *Factbook* authors to analyze the data.

Yet, many publications and think tanks rely on the unreliable CIA *Factbook* numbers, often without explicitly stating the origin of the numbers, which makes

---

[18] Daniel Pipes, "Did the CIA Fiddle With Population Statistics about Iran?" *DanielPipes.org* blog January 5, 2015 (https://www.danielpipes.org/blog/2015/01/did-the-cia-fiddle-with-population-statistics).
[19] See Daniel Pipes, "Did the CIA Fiddle With Population Statistics about Iran?" *DanielPipes.org* blog January 5, 2015 (https://www.danielpipes.org/blog/2015/01/did-the-cia-fiddle-with-population-statistics).

it appear that their publication provides a new, independent source on the relative shares of ethnic minorities in Iran. Many publications also cross reference each other, while still originally using the *Factbook* data. This is misleading and creates the erroneous impression that additional independent sources have conducted assessments and drew conclusions similar to the *Factbook*.

A major focus of the research for this book was an attempt at a more accurate assessment of Iran's ethnic makeup. Four primary sources are the basis of this analysis: (1) statements of Iranian officials, (2) the Iranian government's Values and Attitude Survey, (3) a report by Iran's Council of Public Culture, and (4) comprehensive historical survey data compiled by the Iranian military. In analyzing the data, this study examined demographic data, Iran province population data, and surveys of language use to assess the population of Iran's ethnic groups.

According to these sources, Persians make up less than half of Iran's population. The sources also show that non-Persian groups form overwhelming majorities in most of Iran's border provinces, in contrast to Iran's Persian-dominated center. Ethnic identity and use of local languages are much stronger in the border provinces than among the minorities residing in Iran's center. Likewise, Persian proficiency is much weaker in the provinces than in Iran's central cities.

Among researchers, the most contested issue is the number of Azerbaijanis in Iran. Accuracy is critical, since they are the largest group after the Persians. In addition, the Azerbaijanis are Iran's only minority group in which significant numbers of the group assimilate and intermarry with Persians and reside in Iran's central provinces. Hence, due to the difficulty in determining their assimilation rates there is much debate on their numbers and self-identity, especially in ethnically mixed cities such as Tehran.

The Iranian government's demographic studies likely underestimate the number of Ahwazis. Since the group is concentrated in very strategic regions of the country – Khuzestan and Bandar Abbas, the centers of Iran's oil industry – this underestimation may reflect an intentional effort to obscure the government's potential vulnerability. Khuzestan alone has close to five million inhabitants, and over half of the population is Ahwazi. Thus, the true number of Ahwazis is higher than that reflected in Tehran's data.

Official Statements

While Iran does not publish official statistics on the ethnic background and native language of its citizens, Iranian officials periodically cite internal government data, especially when discussing educational challenges. Education Ministry officials often cite data on the number of speakers of Iran's various languages, since lack of proficiency in Persian among Iran's pupils is a major education challenge. In December 2009, Hamid Reza Haji Babai, then-minister of education and later a member of Iran's parliament, reported that 70 percent of Iran's pupils are bilingual, with Persian still not a primary language after the first grade.[20]

During an official visit to Turkey in January 2012, then-Iranian Foreign Minister Ali Akbar Salehi, in pointing out the commonalities between Turkey and Iran, stated that 40 percent of Iranians speak Turkish,[21] suggesting that 40 percent of the country is ethnically Turkic, since a minute number of Iranians study Turkish as a foreign language.

The Iranian Government's Values and Attitudes Survey

In 2015, Iran's Office of National Projects of the Ministry of Culture and Islamic Guidance, in cooperation with the Ministry of Interior, conducted face-to-face interviews with 14,906 Iranian citizens in all 31 of Iran's provinces, in both rural and urban locations.[22] The 2015 Values and Attitudes Survey asked extensive questions that provide instructive data regarding Iran's ethno-linguistic composition.

When asked which language they speak at home, most non-Persians reported they do not speak Persian at home. The percentages of Turkmen and Baluch who reported speaking their minority language at home were exceptionally high: 92 and 94 percent, respectively. The Baluch and Turkmen also reported the highest percentages desiring to teach their children their native languages. This is a strong indicator of ethnic identity.

---

[20] "Deputy Minister of Education announced 100 hours of Persian-language teaching in preschool for bilingual children," *Iranian Students News Agency* (ISNA), September 2, 2012 (https://www.isna.ir/news/91072213844/); "Unresolved challenges of Education in Iran," *Deutsche Welle*, September 22, 2017 (https://p.dw.com/p/2kSOW).

[21] HarayHarayMenTurkem, "Iran Foreign Minster: 40% of Iranians talk in Turkish," *YouTube*, January 21, 2012 (https://www.youtube.com/watch?v=OFZVGvsw9gk).

[22] Islamic Republic Ministry of Culture and Guidance, Office of National Plans, in collaboration with the Ministry of Interior, National Center for Social Observation, "Third Values and Attitudes Survey," 2015. For background on the survey, see: Islamic Republic of Iran Ministry of Culture and Guidance, Research Center for Culture, Art and Communication, "A Brief Introduction to Iranian National Plan of Values and Attitudes (Third Wave)," November 28, 2017 (https://www.ricac.ac.ir/en/en/7).

Table 2: Language Spoken at Home: Persian vs. Local Ethnic Language

Ethnic Group	Local Ethnic Language	Persian
Persian	15%	85%
Azerbaijani	79%	21%
Lur	85%	15%
Kurd	85%	15%
Turkmen	92%	8%
Arab	82%	18%
Talesh	74%	26%
Baluch	94%	6%
Gilak	70%	30%
Mazani	65%	35%

Language use trends shed interesting light on the scope of Iranian ethnic assimilation. Interestingly, 15 percent of the self-identified Persian respondents reported that they speak a minority language at home. This may indicate that they are partially assimilated ethnic minority community members or from ethnically mixed families. The majority of self-defined Persians who responded that they speak a different language at home reside in Iran's central provinces. The northern province of Mazandaran and southern province Hormozgan also had a high degree of respondents that identify as Persian while reporting that they speak a language other than Persian at home. Hormozgan Province is populated by a large percentage of ethnic Lurs, which are a relatively assimilated group into Iranian identity in Iran. In Mazandaran Province, a high percentage (35 percent) of respondents that self-define as Mazanis, also reported speaking Persian at home.

There is significant variation in the use of Persian between the central and border provinces. Within ethnic groups, residents of provinces where their group forms the majority almost universally speak their ethnic languages at home, while those in mixed provinces have greater variation in the language spoken at home. For instance, 21 percent of Azerbaijani respondents reported speaking Persian at home. Among those individuals, only 12 out of more than 1,000 respondents resided in the main Azerbaijani-populated provinces (Ardabil, East Azerbaijan, Zanjan, and West Azerbaijan). In Persian-dominated provinces, a greater number of Azerbaijanis reported speaking Persian: 60 percent in Tehran Province and 42 percent in Alborz.

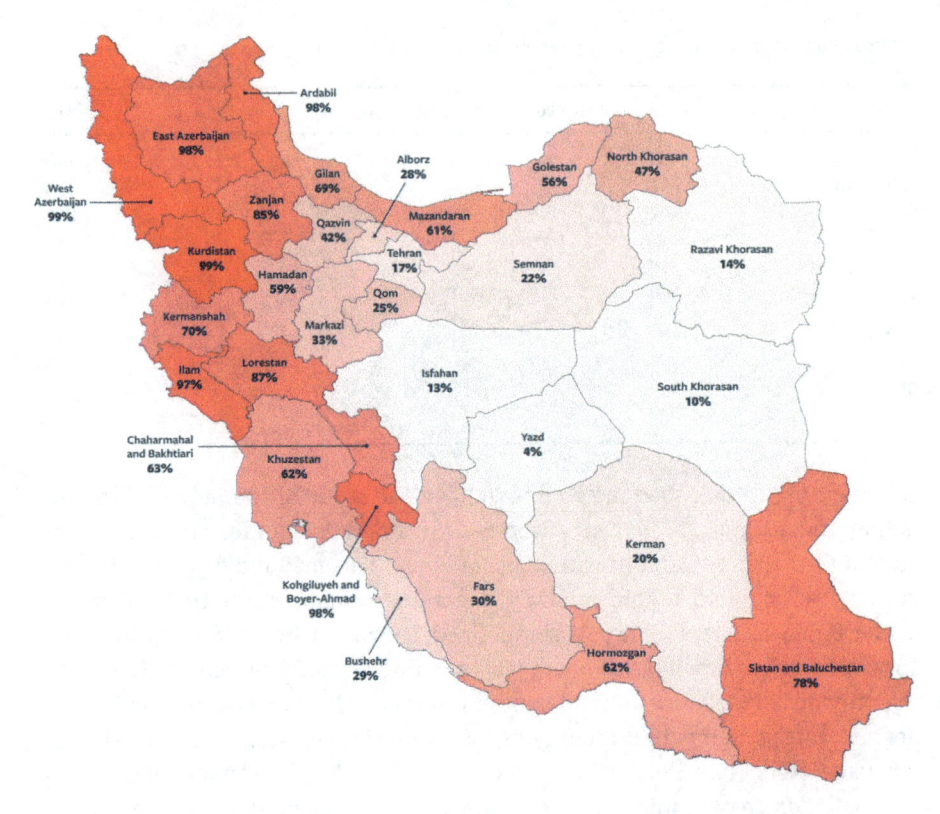

Figure 2: Percentage of Inhabitants with Primary Language Not Persian
Source: "Third Values and Attitudes Survey," Islamic Republic Ministry of Culture and Guidance

A gap in the level of Persian proficiency exists between ethnic minorities who live in rural areas and those who live in urban areas. Forty percent of those who live in urban areas consider their knowledge of Persian "very high," compared to only 21 percent of respondents living in rural areas. Overall, 40 percent of all the survey respondents described themselves as not fluent in Persian.

Table 3: Level of Persian Knowledge

Ethnic Group	To Some Extent or Less	High and Very High
Azerbaijani	43%	57%
Lur	41%	59%
Kurd	34%	66%
Turkmen	54%	46%
Arab	39%	61%
Talesh	35%	65%
Baluch	46%	54%
Gilak	51%	49%
Mazani	48%	52%

A very high percentage of non-Persians who reside in ethnically mixed cities declined to answer the question evaluating their own Persian proficiency level. This likely suggests their embarrassment regarding their knowledge level. For instance, among the Azerbaijanis in Tehran Province, an exceptionally high number of respondents (67 percent) declined to answer the question on the level of their Persian-language proficiency. In the Azerbaijani-populated provinces, by contrast, the overwhelming majority answered this question, suggesting that in those that live in Azerbaijani-majority areas are not ashamed to admit they are not highly fluent in the Persian language:

Table 4: Persian-Language Proficiency Among Azerbaijanis in the City of Tehran, by Age Group

Age	Very Low	Low	To Some Extent	High	Very High	NA	N
15–25	0%	0%	4%	13%	9%	74%	15%
26–35	0%	0%	1%	20%	11%	68%	27%
36–45	0%	0%	6%	13%	9%	72%	17%
46–55	0%	2%	6%	18%	5%	69%	20%
56–65	5%	5%	9%	21%	2%	58%	14%
66–75	4%	13%	21%	13%	4%	46%	8%
Total	**1%**	**2%**	**6%**	**17%**	**7%**	**67%**	**100%**

Table 5: Persian-Language Proficiency Among Azerbaijanis in Four Predominantly Azerbaijani Provinces (Ardabil, East Azerbaijan, West Azerbaijan, Zanjan), by Age Group

Age	Very Low	Low	To Some Extent	High	Very High	NA	N
15–25	1%	4%	22%	41%	23%	8%	21%
26–35	1%	5%	33%	43%	14%	4%	26%
36–45	7%	10%	37%	29%	13%	4%	23%
46–55	15%	13%	37%	25%	7%	3%	14%
56–65	26%	24%	22%	16%	8%	4%	10%
66–75	46%	24%	23%	4%	2%	1%	7%
Total	10%	10%	30%	32%	13%	5%	100%

Azerbaijani Persian-language proficiency varied significantly across different age groups. The younger generations reported greater capability in Persian than the older generations, potentially indicating that the government's Persianization policies have achieved success over time. For example, Azerbaijanis between the ages of 15 and 25 reported being mostly proficient in Persian, in contrast to 40-year-olds and above:

Table 6: Azerbaijanis' Declared Persian-Language Proficiency, by Age Group

Age	Very Low	Low	To Some Extent	High	Very High	N
15–25	1%	3%	18%	43%	35%	21%
26–35	1%	4%	27%	42%	26%	27%
36–45	5%	8%	33%	33%	20%	21%
46–55	10%	10%	33%	31%	16%	14%
56–65	19%	19%	25%	25%	13%	11%
65+	33%	22%	27%	12%	7%	7%
Total	7%	9%	27%	35%	22%	100%

According to the survey, Iran's ethnic groups expressed a strong desire to teach their children their mother tongues. In what is likely an indicator of self-identification, a majority of respondents from all ethnic groups said they feel "highly" or "very highly" committed to teaching their mother languages to their children:

Table 7: Desire to Teach Mother Language to Own Children

Ethnic Group	Very Low	Low	To Some Extent	High	Very High
Persian	5%	5%	33%	36%	21%
Azerbaijani	2%	3%	18%	46%	31%
Lur	4%	6%	27%	44%	20%
Kurd	3%	2%	16%	34%	45%
Turkmen	1%	0%	12%	48%	40%
Arab	2%	3%	28%	32%	36%
Talesh	3%	1%	33%	41%	22%
Baluch	0%	1%	9%	52%	38%
Gilak	4%	7%	30%	50%	9%
Mazani	1%	1%	23%	53%	21%

The data on language trends shed lights on identity trends in Iran. Younger people self-report much higher levels of Persian fluency than the older age groups. Consequently, the regime's efforts to promote Persian among Iran's population are succeeding and this is potentially leading to higher assimilation rates into Iranian identity among young people in Iran than previous generations. At the same time, the percentages of those that want to teach their native tongue to the next generation is very high among Iran's ethnic minorities, even if they have proficiency in Persian, suggesting that ethnic identity persists even when Persian proficiency is attained.

Council of Public Culture Study

From 2008 to 2010, Mansour Va'ezi, secretary of Iran's Council of Public Culture, led a study on the cultural practices and ethnic composition of each of Iran's 31 provinces. The results of the study, published in 2010, reported that Persians comprised 47 percent of the population of Iran. The next-biggest group was the Turks, at 23 percent.[23]

---

23 Secretary of the Council of Public Culture Mansour Va'ezi, Islamic Republic of Iran, بررسی و سنجش شاخص‌های فرهنگ عمومی کشور [Study and evaluation of the indicators of the general culture of the country], 2010.

Table 8: 2010 Iran's Council of Public Culture Study on Ethnic Groups

Ethnic group	Percentage of Total Population, According to 2010 Study
Persians	47%
Turks	23%
Northern	9%
Kurd	8%
Lur	7%
Arab	2%
Baluch	2%

The 2010 study seems to undercount especially the Baluch and Arabs. For instance, according to official Iranian government data, the population of Sistan-Baluchistan Province stood at close to 2.8 million in 2016. Out of these, at least 2 million are Baluch, although the number is likely higher. If the Baluch were only two percent of Iran's population, that would mean that roughly 1.2 million non-Baluch live in Sistan-Baluchistan and that few Baluch live outside the province, both are not likely. In addition, Arabs comprise approximately 70 percent of the population of Khuzestan Province's 4.7 million residents, thus over three million in Khuzestan Province alone. This study also seemed to underestimate the Turkic groups in Iran, which it grouped together (Azerbaijanis, Qashqai, and Turkmen).

Iranian Military Survey

The most detailed historical survey of Iran's villages and towns, conducted by Iran's military, shows that Persians formed less than half of Iran's population even in the mid-twentieth century. From 1949 to 1952, the Iranian Military Geographic Research Headquarters published *Geographic Culture of Iran*, an 11-volume survey of the language and religious composition of almost every town and village in Iran.[24] The lead author, Hossein Ali Razmara, was an instructor at Iran's war college and headed the military's geography department. The survey is very detailed and provides important insights into the composition of Iran's population today. According to this study, the Iranian population stood at 17.15 million people in

---

24 Hossein Ali Razmara, فرهنگ جغرافیائی ایران [*Geographic Culture of Iran*] (Tehran: Iranian Military Geographic Research Headquarters, 1949–1952).

1949,[25] with Persians comprising an estimated 49.5 percent of the population. The study categorized all inhabitants of Tehran and other major cities in central Iran as Persians, since they were likely to be proficient in the Persian language. Thus, the survey overestimated the ethnic Persian population.

According to the study, the ethnic composition of Iran in 1949 consisted of:

Table 9: Iran Ethnic Composition, 1949

Ethnicity	Population
Persians	8,543,586
Turks	4,452,666
Kurds	1,165,087
Lurs	530,285
Baluch	395,257
Arabs	274,423
Turkmen	127,117
Others (small groups and unknowns, including Gilanis [Gilaks, Gilakis], Lakis, Laris, Mazanis, Armenians, Georgians, and Jews)	2,000,000

This detailed historical survey reinforces later studies indicating that Persians make up less than half of Iran's population, since it is highly unlikely that the percentage of Persians grew over the second half of the twentieth century and the early part of the twenty-first century: There has been only modest outmigration among several of Iran's ethnic minorities (Kurds, Baluch, and Turkmen) from their native provinces, limiting their opportunity for cultural assimilation. Moreover, because the study categorized all residents of Tehran and other major central Iranian cities as Persians, it accounted for any assimilation that has subsequently occurred among minorities residing there. Finally, birth rates in Iran's border provinces are higher than in the center, consequently lowering the percentage of Persians in Iran's ethnic composition.

---

25 See also Julian Bharier, "A note on the population of Tehran, 1900–1966," *Population Studies*, Volume 22, Issue 2, 1968 (https://www.tandfonline.com/doi/abs/10.1080/00324728.1968.10405540).

Estimated Numbers of Iran's Ethnic Minorities in 2020

In 2020, Iran's population stood at approximately 84 million. The below assessment is based on the 2010 Iranian Council of Public Culture internal government study on the numbers of Iran's ethnic minorities, with several corrections. One, it corrects for the underestimation of the Baluch and Arab groups. Based on analyzing the populations of Iran's provinces according to the official Iranian 2016 census performed by the Statistical Center of Iran[26] and the Iranian data on Persian proficiency, the percentages of Baluch and Arabs is larger than the percentages presented in the 2010 Iranian data. Alam Saleh, who has conducted extensive field research on the Ahwaz in Iran and specifically in Khuzestan, contends that Ahwaz make up 70 percent of the population of Khuzestan Province.[27] In addition, the below assessment corrects the low numbers of Azerbaijani and other Turks presented in the 2010 data. The 2010 data seems to assume much higher rates of assimilation of Azerbaijanis than in reality and also seems to count the Qashqai as Persians. This 2020 assessment also separates the Turks in Iran into three separate groups: Azerbaijanis, Qashqai, and Turkmen.

Second, the 2020 estimate reflects the lower birth rate of the largely urbanized Persians versus the inhabitants of Iran's provinces.[28] Iran's agricultural households, which have higher birthrates than its urban residents, have a much higher percentage of ethnic minorities than Persians. The percentage of rural households in Iran continues to grow, which means that the numbers of ethnic minorities are growing. Note that rural households of ethnic minorities command a lower rate of Persian fluency than urban households.

---

26 Iran Statistics Center (https://www.amar.org.ir).
27 Alam Saleh, *Ethnic Identity and the State in Iran* (New York City: Palgrave Macmillan, 2013), p. 70.
28 David P. Goldman, "The dangerous, disappearing Persians," *AsiaTimes*, February 1, 2021 (https://asiatimes.com/2021/02/the-dangerous-disappearing-persians/); David P. Goldman, *How Civilizations Die* (Washington, DC: Regnery Publishing, 2011); "Security Forces Fear the Growing Number of Sunnis in Iran," *IranWire*, October 20, 2021 (https://iranwire.com/en/features/67843).

Table 10: Iran's Ethnic Composition, 2020

Ethnicity	Percentage of Iran's population
Persians	37
Azerbaijani Turks	26–29
Northerners	8–9
Kurds	8
Lurs	7
Arabs	6
Baluch	3
Qashqai Turks	1.5[29]
Turkmen	1.5
Others	1

It should be noted that activists of most of the ethnic groups claim much higher percentages than those presented here. For instance, Azerbaijani activist groups claim that the Azerbaijani and tribal Turkic population of Iran is approximately 40 percent. Kurdish activist groups claim that Kurds number 10 million in Iran, thus 12 percent of the population. Ahwazi Arab activists claim that the Ahwazis number close to eight million (9.5 percent). Turkmen groups claim that the Turkmen in Iran number five million (6 percent). Qashqai researchers claim that they number three million in Iran (3.6 percent).

Furthermore, it is important to note that ethnic background does not necessarily translate into self-identification or to politically relevant identities. Many in ethnically mixed urban areas, such as Tehran, may be aware of emanating from a certain ethnic group, while this does not inform their choices or political attitudes. At the same time, researchers must be careful not to project behaviors and attitudes of ethnic minorities in urban ethnically mixed centers onto the ethnic groups that live in the provinces. As seen by the language data, those that continue to reside in the provinces where non-Persians are the majority, uphold high rates of minority language use and thus likely associated cultural identities.

Socioeconomic Indicators for Ethnic Groups

Iran's ethnically populated provinces fare worse on nearly all the major economic and human development indicators than the Persian center. However, among

---

[29] Determining the number of Qashqai is complicated. See discussion in section on "Qashqai Turks."

the ethnically populated provinces, there are sharp differences in levels of economic and human development. Gilan and Mazandaran rank high on the human development index. Some of the Azerbaijani-populated provinces rank near the middle of Iran's provinces, and the Baluch and Kurdish provinces consistently rank at the lowest end.[30] In the words of the premier geographer of Iran, Bernard Hourcade:

> The Persians occupy the central space, in the heart of the national territory... This is an obvious and conscious principle of domination, confirmed by the economic geography of the country which shows the underdevelopment of most of the non-Persian-speaking provinces, whether agricultural and pastoral (Baluchistan, Kurdistan Azerbaijan, Lurestan), or oil like the Arabic-speaking regions of the Persian Gulf.[31]

Most of the ethnically populated provinces have much higher rates of unemployment and higher rates of poverty than the Persian-populated center of the country.[32] And, within provinces, there are many indications of employment discrimination toward ethnic minorities. In Khuzestan, for instance, the Persians and Lurs hold the high-paying jobs in its oil and petrochemical industry. By contrast, the Arabs hold mostly blue-collar jobs. On January 6, 2021, Mohsen Haidari, the Supreme Leader's representative in Ahwaz, claimed that ethnic Arabs hold only five percent of the province's management-level jobs in the oil industry. He noted that when candidates with discernible Arab names apply for well-paying jobs in the sector, they do not receive interviews.[33]

The UN Human Rights Council Special Rapporteur on Iran noted when discussing the mainly Baluch-populated province in Iran:

> Sistan-Balochistan is arguably the most underdeveloped region in Iran, with the highest poverty, infant and child mortality rates, and lowest life expectancy and literacy rates in the country.[34]

---

[30] Asma Sabermahani, Mohsen Barouni, Hesam Seyedin, and Aidin Aryankhesal, "Provincial Human Development Index, a Guide for Efficiency level Analysis: The Case of Iran," *Iranian Journal of Public Health* Vol. 42, No.2, 2013, pp. 149–157 (https://www.ncbi.nlm.nih.gov/pmc/articles/PMC3595646/#/).
[31] Bernard Hourcade, "La recomposition des identités et des territoires en Iran islamique," *Annales de Géographie*, 3, 2004, p. 516.
[32] *Bartarinha*, October 2, 2021 (https://www.bartarinha.ir/fa/news/1158103/).
[33] "Official Confessions: Arabs are Seriously Discriminated in Iran," *Padmaz*, January 6, 2021 (https://padmaz.org/en/?p=268).
[34] Report of the UN Special Rapporteur on the situation of human rights in the Islamic Republic of Iran, UNHRC statement (A/HRC/22/56), February 28, 2013.

Iran's ethnic minority-populated provinces have much lower literacy rates than Tehran Province and the national average.[35] The major gap in literacy rates between Iran's Persian center and its minority provinces is also supported by earlier surveys:[36]

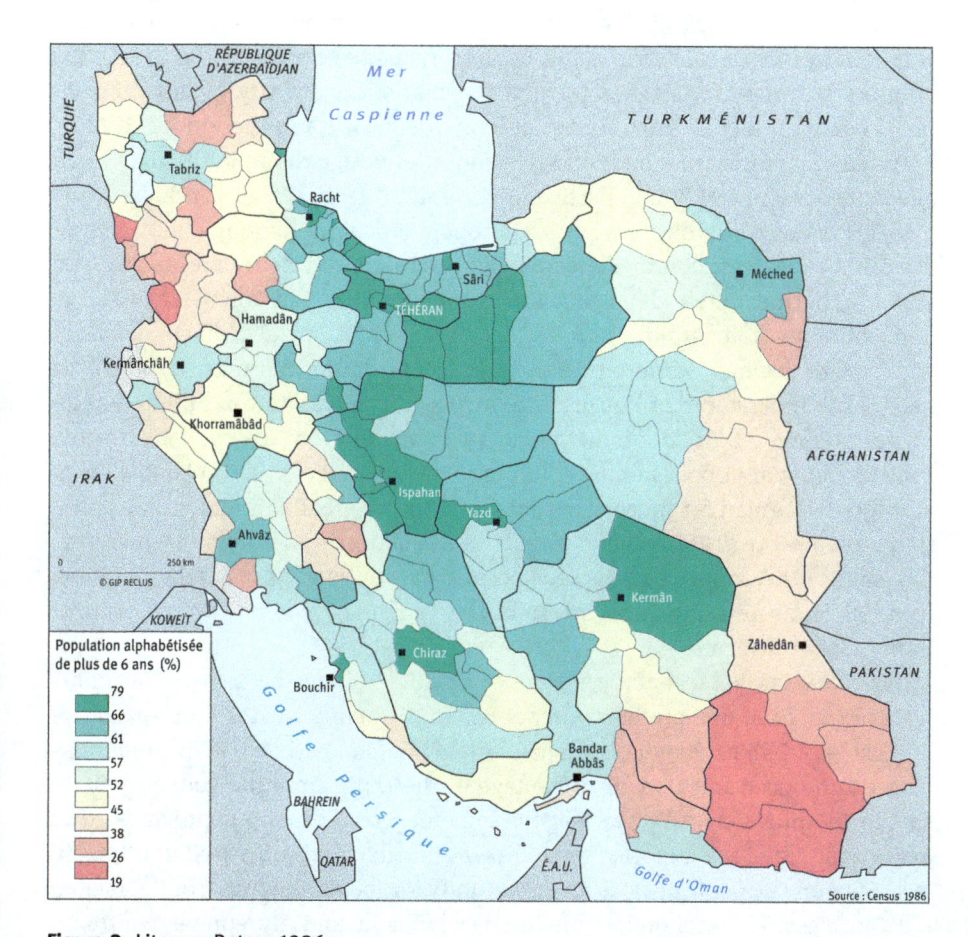

Figure 3: Literacy Rates, 1986
Source: Bernard Hourcade, *Atlas d'Iran* and CNRS, Paris 2021 CartOrient, Centre de Recherche sur le Monde Iranien

---

[35] "Iran's literacy rates improve," *Financial Tribune*, April 5, 2017 (https://financialtribune.com/articles/people/61861/iran-literacy-rates-improv).
[36] Bernard Hourcade et al., *Atlas d'Iran* (Paris: Reclus et Doc., 1998), p. 65.

Different Levels of Services, Infrastructure, Health Services, and Environmental Protection

The provinces of Iran that are inhabited by Persians are the most developed provinces in the country.[37] Iran's central government provides ethnic minorities with fewer government services, infrastructure, health services, and environmental protection than the Persian-populated center of the country. Javaid Rehman, the UN Human Rights Council Special Rapporteur for Iran stated in his 2022 report that "Environmental and land-related issues pose a threat to the right to an adequate standard of living, particularly in minority-populated provinces."[38]

This overlap of ethnic groups and economic/health/environmental grievances could prove particularly dangerous for the ruling regime. Representatives of ethnic minorities often claim that they suffer from the environmental damage and pollution from mining and extracting minerals, metals, oil and natural gas in their regions, while outsiders gain the revenue. This claim is made by many Arab inhabitants of Khuzestan Province, the center of Iran's oil and natural gas production. In addition, Azerbaijanis point out that the copper extracted from the Sungun Copper mining complex is transported over 1,500 kilometers to a factory in Kerman for processing. Subsequently, Azerbaijanis endure the pollution from the extraction while residents of Kerman gain the main revenue from the copper. The copper mine is located in Varzegan city, East Azerbaijan Province, 90 kilometers northeast of Tabriz. It reportedly contains 20 percent of Iran's copper reserves.

Even regime representatives have complained about the transfer of profits from resources in one province to another. The Supreme Leader's representative in East Azerbaijan Province, Hojjatoleslam Mohammad Ali Al-Hashim, has stressed the need for a small percentage of the profit from the cooper mine to stay in the province: "We see that the mineral resources of our province, after extraction, are either exported or sold raw or melted and processed in other cities… Songun Copper [mines] is an opportunity for the development of the region, but the blessings, economic benefits, development and entrepreneurship and employment of this God-given blessing must return to the province."[39] He further "stressed the necessity for the independence of Azerbaijan Copper Industry,"

---

37 Hussein D. Hassan, *Iran: Ethnic and Religious Minorities*, Congressional Research Report, November 25, 2008.
38 United Nations Human Rights Council, "Situation of human rights in the Islamic Republic of Iran," January 13, 2022 (https://www.ohchr.org/en/documents/country-reports/ahrc4975-situation-human-rights-islamic-republic-iran-report-special).
39 *Fars News Agency* (Provinces News Board-East Azerbaijan), February 16, 2022.

noting that the fulfillment of the right of East Azerbaijan in this regard requires serious attention of officials and the independence of Sungun Copper Company and the establishment of the Azerbaijan Copper Company to prevent the export and sale of extractive materials from the province.[40] According to a report from the *Fars News Agency:*

> Provincial officials as well as the representatives of East Azerbaijan in the Islamic Consultative Assembly also believe that the refusal of the officials of the National Copper Industries Company of Iran to accept the establishment of an independent Azerbaijani copper company and creating obstacles in this case is contrary to the approvals of the Supreme Council of Mines, which emphasizes the necessity to transfer all financial accounts of mines to the provinces where they are located and extracted. They say that the obstruction of the formation of an independent Azerbaijani copper company as an example of fulfilling the slogans of the 13th government in the field of social justice originates from the personal profit-seeking and centralized approaches of some officials as well as interest groups in the National Copper Industries Company of Iran.[41]

Regime representatives also at times complain about the disparity of services and state protection between the center and the provinces, for instance in the field of electricity production. Despite having the second largest natural gas reserves in the world, Iran frequently has natural gas shortages. In order to continue to supply heat and electricity during the supply outages, the government fuels some power and heat plants with heavy oil, which creates dangerous air pollution. The regime tends to reserve the clean natural gas for use in Tehran and the center of the country, while using polluting fuel oil in the other provinces. During Friday Prayers at the Imam Khomeini Mosque in November 2021, the representative of the Supreme Leader in Tabriz, Seyyed Mohammad Ali Al-Hashim, criticized Iran's Ministry of Energy for creating the extreme air pollution in Tabriz and called on the Ministry "to eliminate this pollution immediately." He explicitly pointed out the inequality in Tehran's policy: "the representatives of Tabriz in the Islamic Consultative Assembly should ask why the use of diesel fuel is not allowed in other power plants of the country, but in Tabriz this is allowed?"[42]

Members of ethnic minorities claim that Iran's water policies favor the Persian-populated heartland over provinces where they form majorities. In recent

---

40 *Fars News Agency* (Provinces News Board-East Azerbaijan), February 16, 2022.
41 *Fars News Agency* (Provinces News Board-East Azerbaijan), February 16, 2022.
42 "Al-Hashim's serious warning to the Ministers of Energy and Oil for burning heavy oil and pollution made by the Tabriz power plant," *Moj News Agency,* November 19, 2021. (https://www.mojnews.com/fa/tiny/news-406381).

years, Tehran has built large-scale water diversion projects, which have all failed according to Iranian press reports:

> Although the water transfer projects among the basins in Khuzestan, Isfahan, Yazd and Kashan have failed and they have caused problems and even crises in the provinces of origin and destination of the water transfer project, it is not clear why there is such an insistence on re-implementing such water transfer projects with large budgets![43]

Environmental concerns rank high among the most charged issues in Iran. Dissatisfaction over environmental threats regularly spurs anti-regime protests. Khuzestan Province particularly suffers from environmental degradation. The province experiences exceptional air pollution rates. The major measure for air pollution is the number of parts per million of particles smaller than 10 micrometers (PM10) in the air. According to the World Health Organization, Beijing, globally known as a byword for air pollution, has a PM10 rating of 121. Ahwaz, by comparison, has a PM10 rating of 372.[44]

---

[43] "Allocating the budget for 'transferring water to the central plateau of Iran' despite the opposition of the environmental organization," *Tasnim News Agency*, December 23, 2021 (https://tn.ai/2624762).

[44] Alex MacDonald, "Protests over pollution in Iran's Khuzestan Province 'a national threat,'" *Middle East Eye*, February 18, 2017 (https://www.middleeasteye.net/news/protests-over-pollution-irans-khuzestan-province-national-threat).

3 The Islamic Republic's Policies Toward Ethnic Minorities

Both of the governing systems that have ruled Iran for much of the twentieth century and the early twenty-first century—the Pahlavi monarchy and the Islamic Republic—have suppressed Iran's ethnic minorities and not allowed them to use their languages in schools and government institutions. Despite possessing vastly different ideological and strategic orientations, the two regimes granted the Persians a dominant position, including exclusive use of the Persian language in government institutions and schools.[45] Although its Constitution does not formally discriminate against Shia Muslims from different ethnic groups, the Islamic Republic has upheld the hegemony of the Persian language and Persian ethnic group.

Despite claiming that Iran is one big happy multiethnic family, the Islamic Republic goes to great lengths to suppress political activity by ethnic minorities, including by assassinating and executing ethnic political and cultural leaders both in Iran and abroad. In addition, the regime diligently enforces use of the Persian language in schools and government institutions. If the Persian language was universally spoken, there would be no need for enforcement mechanisms.

Ethnic Nationalism—A Twentieth-Century Issue

The dominance of the Persians since the beginning of the twentieth century is an exception to most of Iran's modern history. Up until the twentieth century, Iran functioned as a multilingual empire, with Turkic dynasties leading the country's political and military institutions and Persian speakers dominating cultural life. This changed under the Pahlavi shahs in the early twentieth century, who promoted Persian nationalism as a state ideology.

Technological advances during the twentieth century fundamentally changed the relationship between most states and their subjects or citizens. In Iran, up until the twentieth century citizens outside the capital city and a handful of large cities had few interactions with state institutions. However, technology allowed the central Iranian government a regular presence in the provinces beginning in the twentieth century. For instance, schools were established wide-

---

[45] Alireza Asgharzadeh, *Iran and the Challenge of Diversity: Islamic Fundamentalism, Aryanist Racism, and Democratic Struggles* (New York City: Palgrave Macmillan, 2007).

ly in Iran's provinces in the 1960s. For many, the newly established schools were their first regular exposure to the Persian language. The Pahlavi regime used state schools and other institutions as a tool to assimilate ethnic minorities into Persian society. The Pahlavi shahs also promoted a state ideology that claimed Persian greatness and its superiority over other ethnic groups and used the schools to promote this ideology.

As part of the government-led assimilation process, the Pahlavi regime also forcibly settled large numbers of Iran's nomadic peoples, including the Bakhtiar, Qashqai and Lurs, starting in 1932. Mohammad Reza Pahlavi conducted another round of forced settlement in 1962, nationalized most pastures, and forced tribal leaders into exile. The Islamic Republic continued the process of eliminating the tribal groupings. As part of this process, Khomeini's regime in 1980 arrested and later executed Khosrow Qashqai, a Qashqai leader who returned from exile following the Islamic Revolution. Despite these efforts by successive regimes, Iran still has a large nomadic population,[46] who are mostly non-Persians. Presumably, in these landscapes and high mountains, these groups use almost exclusively their minority languages and preserve their ethnic culture.

Ethnic Minorities During the Islamic Revolution

The events of the Islamic Revolution in Iran weakened central rule over the provinces. As in other periods of modern Iranian history when Tehran's rule faltered, the ethnic minorities took advantage of the power vacuum and attempted to establish various degrees of self-rule. Almost all of Iran's major ethnic minority groups attempted to achieve autonomy or independence after the fall of the Shah.

A wide coalition of groups with often divergent goals were behind the 1979 revolution against the Pahlavi shahs. While they shared antipathy to the Shah regime, most of the groups that supported the revolution did not share the same vision of the post-revolution governing system. Many members of the ethnic groups that participated in the anti-Shah revolt assumed that democracy would follow the fall of the Shah regime and thus that the ethnic minorities would attain greater freedom. Iran's ethnic minorities, which had particularly suffered under the Pahlavi regime, joined the wide movement that emerged in the late 1970s in Iran, to bring down Pahlavi rule. The ethnic minorities had com-

---

[46] Bernard Hourcade, "La recomposition des identités et des territoires en Iran islamique," *Annales de Géographie*, 3, 2004, p. 521.

pounded grievances against the Shah, suffering from the limitations on all of Iran's citizens while also the brutal policies of the Shah regime to eradicate their cultures and language use and killing of their leaders and many members of their cultural elite.

During the revolution, many activists distributed anti-Shah materials in minority languages, including Azerbaijani and Kurdish, and made ethnic-based demands during their protests against the Shah's regime.[47] However, by the first year of the Islamic revolution, the new government acted to resubdue the minorities who violently clashed with the forces of the new regime. During the first year of the revolution, the new regime in Tehran faced open rebellions from the Kurds, Azerbaijanis, Turkmen, and Arabs.

Tabriz, a city that is populated almost exclusively by Azerbaijanis, was an epicenter of the activity that brought down the Pahlavi shahs. The historiography of the Islamic Republic terms the riots that took place in Tabriz in February 1978 as the beginning of the Islamic Revolution that brought Ayatollah Khomeini to power in Iran in 1979. In response to the killing of 162 demonstrators in Qom on January 9, 1978, Ayatollah Kazim Shariatmadari, an ethnic Azerbaijani and native of Shabestar, called for strikes on the fortieth day of mourning for the victims. His call was especially heeded by Azerbaijani followers in Iran. In Tabriz, the accompanying protests turned violent and set off a series of confrontations between the residents of Tabriz and the Shah's forces and a series of 40-day cycles to commemorate the "Tabriz massacre." The Shah cited ethnic separatism as a factor in the Tabriz protests: "in certain geographic regions, there is no alternative but chauvinism. Iran is one of those regions; otherwise, you would disappear and your name would no longer be Iran, but Iranistan."[48]

Members of Khomeini's inner circle attempted to entice Kurdish and Azerbaijani groups to support the Islamic Revolution with commitments that the new regime would allow language rights for ethnic minorities and a degree of regional autonomy. However, soon after the regime consolidated its power, it became clear that it had no intention of granting either regional autonomy or the right to education in native languages.

Many ethnic leaders had assumed that under an Islamic government there would be greater accommodation of Iran's ethnic minorities than under the Pah-

---
[47] Hasan Javadi, "Research Note: Azeri Publications in Iran," *Critique*, No. 8 (Spring 1996), p. 85.
[48] Interview with Mohammad Reza Pahlavi, Tehran Domestic Service in Persian, May 13, 1978 (FBIS-MEA-78–94). It is interesting to note, that in the 2020s, Iranian monarchist supporters refer to this interview very positively and claim that it supports their view that the ethnic minorities need to be suppressed in Iran.

lavis who had built their state ideology on Persian supremacy. Consequently, ethnic group leaders and activists judged that the end of the Pahlavi regime meant that leaders of the ethnic minorities could live safely in Iran. And thus, many of these leaders returned to Iran from exile abroad following the departure of the Shah, such as the Qashqai leader Khosrow Qashqai and the Kurdish leader Abdul Rahman Ghassemlu. Qashqai was subsequently executed in Iran by Khomeini's regime, and Ghassemlu was assassinated after his escape abroad.

Despite promoting an Islamic ideology, Khomeini and his followers retained the Pahlavi's Persian-centric policies. Khomeini's regime promoted Persian dominance, despite the fact that Islam is a universal religion with that does grant special status to any specific ethnic group. In formal statements, Ayatollah Khomeini—the founder of the Islamic Republic of Iran—stated that Islam that does not differentiate between different ethnic groups:

> Islam is not for a special nationality and does not have Turks, Persians, Arabs and non-Arabs. Islam is for everyone so that race, color, tribe and language have no value in this system. The Qur'an is the book of all, so the propaganda whether this is Arab, that is Turk, or Kurd or Persian, is propaganda propagated by foreigners to plunder the treasury that exists in these countries, through separating Muslims.[49]

He blamed foreigners for promoting separate identities among Muslims:

> Islam has come to unite all the nations of the world, including Arabs, non-Arabs, Turks and Persians and to create a great nation, called the nation of Islamic Ummah, in the world. Thus, those who want to dominate these Islamic states and Islamic centers cannot because of the large community that Muslims form, regardless of their tribe. The plan of the great powers and their allies in the Islamic countries is to separate these Muslim groups, among whom God has created brotherhood calling all of the believer brothers. However, they want to separate them through promoting terms such as the Turkish nation, the Kurdish nation, the Arab nation, the Persian nation; even make them enemies. And this is completely contrary to the direction shown by Holy Quran and Islam. All Muslims are brothers and equals, and none of them is separate from the other. And all of them must be under the flag of Islam and monotheism. Those who divide Muslims under the pretext of nationality, sectarianism and nationalism are the armies of Satan (Devil) and the helpers of the great powers and they are those who oppose the Holy Quran.[50]

---

[49] Ayatollah Khomeini's interview with Amal (Lebanon) in 1978, published in *Sahife-ye-Noor* [A collection of Khomeini's speeches and interviews], Vol. 4. Republished by *Hozeh* news agency, January 25, 2018.

[50] *Aparat*, https://www.aparat.com/v/LF6EO/امام_خمینی_-_عرب_و_عجم_و_ترک_و_فارس

Directly following the Islamic Revolution and during the uprisings of Azerbaijanis and Kurds against Khomeini's rule in December 1979, he stated:

> Sometimes the word minorities is used to refer to people such as the Kurds, Lurs, Turks, Persians, Baluch, and such. These people should not be called minorities, because this term assumes that there is a difference between these brothers. In Islam, such a difference has no place at all. There is no difference between Muslims who speak different languages, for instance, the Arabs or the Persians. It is very probable that such problems have been created by those who do not wish the Muslim countries to be united...They create the issues of nationalism, of pan-Iranianism, pan-Turkism, and such isms, which are contract to Islamic doctrines. They plan is to destroy Islam and the Islamic philosophy.[51]

However, despite these declarations that all ethnic groups are equal under Islam, the Islamic Republic placed Persian language and culture at the center of the new regime and the Islamic Republic repressed Iran's ethnic minorities. The new regime banned genuine representatives of the minority groups from participating in government institutions, such as the Assembly of Experts, and banned the political organizations that represented the ethnic minorities.[52]

In the period of the anti-Shah revolution, publication in the minority languages flourished. During this period, many new publications were established in the minority languages. In May 1979, Professor Javad Heyat published the first volume of the journal *Varliq* (existence). Professor Heyat chose the name *Varliq* to indicate that Azerbaijanis and their distinct culture still exist in Iran.[53] Azerbaijanis in Iran began publication of the newspaper *Ulduz* on January 17, 1979, with articles in both Azerbaijani and Persian.[54] Authors called for the granting of language rights. A left-wing journal, *Yoldash* (comrade), was also published in this period in the Azerbaijani language.

Following Khomeini's rise to power, the regime itself began to publish a journal in Azerbaijani, *Islami Birliq* (Islamic Unity). This journal was published in the Azerbaijani language in both Arabic script and Cyrillic. Evidently the new regime chose to publish it also in Cyrillic in an attempt to influence Azerbaijanis in the neighboring USSR, which at the time read Azerbaijani in the Cyrillic script. As the Khomeini regime consolidated power, it became more difficult to publish

---

51 Ayatollah Khomeini, Radio Tehran, December 17, 1979. Accessed via BBC Summary of World Broadcasts.
52 Charles G. MacDonald, "The Kurdish Question in the 1980s," in in Milton J. Esman and Itamar Rabinovich, *Ethnicity, Pluralism, and the State in the Middle East* (Ithaca and London: Cornell University Press, 1988), p. 243.
53 Javad Heyat's interview with the author in 1999.
54 E.Ch. Baaev, "Iuzhnyi Azerbaidzhan v iranskoi revoliutsii 1978–1979 gg, *Cənubi Azərbaycan Məsələləri* (Baku: Elm, 1989), p. 128.

books and media in minority languages. Albeit, under the new regime, publications in languages other than Persian remained far more tolerated than during the Pahlavi period.

During the first year of the revolution, many ethnic-based political movements appeared as well, some of which adopted Islamic names and rhetoric in an attempt to survive under the new regime. Associates and family members of Ayatollah Shariatmadari, the main Ayatollah followed by Azerbaijanis in Iran, established the Muslim People's Republican Party (MPRP, Khalq-e Musulman) on February 25, 1979, comprised mostly of ethnic Azerbaijanis from the northwest provinces and Tehran bazaari of Azerbaijani origin. The party called for autonomy for ethnic minorities within the Iranian state.[55] Ayatollah Shariatmardari's son, Hassan, was one of the leaders of the MPRP.

During the revolutionary period, the communist movements in Iran, in which ethnic minorities predominated also advocated for granting rights to the country's minorities. The April 1979 Plenum of the *Tudeh* party issued a declaration stating:

> The Republic can grow stronger and experience an upswing only if all people in our homeland can participate freely and actively in political and social life, if all religions, traditions and customs, national culture and language of all people are recognized and respected. The granting of administrative and cultural autonomy to all people of the country, within the framework of a united democratic republic, is a necessary condition for implementing national unity, and for protecting the country's independence and territorial integrity.[56]

Khomeini Tricks the Ethnic Minorities by Appealing to Ethnic Sentiments

To attain ethnic support before Khomeini fully consolidated power, his representatives pledged to guarantee minority language and cultural rights under the new government. His emissaries conducted negotiations with representatives of the ethnic minorities on the inclusion in the new Iranian constitutional provisions protecting rights for these groups. Clearly, Khomeini and his inner circle assessed that such guarantees of minority rights were important to most of Iran's ethnic minorities; thus they made this promise as an effort to entice them to support the new regime.

---

[55] For more on additional Azerbaijani groups that were active promoting ethnic and language rights in Iran in the early revolution period, see Brenda Shaffer, *Borders and Brethren: Iran and the Challenge of Azerbaijani Identity* (Cambridge, MA: MIT Press, 2002), pp. 90–95.
[56] Tudeh Central Committee Sixteenth Plenum Declaration, published in *Horizont* (East Berlin), No. 14 (1979), pp. 11–12 (FBIS-MEA-079–070).

The Kurds and many Azerbaijanis hoped the new government would adopt a federal structure that would give the provinces a wide degree of autonomy. Kurdish representatives submitted several demands to Khomeini's representatives, which included the request that Kurds would be administered in a single unit and that "Kurdistan's autonomy would be written into the draft constitution."[57] According to David McDowall, Kurdish representatives demanded autonomy for West Azerbaijan Province, where Kurds were not the majority, and Ilam where Lurs numbered about the same as Kurds.[58]

Khomeini's representatives circulated a draft text of the Constitution in June 1979 which did not offer autonomy, but stated that "Persians, Turks, Kurds, Arabs, Baluch, Turkomans and others will enjoy equal rights."[59] However, in the next draft, circulated in November 1979, the mention of explicit rights of these ethnic minorities was dropped. Khomeini stated at this point, "even to talk about ethnic minorities in the Islamic domain was an offense against true religion."[60]

In the final draft of the Constitution submitted for approval in a December 1979 referendum, mention of Iran's ethnic minorities were limited to: Article 15 which states that the Islamic Republic of Iran will officially permit the use of the "regional and tribal" languages in their press and mass media and will allow teaching "of their literature" in schools. Article 19 of Iran's Constitution states that "all people of Iran, whatever the ethnic group or tribe to which they belong, enjoy equal rights; and color, race, language, and the like, do not bestow any privilege." Note that these clauses do not guarantee the right to education in the native languages. Moreover, even the stated rights in the Constitution have not been upheld in the Islamic Republic.

Rebellions: Tehran Imposes its Rule on the Provinces

During the first year of Khomeini's rule, the regime faced open rebellions from most of Iran's ethnic minorities and its forces engaged to reestablish Tehran's rule in the provinces. A turning point in the relationship between the new government in Iran and the ethnic minorities was the December 2, 1979 constitutional referendum on the Constitution of the Islamic Republic. Most of Iran's ethnic

---

57 David McDowall, *A Modern History of the Kurds* (London: I.B. Tauris, 1997), p. 263.
58 David McDowall, *A Modern History of the Kurds* (London: I.B. Tauris, 1997), p. 262.
59 David McDowall, *A Modern History of the Kurds* (London: I.B. Tauris, 1997), p. 270.
60 David McDowall, *A Modern History of the Kurds* (London: I.B. Tauris, 1997), p. 271.

minority groups boycotted the referendum due to the absence of provisions in the new Constitution that would guarantee them rights. For instance, eighty percent of the Azerbaijanis residing in northwest Iran boycotted the referendum. All the Kurds boycotted the constitutional referendum, with the exception of those in Kermanshah, who are predominately Shia. Kurds also burnt ballot boxes in many locations in Iran.[61] Almost all of Iran's Turkmen boycotted the constitutional referendum. Soon thereafter, some ethnic minorities launched violent rebellions against the new regime.

In parallel, Ayatollah Shariatmadari, the leading Azerbaijani ayatollah, expressed opposition to the Constitution text. He was especially opposed to the *Velayat-e faqih* concept that would turn religious leaders into political leaders, in contradiction to the Shia tradition, where religious figures remain guides only in the theocratic/moral sphere and the political leaders operate in separation from the religious figures. Moreover, Shariatmadari opposed the centralization of all political power in Tehran and supported granting greater rights to local government. This preference for local power may have been rooted in his upbringing among Azerbaijanis and his sense of Azerbaijani identity.[62]

Despite Shariatmadari's opposition to the content of the proposed Constitution, on the day of the referendum, the official Radio Tabriz broadcast a *fatwah* in his name urging locals to vote to approve the Constitution. When the deception became clear to the public, demonstrators came out to the streets in Tabriz to protest the "rigged" referendum and the treatment of Azerbaijanis in the Islamic Republic.[63] The protests continued the following day and on December 5, 1979 an attack was conducted on Shariatmadari's home in Qom, killing one of his guards.

On December 6, a massive demonstration broke out in Tabriz, in response to the deception and the attack on Shariatmadari's home. The demonstrators took control of the communications tower in Tabriz and the Azerbaijan Province governor's office and residence. In addition, the protestors gained control of the Tabriz airport. Iranian army forces stationed in Tabriz refused to confront the demonstrators, and air force units stationed in Tabriz and other soldiers in uniform joined the protests. The rebellion spread beyond Tabriz and the Azerbaijani forces gained control of government buildings and infrastructure in many Azerbaijani-populated cities, including Urmiya and Ardebil. In the town of Germi,

---

61 David McDowall, *A Modern History of the Kurds* (London: I.B. Tauris, 1997), p. 271.
62 For more on Ayatollah Shariatmadari's view on ethnic issues, see Brenda Shaffer, *Borders and Brethren: Iran and the Challenge of Azerbaijani Identity* (Cambridge, MA: MIT Press, 2002), pp. 101–103.
63 Iranian Tabriz Domestic Service in Azerbaijani, December 2, 1979 (FBIS-MEA-79–234).

near Ardabil, the Azerbaijani rebels took control of all the government installations, including the local prison, from which they released all the prisoners and put in their place the local IRGC members.[64]

The Azerbaijani demonstrators demanded local control over appointments of officials in the Azerbaijani-populated province and local media. MPRP representatives stated that their goal was to take control of Azerbaijan Province, and they called for the removal of Khomeini's representative in the province and Tehran-appointed government officials there. Banners displayed at the Tabriz demonstrations also called for the "self-determination of the peoples in Iran," thus their agenda evidently was not just self-rule of the Azerbaijani-populated areas, but of self-rule for other minorities in Iran. Interestingly, these banners calling for rights of all peoples were printed in Persian, perhaps with the goal of attracting the support of other ethnic minorities in the rebellion. Participants in the demonstrations reported that all the speeches were in the Azerbaijani language, and that any speakers that attempted to address the demonstrations in Persian were booed. The MPRP issued a document during the demonstrations that stated that "the rights of the people of Azerbaijan, like the Kurds, will be respected."[65] Thus, they expressed solidary with the Kurdish rebellion that was taking place in tandem.

Ayatollah Khomeini quickly and cleverly acted to quash the Tabriz rebellion. On December 6, 1979 Ayatollah Khomeini arrived at Ayatollah's Shariatmadari's home in Qom. The visit was projected publicly as an act of reconciliation, however, in reality Khomeini threatened Shariatmadari during their meeting. Khomeini stated that if the Azerbaijani rebels did not vacate the Tabriz communications tower within 24 hours, forces loyal to Khomeini would start bombing Tabriz. In parallel, Khomeini loyalists deployed forces in Tabriz, aided by the Tudeh Party forces present in the city. Shariatmadari feared that Tabriz would become a "second Kurdistan," referring to the March 1979 massacre of Kurds who had rebelled against Khomeini's rule. In line with Shariatmadari's typical balanced and moderate approach, he chose to avoid bloodshed and called on the demonstrators in Tabriz to end their rebellion and to vacate the communications tower and government buildings. Shariatmadari's call for the demonstrators to stand down was presented to the public as part of a compromise agreement according to which local Azerbaijanis would retain control of affairs in the Azerbaijani Province and Shariatmadari would be empowered by the central government to approve local appointments. Shariatmadari requested that the

---

64 Author's interview with an eyewitness in Germi.
65 AFP in Spanish, December 6, 1979 (FBIS-MEA-79–237).

protestors relinquish control of the communications tower and other government installations. The Azerbaijani demonstrators agreed to his request and assumed the compromise deal was sincere. This was a turning point in the Khomeini regime's efforts to secure control across Iranian territory.

Upon gaining control of the critical buildings in Tabriz, Khomeini's representatives proceeded to arrest the leading Azerbaijani activists. The public soon understood that Khomeini had not offered Shariatmadari a sincere agreement and that they had relinquished control of the communications tower and other key infrastructure in vain. This revelation triggered a new cycle of violence within which the Tabriz communications tower exchange hands several times during December 1979.

On December 13, 1979, 700,000 demonstrators gathered in Tabriz to protest against Khomeini and against the loss of local power. The demonstrations called for the removal of non-Azerbaijani military forces from the province, rejected the new Constitution, and called for the release of the Azerbaijanis imprisoned by Khomeini's forces.[66]

Khomeini's group deployed additional forces to Tabriz to quell the uprising. During this confrontation, several Azerbaijani activists were executed by the regime's forces. On January 19, 1980 Khomeini loyalists arrested officers and soldiers from the Tabriz Air Base, accusing them of providing arms to the local rebels and plotting to overthrow the Khomeini regime.[67] As Khomeini's forces consolidated power in Tabriz, they continued to execute large numbers of individuals that they considered supporters of the Azerbaijani rebellion. An especially large number of executions of Azerbaijani anti-Khomeini activists took place on May 22, 1980.

Khomeini demanded that Shariatmadari condemn the rebels and call on the MPRP to disband. Shariatmadari issued a cynical reply, stating that there is no need to do so, since the government could just "itself declare all the political parties outlawed, gradually branding them as American, Zionist and anti-revolutionary." Shariatmadari was referring to the Khomeini practice to delegitimize those that disagreed with him as well as the ethnic minorities as foreign agents. This practice of branding as foreign agents ethnic minorities merely seeking rights has continued throughout the Islamic Republic.

The Tabriz rebellion and subsequent treatment of Shariatmadari was a turning point for many Azerbaijanis' relationship with the new Khomeini regime. Is-

---

[66] Nicholas M. Nikazmerad, "A Chronological Survey of the Iranian Revolution," *Iranian Studies*, Vol. 13, Nos. 1–4 (1980), p. 366.
[67] *Tehran Times*, January 21, 1980.

lamic-leaning, conservative Azerbaijanis saw their own ayatollah humiliated and stripped of power. Those who expected that the post-Shah government would end the ban on teaching the languages of the ethnic minorities, and that they could receive equal treatment under the new regime, understood that they had erred.

When Shariatmadari spoke out against the continuation of the Iran-Iraq War after Iran had succeeded in expelling Iraqi forces from the territory of Iran, Khomeini used the incident as an excuse to further limit his activity and influence. Khomeini declared the defrocking of Shariatmadari as an ayatollah (even though he had no authority to do so and there is no formal process of this nature in Shia Islam) and condemned him to house arrest. He was also denied medical care and died under house arrest in April 1986.

In parallel with the Tabriz uprising, the Kurdish anti-Khomeini rebellion continued. Throughout 1979, Tehran failed to reimpose its rule over the Kurdish-populated regions. When it became clear in December 1979 that the new regime had no intention to accommodate their demands, especially for autonomy, the Kurds launched a revolt. Most of the Kurdish factions aimed to achieve autonomy in Iran, while others aimed for all-out independence. Sheikh Ezzedine Hosseini, a leftist-leaning Kurdish religious leader who cooperated with the Kurdish nationalist groups, said: "We want to remain in Iran; there's no question about that...Either President Bani-Sadr agrees to our autonomy demands or we fight. And if that's the case, the Kurds will fight until there is not one scrap of bread left."[68]

In its initial attempt to quell the December 1979 Kurdish rebellion, the regime reportedly killed more than 10,000 Kurds.[69] It took over a decade for Tehran to subdue the Kurds and militarily defeat them. Throughout the 1980s, Tehran conducted a war in Kurdistan to reimpose its rule, at the same time it was fighting Iraq. Human Rights Watch, in its 1997 report, stated that between 1980 and 1992 "more than 271 Iranian Kurdish villages were destroyed and depopulated" in Iran. Between July and December 1993 alone, during a major offensive against Kurdish armed groups, 113 villages were bombed.[70]

Iran's Turkmen also launched a revolt against Khomeini's rule in Iran during the revolutionary period. The Turkmen rebellion is a relatively under-researched historical event, receiving only scant attention in the history books on the period

---

[68] "Iranian Kurds: A continuing revolt against the revolution," *Christian Science Monitor*, June 13, 1980.
[69] David McDowall, *A Modern History of the Kurds* (London: I.B. Tauris, 1997), p. 262.
[70] *Human Rights Watch* 1997, quoted in Alam Saleh, *Ethnic Identity and the State in Iran* (New York City: Palgrave Macmillan, 2013), p. 69.

of the revolution. Turkmen activists, like most other ethnic groups in Iran, called for boycotting the December 1979 constitutional referendum. The Turkmen declared a short-lived independent republic – the Turkmen-Sahra Autonomous State in 1978, when the Pahlavi power had already diminished. Sahra continued to claim independence during the revolution period in 1979. In took the Khomeini regime a year to subdue the Turkmen rebellion.

During the Islamic Republic's March 1979 recapture of the rebel city of Gonbad Kavus, Khomeini's forces killed over 100 Turkmen, including unarmed women and children. Following the completion of the capture of the Turkmen-populated areas, the new regime ordered the execution of hundreds of Turkmen. As the regime consolidated its rule in Iran, additional Turkmen leaders were executed in 1982–83.

The Arabs in Khuzestan also rebelled against the new government in late April 1979. In the process of the new regime quelling the revolt, hundreds of ethnic Arabs were killed. The Baluch also boycotted the December 1979 referendum and revolted against Khomeini's rule in Baluchistan. Khomeini's forces succeeded in quashing their rebellion as well.

In contrast to mainstream historiography on Iran, when central rule has weakened, ethnic groups in Iran have taken advantage of the opportunity and sought self-rule. This is clearly seen by the rebellions of almost all of Iran's main ethnic groups against the rule of the Islamic Republic.

Approach of the Islamic Republic Post-Revolution to Iran's Ethnic Minorities

Despite championing an Islamic ideology that should not differentiate between ethnic groups and languages, the Islamic Republic adopted most of the Pahlavi era measures against ethnic groups. The new regime prohibited the use of minority languages in official settings, such as schools and courts. The regime has diligently enforced the use of the Persian language, even expanding requirements for pupils to arrive at first grade already proficient in Persian. The regime regularly claims that the people of Iran are united in their shared love for the Persian language. However, the regime would not have to resort to widespread and often violent mechanisms to enforce the use of Persian and punishments for teachers that are caught using the minority languages in conversations with pupils, if the use of Persian was so widespread in Iran.

In addition, the Islamic Republic suppresses political activity by ethnic minorities, including by assassinating and executing political and cultural leaders both in Iran and abroad and prohibiting all political and some cultural activity of the ethnic minorities. The Islamic Republic arrests and imprisons, on various national security charges, citizens who join ethnically based political organizations or parties, including those that advocate for their rights as Iranian citizens and do not advocate for separatism or self-rule for their ethnic group.

When faced with challenges from ethnic groups in which a large percentage of the group are Sunni, such as the Kurds, Baluch, and Arabs, Tehran tries to frame the challenge in religious rather than ethnic terms. The regime claims that the perpetrators of anti-regime activity from these groups are motivated by religious goals and describes them as members of the Islamic State, al-Qaeda, or other extremist Sunni organizations. Ethnic minority activists that are Sunni are also often referred to by the regime as *takfiri* (apostates). Tehran prefers to categorize this anti-regime activity as Sunni-based, since Tehran does not want to openly acknowledge the ethnic-based challenges to the regime. This policy also attempts to elicit Western sympathy for Tehran's efforts to address a so-called common extremist challenge. Many Western based academics and regime sympathizers in the West follow the regime line in portraying anti-regime activity as Sunni-based and not ethnic-based.[71] The Western press often also mimics the regime line and refers to anti-regime or violent activity of Baluch, Arabs, and others, as "Sunni extremist" instead of ethnic-based. *New York Times* correspondent Thomas Erdbrink, for instance, described tensions in Sistan-Baluchistan Province as "a hotbed of Sunni resistance against the Shiite Islamic Republic of Iran" instead of Baluch-based anti-regime activity.[72]

Not only does the Islamic Republic deny the ethnic motivation in the anti-regime activity of the minority group, but Tehran also imposes Shia education on those groups that are Sunni. Among Iran's ethnic minorities, the Baluch and Turkmen are predominately Sunni and about half of the Ahwazi and Kurds are Sunni.

The regime often denies the existence of non-Persian groups in Iran. For instance, state media, publications for schools, leading Persian intellectuals, and senior government representatives frequently claim that Iran's minorities are genetically Persian but stopped speaking the Persian language after foreign invaders forced their languages on the Persians.

---

71 For example, see Scherezade Faramarzi, "Iran's Sunnis Resist Extremism, but for How Long?" Atlantic Council, April 2018 (https://www.atlanticcouncil.org/wp-content/uploads/2018/04/Iran_s_Sunnis_WEB.pdf).
72 Thomas Erdbrink, "Iran Executes 16 Sunni Insurgents in Retaliation for an Attack," *New York Times*, October 16, 2013.

Ali Yunesi, who served as an advisor to President Hassan Rouhani and had headed Iran's Intelligence Ministry, made this claim publicly several times. Yunesi said that Iran's Turkish speakers are actually "Persians who were forced to speak *Torki*."[73]

By claiming that the minorities are actually Persian in origin, the government and Iranian intellectuals justify attempts to "return" them to Persian speakers. Members of the ethnic minority often counter this claim by joking that it is amazing how the foreign conquerors spent so much time forcing their language on Iran's highlanders, alluding to the fact that most of Iran's mountain dwellers speak minority languages.

In contrast to those Iranian officials who claim that the Turks in Iran were actually originally Persians, the late IRGC Commander Qassem Suleimani claimed that the descendants of Turkic dynasties that live in Iran are not Iranian. Suleimani claimed: "Turks are aliens and non-Iranians. For hundreds of years (during Turkic rule in Iran), Iran had no history. Non-Iranians like the Seljuks invaded and ruled Iran."[74]

Official educational curricula attempt to assimilate Iran's ethnic minorities by teaching them that they are Persian in origin. For example, in 2020, the Ministry of Education published a magazine for second and third graders claiming that "Azeris" are actually Persians whose language was changed several centuries ago.[75] School materials also depict Iran's Ahwazi population as Persians who neighboring Arabs "Arabized."

Official media in Iran often refer to the minority groups as "Arabic speakers" or "Kurdish speakers" rather than Arabs and Kurds, indicating that they are not separate ethnic groups, but just Iranians that speak a different language than Persian. In addition, the government often refers to Iran's ethnic minorities as "tribes," portraying them not as separate ethnic groups or nations, but Iranians whose cultural traditions recall their pastoral past. For instance, in response to Turkish President Recep Tayyip Erdogan's 2020 poem reading in which he appealed to Azerbaijani Turks in Iran, Ali Shamkhani, the Secretary of Iran's Supreme National Security Council, stated that, "Fear of tribes belongs to a govern-

---

[73] "Iranian MPs of Turkish origin slam Rouhani's aide over Azeri remarks," *Daily Sabah*, April 22, 2018 (https://www.dailysabah.com/mideast/2018/04/22/iranian-mps-of-turkish-origin-slam-rouhanis-aide-over-azeri-remarks).

[74] @ArazNew_org, *Twitter*, April 30, 2021 (https://twitter.com/ArazNews_org/status/1388130177004232707?s=20&t=8f1_ZwO3tfSqdfPLA8hR4g).

[75] Islamic Republic of Iran Ministry of Education, Educational Research and Planning Organization, *Roshd Noamooz*, Series 1, Number 317, September 2020.

ment that confronts them with sword and discrimination, not Iran which is the paradise of tribes."[76]

Most Persians and many members of the ethnic minorities differ on their interpretation of what Iranian identity means. Persians claim Iranian identity is supra-ethnic, not connected to a specific ethnic group. Members of the ethnic minorities say, in contrast, that in reality the Iranian promoted identity is predicated on Persian language and culture. They claim that the version of one nation promoted by Iranian nationalists depends on submission to Persian dominance under the name Iran. Supporting their view is the fact that the only official representations of Iranian culture and the state allowed are those of Persians. For example, the team that represented Iran in the 2020 Tokyo Olympic Games was called the Persian Stars (*Setaregan-e Parsi*), and in previous games was called the Persian Cougars (*Yuz-Haye Parsi*). This is akin to calling a national British sports team "English." While the Persian title is allowed in the Islamic Republic, that of the ethnic minorities is usually prohibited. For example, a private entertainment company started a talent show competition for Azerbaijani speakers in Iran called the "Turk Show." The authorities forced them to change to a generic name of *Ulduzlar* (stars in Azerbaijani) to remove the ethnic group connection in the name.[77]

As part of its policy to eradicate minority cultures and identity in Iran, the government often bars citizens from registering minority names for children and receiving birth certificates for their newborn children with minority names. Government authorities even at times bar registration of modern Arabic names for children. Ahad Jodi, director of the Civil Registry in East Azerbaijan Province, noted that despite these government efforts, 40 percent of names in the province are Turkic ones.[78] In 2021, the government announced a prohibition on the use of non-Persian names for shops and professional organizations in Tehran.

---

[76] "Fear of tribes belongs to a government that confronts them with sword and discrimination, not Iran which is the paradise of tribes," *Iranian Students News Agency* (ISNA) October 23, 2021 (https://www.isna.ir/news/1400080100478/).

[77] Azerbaycan, "Changing the name of the big competition 'Turk show' to 'Ulduzlar' under the pressure of Pan-Persians," *YouTube*, June 24, 2020 (https://www.youtube.com/watch?v=2kKtbQMs2eo); On the website of the show, the original name remains—Turk talent show. But, the new formal name was changed to Ulduzlar (Stars) (http://turktalent.ir); (https://www.gunaz.tv/fa/new/SH.A208-1592991390).

[78] "40 percent of the names in East Azerbaijan are Turkish," *Azar Anjoman News*, January 31, 2021 (https://aazaranjoman.ir/?p=14170).

Figure 4: The Government Removes a Ferdowsi Statue in Salmas Following Protests in 2015

In its efforts to mold minorities into the Persian identity, the regime often promotes Persian symbols and figures that the minorities disdain for their approach toward their groups. For instance, Ferdowsi's *Shahnameh*, one of the most revered works of Persian literature, portrays Arabs and Turks highly negatively. In several cities where minorities dominate, such as Salmas, Ardabil, and Ahvaz, the local government removed statues of Ferdowsi in 2015 following violent demonstrations, though they later returned them on orders from the central government.

At times, the Islamic Republic has implemented policies that aimed to narrow the development gap between the Persian-populated heartland of Iran and the minority-dominated provinces. Tehran's programs had mixed impacts on issues of identity. Aware of the large disparity in economic and infrastructure conditions between the center and provinces, Tehran initiated development programs for Iran's provinces in the 1990s. The programs affected the development of ethnic minority identities in two ways: The programs improved the economic situation and state of infrastructure in ethnic-dominated areas and this helped minorities feel they had benefitted from being part of Iran. This response was observed, for instance, among Iranian Kurds, who had engaged for more than a decade in an all-out war with Tehran. On the other hand, these development programs facilitated regular contact between Persians and the minority groups, such as through providing scholarships for minority students to study in universities in Tehran. For some of the minority members, these encounters strengthened their identity, as they experienced first-hand discrimination and racism and also perceived fundamental differences between the groups. In addition, they observed the inequality between Iran's center and periphery regions.

Tehran Knows

Tehran doesn't openly publish data on Iran's ethnic groups or Persian language proficiency. Iranian officials project the image that Iran is united and often portrays the ethnic minorities as just colorful or tribal Iranians. While they often publicly deny that Iran faces any challenge from its minorities, regime officials periodically make statements and commission internal government studies that indicate otherwise. These statements and studies provide a window into how the regime actually views the ethnicity question. The findings of some of these studies have been published or disseminated among officials and researchers. The studies noted that new developments, such as widespread access to social media and the establishment of the neighboring Republic of Azerbaijan, up-ended earlier assumptions about the bedrock allegiance of Iranian ethnic groups.

Contrary to the official government line, Ali Yunesi, after serving as Iranian minister of intelligence, remarked in 2005, "I see no political threat towards Iran in the future, but if any crisis occurs, it will be ethnic and societal."[79] In November 2008, General Gholamali Rashid, who served as deputy commander-in-chief of Iran's joint armed forces, stated that Kurdistan, Baluchistan, and Khuzestan are hotbeds of armed opposition that Tehran must confront.[80] In discussing the wave of anti-regime protests in November 2019, IRGC Spokesman Brigadier General Ramezan Sharif declared that "secessionists" were involved.[81]

Iran's Interior Ministry periodically conducts internal government studies on popular beliefs and attitudes, including on issues of ethnic identification. A 2004 ministry study concluded that:

---

[79] Alam Saleh, *Ethnic Identity and the State in Iran* (New York City: Palgrave Macmillan, 2013), p. 93.
[80] "General Rashid: We are on the verge of a possible war," *BBC Persian*, November 23, 2008 (https://www.bbc.com/persian/iran/2008/11/081123_ka_rashid).
[81] "Iran warns regional states of consequences if they stoked unrest," *Reuters*, November 23, 2019. (https://www.reuters.com/article/us-iran-gasoline-protests/iran-warns-regional-states-of-consequences-if-they-stoked-unrest-idUSKBN1XX07O).

ethnic identity awareness/commitment among major ethnic groups – that is, the extent to which groups' primordial claim to identity is their ethnicity rather than their national citizenship as "Iranians" – is increasing and is as follows: Azeris 83 percent; Baluch 84 percent; Turkmen 79 percent, Arabs 76 percent, and Kurds 76 percent.[82]

In the mid-2000s, Iran's Center for Strategic Studies conducted several studies on the country's minorities on behalf of the Iranian parliament, the Majles. According to a 2007 report, "the country will face even more serious internal unrest unless the government better addresses the needs of its ethnic minorities."[83]

Iranian scholars employed by government research institutes have also published several studies on specific provinces and ethnic groups. Almost all pointed to a trend of rising ethnic political activity and recommended that the central government improve services and extend rights to these provinces and groups.[84]

Use of Ethnic Minority Languages in Schools and Official Settings

Tehran does not allow Iran's ethnic minorities to operate schools in their languages or to teach their languages in school alongside Persian. In addition, government services in Iran are not offered in minority languages. For example, police interrogations and court appearances must be conducted in Persian, and citizens under investigation do not receive translations to their native languages, potentially paving the way for wrongful convictions.

The Islamic Republic's Constitution formally guarantees equal rights to all "people of Iran," regardless of ethnic or tribal background. "[C]olor, race, language, and the like, do not bestow any privilege," states Article 19. Article 15 designates Persian as the Islamic Republic's official language: "The documents, correspondence, official texts, and schoolbooks must all be in this language and script." Article 15 also states that the use of "regional and ethnic languages in

---

[82] Alam Saleh, *Ethnic Identity and the State in Iran* (New York City: Palgrave Macmillan, 2013), p. 99.

[83] Alam Saleh, *Ethnic Identity and the State in Iran* (New York City: Palgrave Macmillan, 2013), p. 96.

[84] On the Baluch in Iran's official *Journal of Strategic Studies*, see: Morad Kaviani Rad, "Political Regionalism in Iran: The Case of Iranian Baluchestan," *Journal of Strategic Studies*, Volume 10, Issue 1, 2007, pp. 89–121 (https://www.magiran.com/paper/467381?lang=en). On the Kurds, see: J. Haghpanah, *The Kurds and the Islamic Republic of Iran's Foreign Policy* (Tehran: Cultural Research Institution, 2009); "Ethnic Azerbaijan Nationalism: An Overview in Iran," *Strategic Studies Quarterly*, Volume 5, Number 2, 2002, pp. 573–581.

the press, the mass media, and literature at schools is freely permitted." Thus, minority literature formally can be taught, but education in the other tongue is not a protected right.

Arabic has a different status in Iran than the other minority languages. Article 16 of the Islamic Republic's Constitution guarantees the right to study Arabic in grades above elementary school, but Arabic is not allowed as a language of school instruction.[85] Quranic Arabic is taught in Iranian schools to all Iranians. However, spoken Arabic is not taught or permitted as a language of instruction for Arab citizens of Iran. Modern spoken Arabic and Quranic Arabic are vastly different.

Individuals that have undergone police interrogations in ethnically populated regions in Iran reported the almost comical nature in which the authorities uphold the mandate to only use Persian in official settings, while they need to communicate and interrogate suspects and others with which they share a native language. The local languages are commonly used in conversations, interrogations, and in police stations in the ethnically populated provinces. However, in written documents, the questions and answers appear only in Persian. The police officers usually speak in their mother tongue when they talk to their colleagues on the phone (even when they are talking to superior authorities), but when they talk on the police wireless system, they must speak in Persian. Reportedly, if they speak in their mother tongue, they will be punished. If the accused is not proficient in Persian, the police, interrogator or prosecutor will ask him questions in his native language and translate his answers into Persian in the interrogation report. The suspect must then sign a text that he is unable to read, that the suspect does not know whether the answers are translated accurately.[86]

The fact that half of Iranian pupils are not educated in their native tongue creates an educational challenge and disadvantages the non-Persian pupils. Accordingly, the minority provinces fill the lowest ranks of Iran's educational levels. Khuzestan, for instance, is ranked twenty-eighth in education among Iran's 31 provinces. This is not surprising when only 20 percent of the minorities residing in the province report speaking Persian at a high level.

Children and their families report that teachers regularly humiliate minority children due to their accents and lack of proficiency in Persian and insult their local cultures, which results in high drop-out rates among minorities. In addition, many minority children are held back grades because they cannot pass Persian proficiency tests.

---

85 Pupils in Iran study Quranic Arabic from middle school through high school.
86 Author's interview, May 2022.

Various officials in Iran's education system have pointed out the negative consequences of prohibiting the ethnic minority children from study in their native languages. For instance, Ali Asghar Fani, minister of education under President Rouhani, stated that teaching the ethnic languages should be a priority of the ministry. He referred to the constitutional provision that allows teaching of minority languages alongside Persian: "We must implement Article 15. A series of plans have been made during Mr. Khatami's period, but have finally been stopped. These programs should now be re-examined. Teaching ethnic languages in schools is my priority."[87] Despite these declarations, the government made no policy changes that would allow for the teaching of minority languages.

In the early part of Rouhani's tenure as president, he flirted with fulfilling some of his campaign promises to allow the ethnic minorities some use of their languages. For instance, Tehran allowed the opening in Ilam Province of a center that gave courses in Kurdish. However, the government quickly closed down the center when it saw the large number of participants that showed up for the courses.[88] Members of Iran's Persian Language and Literature Academy also strongly criticized Rouhani's exploration of allowing the ethnic minorities to study their languages alongside Persian. Salim Neysari, a member of the academy, called the plan "very dangerous. In a meeting with Iranian education minister, Ali Asghar Fani, members of the academy expressed concern about teaching regional (ethnic) languages, viewing it as a serious threat to the Persian language."[89]

In fact, over the years, the Islamic Republic government prohibitions against minority languages have become harsher. The government has prosecuted teachers for providing private lessons to students in their mother tongues. In 2021, Tehran sentenced one teacher, Zahra Mohammadi, to 10 years in prison for giving private lessons in Kurdish language to children in Kurdistan Province, in Sanandaj.[90] Many teachers were reprimanded and even fired in 2020–2022 during the period of online education due to Covid-19 shutdowns of schools, when it became apparent through observation of the online lessons that teachers were conversing with students in the minority languages, and not in Persian as obligated by the state. Despite government prohibitions, online teaching revealed that

---

[87] *Jamaran News*, October 4, 2013 (https://www.jamaran.news/fa/tiny/news-32094).
[88] "Iranian Authorities Close Down Kurdish Language School," *Rudaw*, September 13, 2019. (https://www.rudaw.net/english/middleeast/iran/16092013).
[89] "Teaching mother tongues in the provinces smells like conspiracy," *Mehr News*, January 27, 2014. (https://www.mehrnews.com/news/2222873/).
[90] United Nations Human Rights Council, "Situation of human rights in the Islamic Republic of Iran," January 11, 2021, p. 9 (https://undocs.org/pdf?symbol=en/A/HRC/46/50).

teachers throughout Iran were still using languages other than Persian in many locations.

Tehran has also subjected teachers to language demands. According to Iran's Ministry of Education, applicants with "thick accents" are not qualified to serve as teachers. Thus, teaching is *de facto* limited to highly proficient Persian speakers.[91]

While Tehran has long barred schools and government institutions from using minority languages, before 2019 the regime took few measures to obstruct minority-language use in informal settings, such as in homes. In May 2019, however, Iran's Ministry of Education announced that five-year-old and six-year-old children would be required to take proficiency tests in the Persian language.[92] Tehran would then bar children who fail the test from attending regular schools, placing them instead in special education schools for children with disabilities that would classify these children as "slow learners" or hearing impaired. This policy effectively forces families to begin teaching and speaking Persian at home. The government allocated funds to establish pre-school centers to teach the minority children Persian.

In contrast to the increased prohibitions in schools, Tehran has allowed several universities in the provinces to offer local languages and literature as an academic discipline. However, university instruction is not offered in minority languages. For instance, since 2016, the University of Tabriz has offered B.A.-level degrees in Azerbaijani language and literature.[93] Since 2015, a degree in Kurdish language and literature has been available at the University of Kurdistan in Sanandaj. The Islamic Republic has never banned the study of Arabic in universities. In the Azerbaijani language and literature degree program at the University of Tabriz, Persian language textbooks are still used for many of the courses, such as linguistics and literary history.

---

91 "Iran Says Women Who Are Infertile Or Have 'Too Much Facial Hair' Can't Be Teachers," *Radio Free Europe/Radio Liberty*, August 24, 2017 (https://www.rferl.org/a/iran-education-ministry-teachers-rules-women-infertile-too-much-facial-hair/28694884.html).
92 "Persian-language adequacy test to assess the health of new students on the agenda," *Iranian Students News Agency*, May 29, 2019. (https://www.isna.ir/news/98030803377/).
93 "First graduation ceremony of students of Faculty of the Azerbaijani Language and Literature of Tabriz University Held," *APA*, September 23, 2020
(https://apa.az/en/asia-news/First-graduation-ceremony-of-students-of-Faculty-of-the-Azerbaijani-Language-and-Literature-of-Tabriz-University-held-330947); "Azerbaijani language, literature to be taught in Tabriz University," *News.Az*, August 18, 2016.

Criminalizing Use of Minority Languages and Government Promotion of Persian

As pointed out in the demography chapter, native Persian speakers comprise less than half of Iran's population. The Iranian government actively promotes use of the Persian language among all Iranians and has criminalized non-use of Persian in certain circumstances. The active measures to impose use of Persian have increased in the 2020s. The government's activity to promote the use of Persian actually is an acknowledgement that Iran faces a language challenge. Iran's Minister of Culture and Islamic Guidance, Mohammad Mehdi Esmaili stated in 2022 that the Persian language is supported and loved "even in the border areas of the country," indirectly referring to Iran's ethnic minorities.[94] This is not reflected in the low levels of Persian fluency in the border provinces.

As part of its policy to promote use of the Persian language, the government of Iran has set up mechanisms to report violations of not using the Persian language and script. The Ministry of Culture and Islamic Guidance implements plans and has tasked government agencies with upholding the use of the Persian language throughout the country.

The Minister of Culture and Islamic Guidance has stated that the government is ready to use police force to enforce use of Persian: "Where information and culture building are not effective, we will use police forces to preserve language and literature."[95] Mahmoud Shaloui, advisor to the Minister and Secretary of the Coordinating Council for the Protection of the Persian Language said, "The police force has also had good cooperation in dealing with violators from the usage of Persian language, and it is necessary to subtly institutionalize the law of care for Persian language and script in the society as well as the boards on the city level."[96]

At the Ministry of Culture and Islamic Guidance, a task force on Persian language examined "violations by businesses" of Persian language rules.[97] Iran's Minister of Culture and Islamic Guidance stated in 2021: "Persian language

---

[94] "The Minister of Culture thanks the IRIB for protecting the Persian language," *IRIB News Agency*, March 7, 2022 (https://www.iribnews.ir/fa/news/3380685/). Also, at https://iranwire.com/fa/news/tehran/57695).
[95] @baydaqnews, *Twitter*, March 8, 2022 (https://twitter.com/baydaqnews/status/1501122135607197696?s=20&t=kIDjILlB8DQ0EUL3EVrnVg).
[96] "Launching a warning system for not using Persian language and script according to the order of the Minister of Culture," *Fars News*, October 18, 2021 (http://fna.ir/4bmar).
[97] "Launching a warning system for not using Persian language and script according to the order of the Minister of Culture," *Fars News*, October 18, 2021 (http://fna.ir/4bmar).

and literature are so important that if there is a need to set stricter laws in its set of law, we will do it, because it is considered as one of the manifestations of national pride."[98] Iran's Minister of Culture and Islamic Guidance, Mohammad Mehdi Esmaili, stated during a meeting devoted to "protection of Persian language and literature" that protection of Persian is one of the main concerns of the Ministry of Culture and that the "Supreme Leader emphasizes the protection of Persian language and literature in his various meetings with the regime's officials."[99] Esmaili stated that four arms of government cooperate—"The Ministry of Culture and Islamic Guidance, The Radio and Television Authority, the municipalities and the police to protect the Persian language infrastructure."

In addition to deploying police to enforce use of Persian, the President of the Academy of Persian Language and Literature has encouraged use of cultural celebrations to "increase the esteem of the Persian language in society." He claimed that cultural events will lead to "a decrease in violations by businesses as well as non-use of Persian language will also decrease."[100]

While formally cultural works and activity are allowed in languages other than Persian, in reality the government works to suppress it. Minister Esmaili stated that "it is important to be vigilant in the field of cultural productions: In publishing books, press or film productions, the Persian language should be carefully and obsessively protected as the national-Iranian identity."[101]

Incarceration and Execution Rates

Iran's ethnic minorities are subject to disproportionately high rates of incarceration and execution. This trend is documented biannually by the UN Human Rights Council's special rapporteur on human rights in Iran.[102] For instance,

---

[98] Launching a warning system for not using Persian language and script according to the order of the Minister of Culture," *Fars News*, October 18, 2021 (http://fna.ir/4bmar).
[99] "The Minister of Culture thanks the IRIB for protecting the Persian language," *IRIB News Agency*, March 7, 2022 (https://www.iribnews.ir/fa/news/3380685/). Also at *IranWire* https://iranwire.com/fa/news/tehran/57695).
[100] Launching a warning system for not using Persian language and script according to the order of the Minister of Culture," *Fars News*, October 18, 2021 (http://fna.ir/4bmar).
[101] "The Minister of Culture thanks the IRIB for protecting the Persian language," *IRIB News Agency*, March 7, 2022 (https://www.iribnews.ir/fa/news/3380685/). Also at *IranWire* https://iranwire.com/fa/news/tehran/57695).
[102] United Nations Human Rights Council, "Situation of human rights in the Islamic Republic of Iran," January 13, 2022 (https://documents-dds-ny.un.org/doc/UNDOC/GEN/G22/005/44/PDF/

Kurdish political prisoners charged with national security offenses constitute almost half of Iran's political prisoners.[103] Kurds reportedly account for 70 percent of judicial executions despite comprising 10 percent of the national population. In his spring 2021 report, Special Rapporteur Javaid Rehman, stated that he is "alarmed at reports of executions and enforced disappearances of ethnic minority political prisoners," and that "the imprisonment of individuals from ethnic and religious minorities for practicing their culture, language or faith is an ongoing concern."[104] In his 2022 report, Rehman noted: "An increase in the execution of individuals from minority communities had also been observed, with over 40 Baluchi and over 50 Kurdish individuals executed between January 1 and November 17, 2021."[105]

The regime often charges ethnic minority activists and cultural figures with various national security violations in order to suppress their activities. These include charges such as defamation of the state, "war against God," and anti-Islamic propaganda.[106] The regime often coerces the prisoners to make public "confessions" prior to their executions.

In the wave of anti-regime demonstrations since November 2017, ethnic minority groups have been particularly active and subject to the most extreme crackdowns. In his January 2020 report, Rehman stated that during the November 2019 crackdown on protests, the death rate was highest in provinces inhabited by minorities. "Dozens of activists from ethnic minorities, including Kurds and Azerbaijani Turks, were reportedly summoned or arrested following the protests," he reported.[107] In particular, the regime treated Arabs harshly during and after the 2017–2018 protests, leading to a high death count among this group, and specifically at least 84 deaths in Khuzestan.

G2200544.pdf?OpenElement); United Nations Human Rights Council, "Situation of human rights in the Islamic Republic of Iran," January 30, 2019 (https://undocs.org/en/A/HRC/40/67).

103 "UN Special Rapporteur says half of Iran's political prisoners are Kurds," *Kurdistan24*, August 20, 2019 (https://www.kurdistan24.net/en/news/dc2df5b1-52bd-4f9d-9b87-deef25816a98).

104 United Nations Human Rights Council, "Situation of human rights in the Islamic Republic of Iran," January 11, 2021, p. 9 (https://undocs.org/pdf?symbol=en/A/HRC/46/50).

105 United Nations Human Rights Council, "Situation of human rights in the Islamic Republic of Iran," January 13, 2022 (https://documents-dds-ny.un.org/doc/UNDOC/GEN/G22/005/44/PDF/G2200544.pdf?OpenElement).

106 For example, Nazila Fathi, "Iran Accuses Five of Warring Against God," *New York Times*, January 8, 2010.

107 United Nations Human Rights Council, "Situation of human rights in the Islamic Republic of Iran," January 28, 2020 (https://www.ohchr.org/Documents/Countries/IR/Report_of_the_Special_Rapporteur_on_the_situation_of_human_rights_in_the_Islamic_Republic_of_IranA4361.pdf).

In the 2010s and 2020s, international human rights organizations, such as Human Rights Watch, have given scant coverage to violations of the human rights of Iran's ethnic minorities. This contrasts with these organizations' policies in the 1990s and early 2000s, when they extensively covered the issue. It seems that as the U.S. and Europe have moved toward reconciling with the Islamic Republic, main human rights organizations have reduced their coverage of Iran's human rights violations, and especially the ethnic issue, in order to help facilitate a deal on the Iranian nuclear program.

Suppression of Protests and Other Political Activity

The Islamic Republic does not allow political activity promoting the cultural and language rights of ethnic minorities. Even when groups assert rights already guaranteed by the Islamic Republic's Constitution or work to promote rights as Iranians, the government brands them as "separatists." Western press often repeats the "separatist" labeling in their reporting on political activity in Iran of ethnic minorities, even in cases when the groups are aiming to improve their rights within Iran and have no aims for secession.

Membership in ethnically based political organizations is also prohibited. Leaders and members are subject to national security and defamation offenses, long prison terms, and even execution. In his July 2019 report, Rehman contended that minorities suffer systematic oppression:

> Human rights violations affecting many of the ethnic and religious minority groups include the arbitrary deprivation of life and extrajudicial executions; a disproportionate number of political prisoners; arbitrary arrests and detention in connection with a range of peaceful activities such as advocacy for linguistic freedom, organizing or taking part in peaceful protests and being affiliated with opposition parties; incitement to hatred and violence; the forced closure of businesses and discriminatory practices and denial of employment; and restrictions on access to education and other basic services.[108]

Despite formally tolerating ethnic cultural societies, the regime at times arrests and convicts their members and cultural figures for national security and defamation violations. One of the most prominent Azerbaijani political prisoners is Abbas Lesani, a poet and writer who promoted use of the native language of Iran's Azerbaijanis. Tehran has held him in an Ardabil prison since July 2018

---

[108] United Nations Human Rights Council, "Situation of human rights in the Islamic Republic of Iran," July 18, 2019, paragraph 29 (https://digitallibrary.un.org/record/3823681?ln=en).

and for several prison sentences prior to that.[109] The judiciary sentenced him to eight years for "making propaganda against the Islamic Republic" and "forming a group to disrupt the country's security." At his 2019 appeal, the court lengthened Lesani's sentence to 15 years, followed by two years in exile.

To suppress the minorities, Tehran has gone as far as to import foreign militias to Iran. In the spring and summer of 2019, massive floods in Khuzestan Province led to hundreds of deaths and caused thousands to lose their homes and farmland. To quell the subsequent protests and maintain public order, Tehran deployed foreign militias from Lebanon and Iraq, including Iraq's Popular Mobilization Units (Hashd al-Shaabi) and Lebanese Hezbollah, to the region.[110]

Assassinations of Leaders of Ethnic Movements Abroad

Since the early days of the Islamic Revolution in Iran, Tehran has regularly assassinated anti-regime expatriates.[111] Leaders and representatives of Iran's ethnic minorities, especially those living in Europe, have been common targets. In Iran's most high-profile assassination operation in Europe, the regime in 1992 killed Sadiq Sharafkindi, the general secretary of the Kurdish Democratic Party of Iran, and three of his colleagues at the Mykonos Restaurant in Berlin.[112] German courts concluded that the government of Iran was directly responsible for the murders.[113]

The Islamic Republic continues to assassinate ethnic minority leaders and activists outside of Iran, especially those based in Europe. In the late 2010s, Ira-

---

109 Abbas Lesani served several prison sentences prior to this conviction, totaling close to six years prior to the 2018 sentence.
110 Golnaz Esfandiari, "Iraqis to the Rescue? Iranians wary of paramilitary forces sent for 'flood relief' efforts," *Radio Free Europe/Radio Liberty*, April 16, 2017 (https://www.rferl.org/a/iranians-wary-iraqis-paramilitary-forces-sent-for-flood-relief-efforts/29884709.html); "Following Iraqi Shiite Militias, Hezbollah Shows Up In Iran 'For Flood Relief,'" *Radio Farda*, April 17, 2019 (https://en.radiofarda.com/a/following-iraqi-shiite-militias-hezbollah-shows-up-in-iran-for-flood-relief-/29885674.html).
111 U.S. Department of State, Office of the Spokesperson, "Iran's Assassination's and Terrorist Activity Abroad," May 22, 2020 (https://2017-2021.state.gov/irans-assassinations-and-terrorist-activity-abroad/index.html).
112 *The Criminal System: The Mykonos Documents*, Eds. Abbas Khodagholi, Hamid Nowzari, and Mehran Paydande (Berlin: Nima Books, 2000).
113 Parviz Dastmalchi, *The Text of the Mykonos Judgment* (Berlin: Azad Press, 2000); William Drozdlak, "German Court: Tehran ordered exile killings," *Washington Post*, April 11, 1997 (https://www.washingtonpost.com/archive/politics/1997/04/11/german-court-tehran-ordered-exile-killings/0a33d5cc-6f2c-40ed-aa3b-7b30ce21d767/).

nian assassination operations against Iranian ethnic minority activists in Europe included:
- In June 2020, Sadegh Zarza, a former leadership member of the Democratic Party of Iranian Kurdistan, survived an assassination attempt in the Dutch city of Leeuwarden.[114]
- In June 2020, Danish courts convicted Mohammad Davoudzadeh Loloei, a Norwegian citizen of Iranian origin, for a plot to kill in 2018 a leader of the Arab Struggle Movement for the Liberation of Ahwaz (ASMLA) who resides in Ringsted, Denmark.[115]
- In September 2017, Ahmad Mola Nissi, a Dutch citizen of Iranian origin who founded the Arab Struggle Movement for the Liberation of Ahwaz (ASMLA) organization, was shot dead at his doorstep in The Hague, Netherlands. The Dutch government accused the Iranian regime of carrying out this assassination. ASMLA is viewed by the Iranian regime as a terrorist organization.[116]

Tehran has also kidnapped or demanded handovers of several ethnic activists visiting or living in neighboring countries. In October 2020, for instance, the regime kidnapped Habib Chaab, a Swedish citizen of Iranian origin while he was visiting in Istanbul. Chaab is an Ahwazi Arab activist. Iranian authorities claimed that Chaab led ASMLA's Swedish chapter. The Iranians used drug trafficking rings to capture Chaab in Istanbul and bring him to Iran.[117]

---

[114] "Iranian dissident wounded in stabbing in the Netherlands, says report," *Reuters*, June 20, 2020 (https://www.reuters.com/article/uk-netherlands-iran-stabbing/iranian-dissident-wounded-in-stabbing-in-the-netherlands-says-report-idUKKBN23R0OD).

[115] Sune Engel Rasmussen, "Denmark accuses Iran of planning attack near Copenhagen," *Financial Times*, October 30, 2018; "Trial Exposes Iran-Saudi Battle in Europe," *The Wall Street Journal*, June 26, 2020 (https://www.wsj.com/articles/trial-exposes-iran-saudi-battle-in-europe-11593158091); "Norwegian found guilty of spying for Iran in Denmark," *Reuters*, June 26, 2020 (https://www.reuters.com/article/us-denmark-security-iran/norwegian-found-guilty-of-spying-for-iran-in-denmark-idUSKBN23X1EX).

[116] "Dutch foreign minister: Iran behind two political killings," *Reuters*, January 8, 2019 (https://www.reuters.com/article/uk-netherlands-iran-kilings-idUKKCN1P2193); Laurie Mylroie, "Leader of Ahwaz Movement murdered in Netherlands," *Kurdistan24*, September 11, 2017 (https://www.kurdistan24.net/en/news/05dbe63c-799d-4f5f-9fdc-71294fe58258).

[117] "Iran Intelligence Ministry Nabs Ringleader of Saudi, Israeli-Sponsored Terror Group," *Tasnim News Agency*, November 12, 2020 (https://www.tasnimnews.com/en/news/2020/11/12/2388122/iran-intelligence-ministry-nabs-ringleader-of-saudi-israeli-sponsored-terror-group); Kareem Fahim and Erin Cunningham, "Turkey says Iranian intelligence was behind elaborate plot to kidnap opponent in Istanbul," *Washington Post*, December 13, 2020 (https://www.washingtonpost.com/world/middle_east/iran-intelligence-turkey-kidnap-plot/2020/12/12/818e0c30-3b2c-11eb-8328-a36a109900c2_story.html).

Tehran has also assassinated Iranian Kurdish activists, who reside in or were visiting Iraqi Kurdistan. For example, the Kurdistan Democratic Party said that in August 2021 an Iranian-sponsored assassin killed a member of its Central Committee, Musa Babakhani, in Erbil. Babakhani was a native of Kermanshah, Iran.[118] In addition, Tehran has pressured Erbil to turn over Iranian Kurdish activists who escaped to Iraqi Kurdistan. In 2020, Erbil acquiesced and handed over several Iranian Kurds.[119]

Province Gerrymandering, Settler Programs, and Place Names

Tehran gerrymanders the borders of its provinces in an attempt to prevent provinces from being dominated by a particular ethnic minority and in order to divide ethnic groups up among several provinces. This was the case in East Azerbaijan, which Tehran in 1993 divided into two provinces with the creation of the new Ardabil Province. The Pahlavi dynasty practiced this policy as well: In 1937, the Reza Shah government split off the Azerbaijanis in Zanjan and Qazvin from Azerbaijan State (*ayallet*). In addition, in 1935, Reza Shah split the Arab-dominated region, commonly known as al-Ahwaz, among several provinces.

In late 2021, the regime discussed breaking up Sistan-Baluchistan, which would have spread the Baluch among different provinces.

Iran also has conducted government settler programs to incentivize Persians and other non-local groups to move into relatively monoethnic areas inhabited by non-Persians.[120] For decades, Tehran has encouraged Persians and other groups to move into the strategically important Khuzestan Province, the center of Iran's oil production.[121] On April 15 of each year, the Ahwazi Arabs hold anti-regime protests called the "Day of Rage" to commemorate the first wave of violent demonstrations that took place on April 15, 2005 against this settler policy. This wave of 2005 demonstrations stemmed from a leaked document out-

---

118 Rawad Taha, "Iranian opposition party accuses Tehran of assassinating one of its leaders in Erbil," *Al-Arabiya News*, August 7, 2021 (https://english.alarabiya.net/News/middle-east/2021/08/07/Iranian-opposition-party-accuses-Tehran-of-assassinatin).
119 "Activists: Iraq's Kurdish Region Becomes Less Safe for Iranian Dissidents," *Voice of America*, May 13, 2020 (https://www.voanews.com/extremism-watch/activists-iraqs-kurdish-region-becomes-less-safe-iranian-dissidents).
120 China has also used this policy of encouraging migration of Han Chinese to Tibet and Xinjiang, in order to dilute the predominance of Tibetans and Uyghurs in these regions.
121 "Iran: Interview with Human Rights Special Rapporteur on adequate housing, Miloon Kothari," *ReliefWeb*, August 9, 2005 (https://reliefweb.int/report/iran-islamic-republic/iran-interview-human-rights-special-rapporteur-adequate-housing-miloon).

lining government plans to move Persians and other non-Arabs to Khuzestan. Mohammad Ali Abtahi, an advisor to President Mohammad Khatami, developed the plan. His plan became known as the "Abtahi Document." At the annual April 15th "Day of Rage" Ahwazi protests marking the Abtahi Document, the regime's security forces regularly kill protestors.[122]

The UN Human Rights Council special rapporteur on Iran has reported that Iran continues to attempt to dilute the Arab population in Khuzestan and adjacent areas. In his spring 2021 report, Rehman referred to the Ahwazis and stated that he is "concerned at reports of forced evictions in ethnic minority areas."[123]

As part of this settlement policy, the regime encourages ethnic Lurs to move to Khuzestan, and offers them good jobs in the province. Tehran likely aims to encourage conflict between the local Ahvaz and the Lur settlers and thus strengthen its control over the province.

In addition to Khuzestan, Tehran has also implemented settler policies in locations where Baluch form the majority of the population. Baluch activists claim that Tehran has encouraged migrants to move into major Baluchi cities such as Zahedan, Chabahar, Iranshar, and Khash in order to dilute the Baluch majority.[124]

Turkmen activists based in the west claim that in the Turkmen-populated city of Gonbad-Kavus, hundreds of housing units have been built for non-Turkmen Shia who have been imported to the city, in an attempt to change the demographic balance there, as well as the sectarian balance.[125]

The regime has also systematically changed the names of geographic areas in Iran from local languages to Persian. For instance, Khorramshahr is known in Arabic as al-Mohammarah, Susangerd as Khafajia and Mahshar as Maa'shoor. Azerbaijani location names were also changed. For instance, authorities changed Sa'in Qala to Shahin Dej and Aci Chay to Talkhe Rud.

Gubernatorial Appointments and Their Language Policies

Iran is divided into 31 provinces (ostan). The governors are not elected, rather the central government in Tehran appoints the provincial governors. The ethnic fac-

---

[122] For instance, in 2011, see "Iran: Outside the spotlight, Arab uprising smolders in country's southwest," *Los Angeles Times*, April 30, 2011.
[123] United Nations Human Rights Council, "Situation of human rights in the Islamic Republic of Iran," January 11, 2021, p. 9 (https://digitallibrary.un.org/record/3899852?ln=en).
[124] "Iran," *Human Rights Watch* Report, 1997, p. 6.
[125] Author's interview, April 2022.

tor plays a large role in Tehran's policy of appointing governors and most of Iran's governors are either Persian or Lur. In the case of other ethnicities, the governors rarely are appointed to rule provinces that share their background. The first Pahlavi monarch, Reza Shah, instituted a similar policy of gubernatorial appointments using them as a device to control the provinces and report on potential mutinous developments among Iran's ethnic minorities.[126]

This research looked at Tehran's policy in appointing governors to the provinces from an ethnic perspective. Between 2010 and 2020, more than 60 percent of governors appointed to Iran's provinces were Persian or Lur (54 of 138 governors [39 percent] appointed from 2010 to 2020 were Persian, and 32 were Lur [23 percent]). Lurs make up the greatest share of governors after Persians, while the group comprises only about seven percent of Iran's population. During 2010–2020, Tehran appointed no Baluch or Turkmen as governors, and only one Arab and seven Kurds. The regime has declined to appoint any Sunni governors. Thus, governors selected from groups which are comprised of both Shia and Sunni members, such as the Kurds and Arabs, have only been Shia. Most of Iran's governors appointed from 2010–2020 had served in the IRGC or other security agencies, or Iran's Ministry of Interior, prior to their appointments.

Appointment of non-local governors prevents the emergence of local power centers in Iran. In the cases when Tehran appoints an ethnic minority member to serve as a governor, the center generally appoints governors to lead provinces with which they do not share ethnic ties. For instance, only one Kurdish governor has ruled a region with a mostly Kurdish population. In addition, the one Arab governor appointed in the last 10 years was not appointed to serve in Khuzestan, which has an Arab majority, but rather in Hormozgan. In addition, to a large Arab population, Hormozgan has significant Persian and Lur populations. In cases where the appointed governor shares the ethnicity of the governed province, the governor usually hails from another region.

According to this 2010–2020 survey of governor appointments, in cases where a province is ethnically diverse and the Persians count for one of the two largest groups, Tehran appoints governors either of Persian origin or another ethnic group, but not from the second ethnic group that is close in size to the Persians. In the case of South Khorasan Province, Persians and Sistanis are the two largest ethnic groups there. Tehran has appointed Persian governors to South Khorasan but no Sistani origin governors to this province.

---

[126] Farhad Kazemi, "Ethnicity and the Iranian Peasantry," in Milton J. Esman and Itamar Rabinovich, *Ethnicity, Pluralism, and the State in the Middle East* (Ithaca and London: Cornell University Press, 1988), p. 205.

With regard to the policy of sending governors to serve in provinces with which they do not share ethnic ties, the Azerbaijani majority provinces—East Azerbaijan, West Azerbaijan, and Ardabil—are an exception and close to 70 percent of the governors of these provinces during 2010–2020 were of ethnic Azerbaijani origin. All the governors serving in East Azerbaijan Province during the decade of study have been ethnic Azerbaijanis. However, in provinces where the numbers of Persians and Azerbaijanis are close, such as Hamedan, the central government appoints mostly Persian governors or Lur governors. In the case of Hamedan, for instance, the central government has not appointed a single Azerbaijani governor in the last 10 years. In addition, in provinces where Azerbaijanis are the second largest ethnicity or Azerbaijanis had a considerable population, an Azerbaijani origin governor was not usually appointed.

Tehran also seems to have a policy of sending non-Persians to govern other minority ethnic groups, potentially in order to create discord among the minorities. In this 10-year survey, rarely has Tehran appointed Persian-origin governors to provinces primarily populated by ethnic minorities. For instance, over the past decade, the Kurdish provinces were mostly governed by Lurs, potentially to direct Kurdish dissatisfaction with the government toward the Lurs instead of Tehran.

In most provinces, the governors speak Persian in work meetings and with the wider population. In the period under study, only one governor, Jasem Jaderi, the former governor of Hormozgan Province (November 2013–September 2017), reportedly used both Arabic and Persian in communication with locals. However, in official meetings, Persian was the language of communication. In Gilan, there are reports that two governors have used a combination of Gilaki language and Persian in communication with locals.

The exception is East Azerbaijan Province. During 2010–2020, as pointed out, all governors appointed to this province have been ethnic Azerbaijanis. These governors frequently use the Azerbaijani language to speak at work, while all documents are written in Persian. The governors also converse in the local language with the populations of East Azerbaijan, Ardabil, and West Azerbaijan.[127] In Tabriz, even in official meetings, the governors and staff converse in the Azerbaijani language. However, in other provinces, reportedly, Azerbaijani-origin governors rarely communicate in the Azerbaijani language in public settings with Azerbaijanis residing there.

---

127 Interviews with individuals residing in Tabriz, December 2020.

There are reports of the use of both the Lur language and Persian in official meetings in Lur-majority provinces—Lorestan, Kohgilouyeh va Boyer-Ahmad, and Chaharmahal va Bakhtiari.

Electoral Appeals to Ethnic Minorities

From the late 1990s, candidates in Iran's presidential and parliamentary elections have attempted to gain support among ethnic minority voters by promising to uphold and expand language and cultural rights and by distributing election materials in the minority languages. This reflects the candidates' perception that ethnic minorities want greater language and cultural rights, and that promises to uphold these rights will garner their support. The fact that the candidates perceive that voters want expanded language and cultural rights is telling. These appeals to ethnic sentiments have taken place in all presidential election rounds in Iran over the last three decades.

For instance, during his first presidential bid in 1997, Khatami pledged to uphold Articles 15 and 19 of Iran's Constitution. His campaign also produced and distributed election materials in the Kurdish and Azerbaijani languages.[128] Khatami further promised to establish municipal elections. This idea attracted some support from ethnic minorities because it would grant them greater local influence over policies.

During Iran's 2009 presidential elections, Mir Hossein Mousavi, an ethnic Azerbaijani, during visits to Azerbaijani-populated provinces gave speeches in the local language and read well-known Azerbaijani poems at his rallies.[129] He also hired local Azerbaijani singers to compose lyrics in Azerbaijani for his campaign songs.[130]

In his election campaigns, President Rouhani published election materials in minority languages, and promised implementation of language rights, including explicitly pledging to implement Article 15 of the Islamic Republic Constitution. He also pledged to establish an Academy of Azerbaijani language and liter-

---

[128] Brenda Shaffer, "Iran, Nationalism," *Encyclopedia of Nationalism*, Ed. Alexander Motyl (San Diego, CA: Academic Press, 2001), p. 237.
[129] Iran Resaneh, "Mir Hossein Mousavi's trip to Tabriz and his speech in the Azeri language" *YouTube*, May 26, 2009 (https://www.youtube.com/watch?v=JbRJnd8Ojxo).
[130] "Mir Hossein's campaign song with Shariyari's voice," *Mehr News Agency*, May 26, 2009 (https://www.mehrnews.com/news/885856/سرود-انتخاباتی-میر-حسین-با-صدای-رحیم-شهریاری).

ature in East Azerbaijan.[131] His campaign promises on languages rights were not fulfilled after the election. To be sure, Rouhani did appoint the first presidential advisor on ethnic and religious minority rights.[132] However, he chose Ali Yunesi for this job. The appointment did not generate enthusiasm, as Yunesi had served previously as Iran's minister of intelligence and viewed Iran's ethnic groups as a national security threat.

Ethnic Minority Activity in Iran's Parliament

The Islamic Republic allows ethnically based associations to operate in the Iranian parliament. Parliamentarians from Iran's majority-minority provinces are also permitted to air demands related to the regions they represent.

In 1993, parliamentarians from the Azerbaijani provinces formed the Assembly of Azerbaijan Majles Deputies faction. The faction focused on promoting issues of concern to those provinces and expanding relations with the newly independent Republic of Azerbaijan.[133] Two decades later, in 2016, Azerbaijani parliamentarians formed the Faction of Parliamentarians from Turkic Regions.[134] Over 100 Majles members attended the faction's first meeting on October 30, 2016. Attendees represented 34 percent of the parliament's seats. Reportedly, when members of this faction met with intelligence minister nominee Mahmoud Alavi, they demanded education in their mother tongue, in keeping with Article 15 of Iran's Constitution. They also demanded that Tehran stop treating the request for native language use in education demand as a "security issue."[135]

During the period of President Khatami, Kurdish members of parliament also formed a Kurdish faction in the Majles for a brief period.[136] During this

---

[131] "Azerbaijani to build language and literature academy in Iran," *Azernews*, November 7, 2013 (https://www.azernews.az/region/61364.html).
[132] "Can Rouhani's ethnic minority oriented policies be successful?" *Trend*, February 6, 2014 (https://en.trend.az/iran/2238868.html); "Iran's Ethnic Minorities," *The Economist Intelligence Unit*, April 23, 2014 (http://country.eiu.com/article.aspx?articleid=1121746896&Country=Iran&topic=Politics).
[133] Brenda Shaffer, *Borders and Brethren: Iran and the Challenge of Azerbaijani Identity* (Cambridge, MA: MIT Press, 2002), p. 180.
[134] "Iranian Turks' new parliamentary faction breaking more taboos," *Trend*, October 31, 2016 (https://en.trend.az/other/commentary/2679141.html).
[135] "Ethnic issues emerge as pivotal in Iran's policy making," *Trend*, August 15, 2017 (https://en.trend.az/iran/politics/2787142.html).
[136] Nazila Fathi, "Kurds in Iran Cheer Iraqi Neighbors' Efforts for Greater Voice," *New York Times*, November 14, 2004.

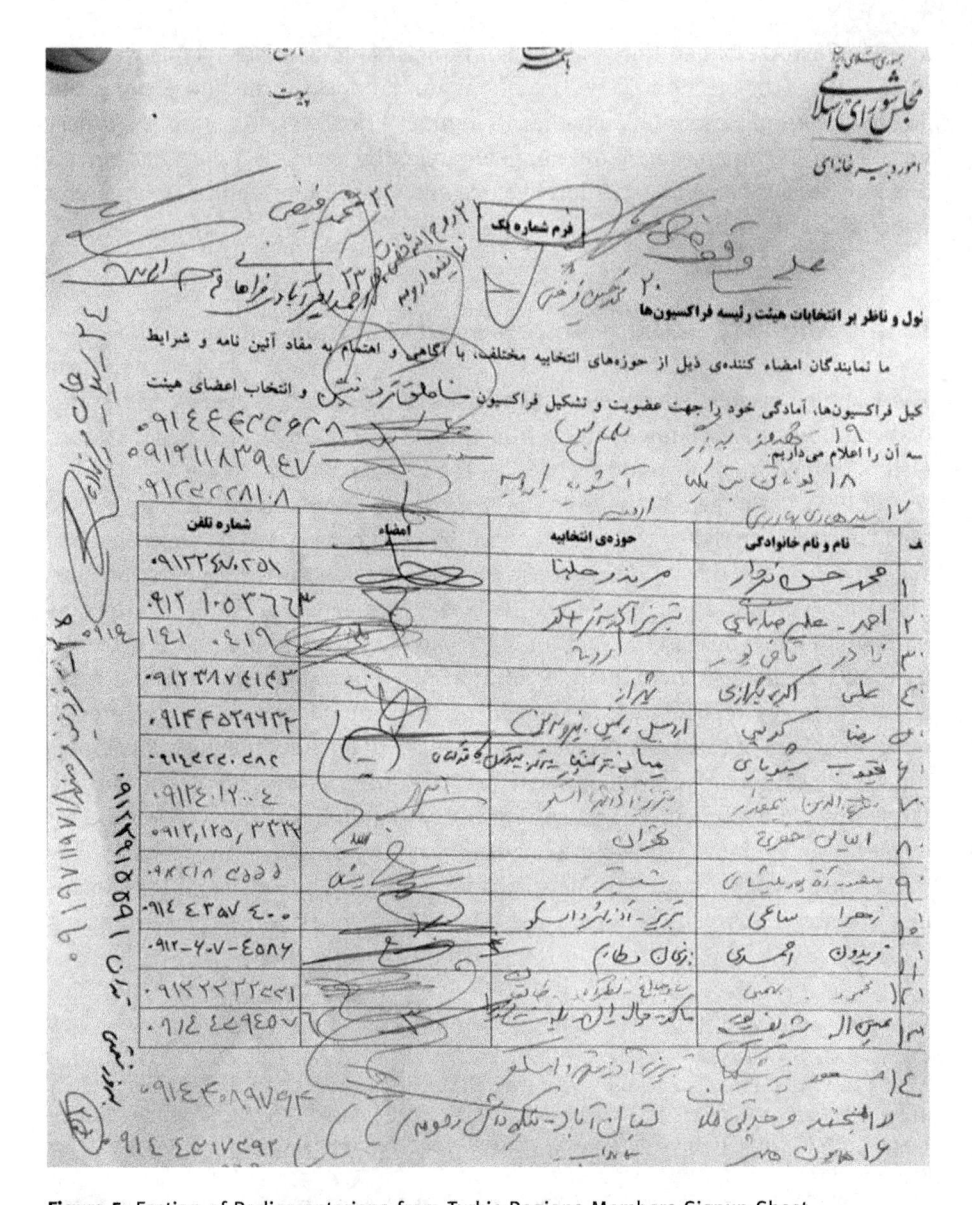

Figure 5: Faction of Parliamentarians from Turkic Regions Members Signup Sheet

time, they campaigned and achieved a significant increase in government budget allocations to the Kurdish-populated provinces. A member of parliament also spoke for the first time in the Kurdish language in the legislative body, and the bloc campaigned for the right to teach Kurdish language and literature as a subject in universities in the Kurdish-populated provinces.[137]

Not all in Iran's power elite are happy about ethnic factions operating in Iran's parliament. In 2001, during Khatami's tenure, the Iranian daily *Entekhab* warned about the emergence of "language based and tribal coalitions" in the Majles. The commentary stated that some parliamentarians have "placed their regional interests above national interests." According to the editorial, the deputies did not vote for cabinet members along policy or ideological lines; rather, they voted for cabinet members because of common regional or linguistic roots. To *Entekhab* this demonstrated the weakness of Iran's party system, which "enables the deputies to act not according to the national interest."[138]

Majles members have weighed in on issues affecting Iran's ethnic groups in the regions they represent. On the eve of planned Iranian executions of several young Kurdish men in 2010, Abdoljabar Karami, a member of parliament who represents Sanandaj, the capital of Iran's Kurdistan Province, tried to stop the executions.[139] Karami also attempted to allow families to recover the bodies of executed young Kurds for burial.[140]

In addition, ethnic minority Majles members have fought against name changes or divisions of provinces that affect the groups they represent. For example, Majles members of Azerbaijani origin openly opposed Tehran's October 1992 decision to split East Azerbaijan Province and remove the name Azerbaijan from the newly created province, Ardabil.[141]

In addition, a parliament member from Ahwaz, Sharif al-Husseini, publicly backed the protestors in Ahwaz in October 2013 against Tehran's continued diversion of the Karun River, which had aggravated water shortages in Khuzestan.[142] In November 2021, Jalal Mahmoudzadeh, a member of parliament repre-

---

[137] Nazila Fathi, "Kurds in Iran Cheer Iraqi Neighbors' Efforts for Greater Voice," *New York Times*, November 14, 2004.
[138] *Entekhab* quoted in *Radio Free Liberty/Radio Europe* Iran Report, Vol. 4, No. 39, October 15, 2001.
[139] Nazila Fathi, "Relatives of Kurds Executed in Iran Are Denied the Remains, and 2 Are Arrested," *New York Times*, May 11, 2010 (https://www.nytimes.com/2010/05/12/world/middleeast/12iran.html).
[140] Nazila Fathi, "Relatives of Kurds Executed in Iran Are Denied the Remains, and 2 Are Arrested," *New York Times*, May 11, 2010.
[141] Brenda Shaffer, *Borders and Brethren: Iran and the Challenge of Azerbaijani Identity* (Cambridge, MA: MIT Press, 2002), pp. 174–176.
[142] "Iran: Ahwaz residents protest against Karun River diversion," *Al-Arabiya*, October 26, 2013 (https://english.alarabiya.net/en/News/middle-east/2013/10/26/Iran-Ahwaz-residents-protest-against-Karun-River-diversion-).

senting Mahabad city, which is mainly populated by Kurds, protested in the Majles against the regime's frequently killing of Kurdish *kolbars* (porters) that transport goods between Iran and Turkey and Iran and Iraq (Iraqi Kurdistan region).[143] Mahmoudzadeh called on Tehran to formalize this transport work so that the Kurdish workers would be out of harm's way. At least 50 Kurdish *kolbars* are killed annually on Iran's borders.

Majles members from the ethnically populated provinces have also complained about the lack of representation of the ethnic minorities in the government and broader discrimination. In September 2001, the deputies from Kurdestan Province went so far as to resign *en masse* to protest discrimination against Kurds. In explaining the resignation, deputy Mohammad-Rezai said that more than 80 percent of the province's residents live below the poverty line and the state universities grant very few places to students from Kurdistan.[144] In their letter of resignation, Bahaeddin Adab of Sanandaj, Jalal Jalali of Sanandaj, Masood Hosseini of Qorveh, Mohammad Mohammad-Rezai of Bijar, Abdullah Sohrabi of Marivan, and Salaheddin Alaie of Saqez "criticized President Khatami for not paying attention to their co-ethnics' plight."[145]

In addition, in 2006, Kurdish origin legislator Bahaeddin Adab asked rhetorically in an interview with the Associated Press: "How can it be that there is not one person qualified to serve as vice president, minister or deputy minister from Iran's Kurdish minority of 10 million people?"[146] Following the arrest of seven Kurdish activists accused by the regime of "separatist agitation" Kurdish legislator Amin Shabani complained of discrimination in a speech to parliament: "Kurds have never been able to enjoy political power in Iran's history."[147]

Majles members representing areas inhabited by Iran's ethnic minorities have at times voiced support for minority language rights. During a visit by Khatami to Mahabad in West Azerbaijan Province, Majles delegate Rahman Behmanesh requested greater language rights for Kurds. He also proposed that "Khatami's administration prepare the ground to establish an academy for the Kurdish

---

143 Khazan Jangiz, "Kurdish MP in Iran: 'Why don't you stop killing and injuring kolbars?'," *Rudaw*, November 11, 2021 (https://www.rudaw.net/english/middleeast/iran/171120211).
144 *Radio Free Europe/Radio Liberty* Iran Report, Vol. 4, No. 39, October 15, 2001; "Report on the situation of human rights in the Islamic Republic of Iran, prepared by the Special Representative of the Commission on Human Rights," Mr. Maurice Danby Copithorne, E/CN.4/2002/42, January 216, 2002, p. 19.
145 *Radio Free Europe/Radio Liberty* Iran Report, Vol. 4, No. 39, October 15, 2001.
146 *Associated Press*, April 10, 2006. In contrast to the parliamentarian's claim, an ethnic Kurd, Bijan Zangeneh, has served in several ministerial positions in Iran.
147 *Associated Press*, April 10, 2006.

language and a college to teach that language, and to publish Kurdish dailies and weeklies."[148]

Following a wave of Azerbaijani protests in 2006, parliamentarians Akbar Alami from Tabriz and Nouraddin Pirmozzen from Ardabil delivered speeches before the Majles, protesting the regime's treatment of the Azerbaijani minority. Referring to the derogative Persian practice of calling Turks "donkeys," Alami also read Shahriyar's famous poem "Are you a donkey or me?"[149]

Majles members have sent letters of protest and petitions to the government on issues relating to their minority ethnic groups. In 2018, for instance, 50 Azerbaijani members of Iran's parliament sent a letter to Rouhani protesting remarks of his advisor for minorities, Ali Yunesi. Yunesi had stated that Turks in Iran are actually "Turkish-speaking Persians" and that they, unlike other Turks, "only began speaking Turkish 300 years ago."[150] In addition, a Majles member from Ardabil, Sodeif Badri, announced that Majles members had signed a petition requesting implementation of Article 15 of the Iranian Constitution.[151]

Iranian Majles deputies from the Azerbaijani provinces led campaigns aimed at limiting Iran's cooperation with Armenia[152] and participated in demonstrations against Armenia's occupation of lands of the Republic of Azerbaijan.[153] In April 1993, Kamel Abedinzadeh, an Azerbaijani deputy from Khoy, even spoke in the Azerbaijani language in the Majles when he condemned Armenian actions against Azerbaijan. He also issued press releases for publication in *Hamshahri* and other journals on this issue.[154] Following the fall 2020 war between Armenia and Azerbaijan, Ahmed Alireza Beygi, a Majles member from Tabriz, criticized Tehran, stating that Iran did not do enough to support Azerbaijan in the war and that Turkey filled this void. Beygi issued this statement at the height

---

148 *IRNA*, September 19, 2000 (https://www.irna.ir/news/5642678/).
149 yaranealami, "Akbar Alami's speech about the incident in Azerbaijan," *YouTube*, April 22, 2009 (https://www.youtube.com/watch?v=3cEihAz4aP8).
150 "Iranian MPs of Turkish origin slam Rouhani's aide over Azeri remarks," *Daily Sabah*, April 22, 2018. (https://www.dailysabah.com/mideast/2018/04/22/iranian-mps-of-turkish-origin-slam-rouhanis-aide-over-azeri-remarks)
151 "Member of parliament: the plan to teach in the mother tongue in the country's schools is ready," *Asriran*, April 17, 2018 (https://www.asriran.com/fa/news/604428/); "İran'da 'Azeriler Farstır' açıklamasına tepki," *Anadolu Agency*, April 22, 2018 (https://www.aa.com.tr/tr/dunya/iranda-azeriler-farstir-aciklamasina-tepki-/1125454).
152 See, for example: "Ahmad Hemmati, Deputy from Meshkinshahr," *Resalat*, April 19, 1993, p. 5.
153 Brenda Shaffer, *Borders and Brethren: Iran and the Challenge of Azerbaijani Identity* (Cambridge, MA: MIT Press, 2002), p. 192.
154 *Resalat*, April 14, 1993, p. 5.

of a spat in 2020 between Turkey and Iran over Turkish President Recep Tayyip Erdogan's perceived support for Azerbaijanis in Iran.[155]

In an Iranian parliamentary session following Armenian Prime Minister Nikol Pashinyan's February 2019 visit to Iran, a parliament member from Urmia, Ruhulla Hezretpur, denounced the visit and Armenia's occupation of Azerbaijani lands. He also condemned the fact that the visit had taken place during the anniversary of the 1992 Khojaly massacre of Azerbaijanis by Armenians. He pointed out that according to Supreme Leader Ali Khamenei, "Karabakh is an Islamic land. Now I ask, what is the difference between Palestine and Karabakh?"[156] Hezretpur also read a nationalist poem in the Azerbaijani language, leading some Majles members to boo him for speaking in a language other than Persian.

Iranian officials of ethnic Azerbaijani origin and parliament members from the ethnic Azerbaijani-populated regions of Iran also expressed views on the conflict that contradicted Tehran's official policy which did not criticize Armenia. In a September 2010 interview for a news service in Azerbaijan, Iran's Vice-President for Parliamentary Affairs Sayyed Mohammad-Reza Mir-Tajeddini stated that:

> Nagorno-Karabakh is Azerbaijani territory. We cannot support an Armenian policy of aggression and occupation that aims to separate the region from Azerbaijan. […] As part of my activities as a MP from Tabriz, I wrote an article about the situation with the Agdam mosque and denounced this fact. Several other members joined me. Naturally, we condemn any disrespect to Islam. A mosque is a symbol of religion and faith. The mosques in Karabakh are not an exception. Our theologians condemn the desecration of mosques.

Portrayal of Ethnic Minorities by Iranian State Media

Iranian media frequently portray ethnic minorities negatively and mock their accents and culture. Persian Iranians play down this ethnic mockery, saying that Iranians enjoy joking about each other. However, members of the minority groups, which are the target of this ridicule, often perceive it differently and point out that the mocking only targets the minorities.

---

155 "Ankara filled void when Tehran failed to support Baku, Iranian lawmaker says," *Daily Sabah*, December 14, 2020 (https://www.dailysabah.com/politics/diplomacy/ankara-filled-void-when-tehran-failed-to-support-baku-iranian-lawmaker-says).

156 Azerbaycan, "Urmia representative protests Iran hosting Armenian occupier during anniversary of massacre of Azerbaijanis" *YouTube*, May 17, 2019 (https://www.youtube.com/watch?time_continue=25&v=POi43CQQssY).

The mocking of ethnic groups, including in mainstream official outlets, has set off mass protests, which in turn have led to arrests, deaths, and injuries during ensuing regime crackdowns. The extreme responses reflect broader animosity toward the regime's discriminatory policies and general Persian cultural hubris toward minorities.

Iran's officially approved cultural sphere, such as films and TV, frequently applies negative stereotypes to Iran's ethnic minorities, portraying Arabs as primitive and extremist[157] and Azerbaijanis as stupid. Sometimes the broadcasts that insult Arabs are targeted at the populations of the neighboring Arab countries but in the process also anger Iran's Ahwazi Arabs.[158] Ahwazis in Iran point out the irony in the Iranian media's depiction of Gulf Arabs as greedy, wealthy sheikhs, while Tehran itself takes Khuzestan's oil wealth and leaves the native Arab population there in extreme poverty.[159]

The official Islamic Republic of Iran Broadcasting (IRIB) has often presented ethnic minorities in a very negative light, which has triggered mass public reactions from Iran's ethnic groups. IRIB set off the first major post-revolutionary upsurge among the Azerbaijanis, a turning point of the Azerbaijani national movement in Iran. On May 8, 1995, the Iranian paper *Ahrar* reported that IRIB[160] had conducted a survey of Iranian attitudes toward "Turk" citizens in Iran. Among the 11 questions in the survey were:

Are you willing to marry a Turk?
Would you allow your daughter to marry a Turk?
Are you willing to participate in religious ceremonies (like Ashura) together with Turks?
If you bought a house, would you be willing to be a neighbor of a Turk?
Are you willing to live in a neighborhood or city where there is a Turk majority?
Are you willing to be friends with a Turk?
Are you willing to go to the home of a Turk as a guest?

---

[157] See, for example: "Photo / Grim Mohammad Reza Sharifinia in the role of ISIL," *Mashregh News*, June 7, 2018 (https://www.mashreghnews.ir/photo/872753/).
[158] For example, this article in the newspaper *Hamdali* states that Arabs have advanced from burying women alive to ministers in the UAE government: "Arab women from cradle to the grave to the ministry" *Aftab News*, October 20, 2017 (https://aftabnews.ir/fa/news/483690/).
[159] Rahim Hamid, "Iran's Institutional Racism" (unpublished paper, 2021).
[160] At the time, Ali Larijani headed the Iranian National Radio and Television Broadcasting Authority. He later went on to become speaker of Iran's parliament and one of the most influential figures in the Islamic Republic.

The results revealed Persian society's extremely negative attitudes toward the group, with most respondents reporting a desire not to interact with Iran's Azerbaijanis.

Islamic Republic of Iran Broadcasting (IRIB) Public Opinion Unit Survey:
"Social distance" project
1) Where are you from? (a–Persian | b–Kurdish | c–Lur | d–Baluch | e–Northern (Gilak-Mazani) | f–other)
2) Where is your father from? (a–Persian | b–Kurdish | c–Lur | d–Baluch | e–Northern (Gilak-Mazani) | f–other)
3) Marital status? a–Single | b–married
4) If you plan to get married one day, would you like to marry a Turkish person?
5) In a case you have a daughter and one day she wants to get married, would you like to let her marry a Turkish man?
6) If you want to participate in some special ceremonies such as Ashura and Tasu'a, would you like to participate in gatherings of Turks?
7) If you want to buy a house and you see the wall-to-wall neighbor or the neighbor in the adjacent apartment is a Turk, would you like to live in their neighborhood?
8) Would you like to work in an office room together with a Turk co-worker?
9) Would you like to get housing in a neighborhood where the majority are Turks?
10) Would you like to live in an Azeri-speaking city?
11) Would you like to hang out with a Turkish person, invite her/him to your home or go to her/his home?

The IRIB survey triggered a wave of Iranian Azerbaijani protests beginning on May 9, 1995. University students led the protests, which focused on racism in Iranian society as well as on IRIB's motives in conducting and publishing such a divisive survey. The demonstrations began at Tehran University. Azerbaijani students assumed that Persian students would join them, but they did not. In response to the lack of solidarity, Azerbaijani university students established their own student union—the Azerbaijani Academic Society (ABTAM). Up until then, there had been no separate student unions based on ethnicity. Protests followed in Tabriz and cities with large Azerbaijani populations.[161] At Tabriz University, some 2,000 students participated in the initial May 9 demonstrations.

In addition, Azerbaijani university students conducted a letter-writing campaign to the offices of Iran's president, the Majles, the Friday sermon leaders, and the governors of East Azerbaijan, Zanjan, and Ardabil Provinces. The letters condemned the survey and called for the right to use and study the Azerbaijani language at the University of Tabriz.[162] The newly founded Azerbaijani Students Union also sent a letter to the Azerbaijani Majles deputies, complaining about the Iranian media's penchant for "mimic[king] and defam[ing] the culture and language of the Azerbaijani Shia."

Since 1995, Azerbaijani university students in Iran have unofficially marked May 9 as Azerbaijani Student Day by holding events extolling their culture and condemning discrimination.[163] The Azerbaijani Academic Society (ABTAM) continues to conduct activities in defense of the cultural, economic and political rights of Azerbaijanis. ABTAM holds cultural events such as festivals, student camps, and literature readings. The society publishes student magazines, reports and open letters on issues related to Azerbaijanis in Iran.

As internet use became widespread in Iran in the 2000s, derogatory publications had an even wider political impact, frequently sparking violent demonstrations and clashes with security forces. Among the examples of racist publications that set off cycles of violence is the infamous cockroach cartoon. On May 12, 2006, the official government newspaper *Iran* published a cartoon of a cockroach that cannot understand a child speaking to it in Persian. In the cartoon, the parents explain to the child that the cockroach does not understand him, "because he speaks Azeri." The cartoon shows the cockroach saying *"namana,"* which means "what?" in Azerbaijani, a word widely known to Persians, as they often mimic the pronunciation when teasing Azerbaijanis. The parents advise the child not to give the cockroach any food and to starve it and suggest other ways to destroy the cockroach.

This publication triggered more than a week of mass protests that broke out on May 22, 2006 in a dozen cities with large Azerbaijani populations. The demonstrations started at Tabriz and Tehran universities and spread. The demonstrations in Tabriz, which were the largest, turned violent, targeting and damaging

---

[161] Brenda Shaffer, *Borders and Brethren: Iran and the Challenge of Azerbaijani Identity* (Cambridge, MA: MIT Press, 2002), pp. 179–180.
[162] Brenda Shaffer, *Borders and Brethren: Iran and the Challenge of Azerbaijani Identity* (Cambridge, MA: MIT Press, 2002), pp. 179–180.
[163] "Letter of the Azerbaijani Students Studying in Tehran Universities to the Azerbaijani Deputies of the Iranian Majles," Azerbaijani Student Union, May 1995 (original document).

Figure 7: Cockroach Cartoon
Source: *Iran* newspaper, May 12, 2006

government buildings. In quelling the demonstrations, the regime killed at least seven people (including four in Naghadeh, West Azerbaijan Province) and arrested and jailed hundreds more. Azerbaijani nationalist organizations claim 20 were killed. Mohammad Ali Qasemi, a researcher at the government-sponsored

Presidential Institute for Strategic Studies, wrote, "Those protests were a manifestation of accumulated dissatisfactions."[164]

In November 2015, a racist episode on IRIB TV-2 again set off demonstrations of Azerbaijanis in Iran.[165] On a children's program called *Fetilehha* ("The Wicks"), a stench in a hotel is blamed on an Iranian Azerbaijani tourist who, according to the manager, used a toilet brush to brush his teeth. The show also mocked Turkic accents in Persian. The broadcast triggered a demonstration that culminated in government forces killing a demonstrator in Urmia.[166] Media outlets in the Republic of Azerbaijan also condemned the show.[167]

Similar demonstrations erupted in March 2018, this time among Ahwazis.[168] A children's program on IRIB TV-2 displayed a young boy placing dolls dressed in the traditional clothing of ethnic minority groups on a map of Iran. Yet the boy did not represent the Ahwazis. Instead, he placed two dolls in Lur clothing on Ahwaz's place on the map.[169] This was likely intended to stir inter-communal tensions between the Lurs and Ahwaz. The demonstrations lasted several days. Protestors chanted nationalist slogans, including against Iran's policies of settling non-Arabs in Khuzestan: "Ahwaz belongs to Ahwazis!" and "We die for Ahwaz, no place for settlers!" The Ahwazis referred to their demonstrations as an "intifada."[170]

---

164 Mohammad Ali Qasemi, "New Societal Movements: The Case of Azerbaijan," Presidential Institute for Strategic Studies, Tenth Year, Number 1, 2007.
165 "Iranian television show sparks outrage among Azeris," *Anadolu Agency*, November 12, 2015. (https://www.aa.com.tr/en/world/iranian-television-show-sparks-outrage-among-azeris/472509).
166 "Azeris hold protest over racial slur," *Radio Free Europe/Radio Liberty*, November 9, 2015. (https://www.rferl.org/a/azeris-hold-protest-in-iran-over-racial-slur/27354275.html); "Iran's Azeris protest over offensive TV show," *BBC News*, November 9, 2015 (https://www.bbc.com/news/world-middle-east-34770537).
167 "YAP Güneydə baş verənlərə reaksiya verdi [YAP reacts to what happened in the South]," *Musavat*, November 12, 2015 (https://musavat.com/news/gundem/yap-guneyde-bash-verenlere-reaksiya-verdi_304663.html); "Iranian Azerbaijanis rise up against Tehran," *Haqqin.az*, November 8, 2015 (https://haqqin.az/news/56724).
168 "In southern province, Iran's Arabs report crackdown as regional tension simmers," *Reuters*, May 3, 2018. (https://www.reuters.com/article/uk-iran-rights-arrests-idUKKBN1I41IF).
169 Shima Silavi, "Arab Ahwaz citizens protest against Iran's IRIB media corporation," *Al-Arabiya*, March 28, 2018 (https://english.alarabiya.net/media/digital/2018/03/28/Iran-s-Ahwaz-citizens-protest-against-IRIB-media-corporation).
170 Ahwazna, "The dignity *intifada*: Demonstrations in Al-Ahwaz condemning the targeting of the Ahwazi Arab identity," *YouTube*, March 13, 2018 (https://www.youtube.com/watch?v=wYON5XsuZgE). The Palestinians use the term "intifada" to refer to their coordinated uprising in the late 1980s and early 1990s against Israeli rule.

The demonstrators also protested the government's environmental damage to the region, which suffers from water shortages and severe health threats to residents. Reportedly, the government security forces killed 50 demonstrators and arrested over 300.[171] The government closed the Tehran bureau of *Al Jazeera* after the network reported about the Ahwaz protests[172] and during the demonstrations Tehran closed down its broadcasts.[173]

Iranian Majles members from Kurdish provinces have complained about the official media's mockery of Kurdish citizens.[174] Kurds were especially angered by an interview with Kurdish intellectual Fariborz Azizi broadcast on January 17, 2021, by Mohammad Jafar Khosravi, host of a popular Iranian state television show. Khosravi mocked the guest's traditional clothing, saying that he looked like a shepherd ("*chupan*"), which is derogatory in Iran. The guest retorted: "This is Kaveh Ahangar's dress and a symbol of freedom from the clutches of tyranny." Kaveh Ahangar is a venerated figure from ancient Iranian mythology who led an uprising against a foreign ruler.[175] The Kurdish guest's point seemed lost on the show's host.

Iranian officials and prominent cultural figures also frequently engage in the mocking of ethnic minorities, similar to the practice of the Iranian press. In May 2009, a video caught former President Khatami's mocking Azerbaijanis and set off a string of rallies organized by Azerbaijani university students, reportedly attended by hundreds of students in several cities. The protests were held in multiple locations in Iran, including Tehran University, Sama University in Urmia, Shahid Rajei University in Tehran and Tarbiyat Moallem University in Karaj. The range of universities illustrates that the leaders likely had a strong organizational capacity on the ground.[176]

---

171 "Iran: Reports of Ethnic Violence Suppressed," *Human Rights Watch*, May 9, 2005 (https://www.hrw.org/news/2005/05/09/iran-reports-ethnic-violence-suppressed).
172 "Iran: Reports of Ethnic Violence Suppressed," *Human Rights Watch*, May 9, 2005 (https://www.hrw.org/news/2005/05/09/iran-reports-ethnic-violence-suppressed).
173 "Fallout from Ahvaz unrest could lead to televised confessions," *Radio Free Europe/Radio Liberty* Iran Report, Vol. 8, No. 17, April 25, 2005.
174 "Kurdish MPs protest against insulting Kurdish dress on broadcast," *Asriran*, January 18, 2021 (https://www.asriran.com/fa/news/765858/).
175 "Kurdish MPs protest TV's hosts insulting Kurdish dress," *Deutsche Welle*, January 18, 2021 (https://p.dw.com/p/3o5fr)
176 "Azeri-Rights Protesters Demand Khatami Apology," *Radio Free Europe/Radio Liberty*, May 24, 2009; "Detentions After Azeri Rights Chants Disrupt Iran Rally," *Radio Free Europe/Radio Liberty*, May 22, 2009.

The government practice to mock the ethnic minorities builds upon a wider Iranian societal negative attitude toward ethnic minorities who retain discernible elements of their native languages and cultures. A study of attitudes of Tehran residents revealed "the less the Tehrani interviewees were able to recognize an accent, the more they associated the speakers of that accent with positive traits. Furthermore, most of the evaluations linked the accented speakers with lower social and education levels."[177]

Instigation of Conflict Between Ethnic Groups

While many members of Iran's ethnic minorities harbor grievances toward Tehran and Persian dominance in Iran, they also have objections toward each other. In shared provinces inhabited by large numbers of different minority ethnic groups there are often clashes over land, water supplies, place names and more. In addition, representatives of ethnic groups accuse each other at times of colluding with Tehran in order to improve their own group's access to resources.

As part of its policy toward Iran's ethnic groups, Tehran masterfully instigates and exacerbates conflict between Iran's ethnic minorities. The regime also exploits conflicts and cleavages between minority groups in Iran that live near each other or in mixed regions. Primary examples are conflicts between Azerbaijanis and Kurds, especially in West Azerbaijan Province, which both groups inhabit, and between Arabs and Lurs in Khuzestan and adjacent territories.

Also, when a crime is committed by an individual from one ethnic group toward a member of a rival group, Iranian media and social media amplify the event, in an attempt to rile up inter-group conflict. In addition, Tehran's government appointment policy often aims to generate public animosity toward the governor's ethnic group, instead of Tehran. For example, in 2021, there were several instances of conflict between Kurds and Azerbaijanis in their shared West Azerbaijan Province. From 2017, West Azerbaijan Province has had a Kurdish governor whose policies seem to further the tension between Kurds and Azerbaijanis in the province. To widen cleavages among the groups, the regime employs primarily Azerbaijanis to police Kurds in West Azerbaijan Province.[178]

---

[177] Shahriar Mirshahidi, "I find you attractive but I don't trust you: the case of language attitudes in Iran," *Journal of Multilingual and Multicultural Development*, Volume 38, Number 2 (2017), pp. 146–159.

[178] Author's interview with Rahim Rashidi, August 2020.

The regime also amplifies disputes between ethnic groups on the borders and names of Iran's provinces, in multiethnic regions. For instance, in 2014 Iranian press gave extensive coverage to the proposal of a Kurdish member of the Majles, Osman Ahmadi, to turn part of West Azerbaijan Province into a new "Northern Kurdistan" province.[179] This proposal drew strong criticism from Azerbaijani-origin Majles members and mutual accusations. Conflict between Kurds and Azerbaijanis serves Tehran's agenda to retain power and control.

---

179 Frud Bezhan, "Northern Kurdistan' Gets Icy Response In Iran's West Azerbaijan Province" *Radio Free Europe/Radio Liberty*, January 10, 2014 (https://www.rferl.org/a/iran-provinces-kurds-azeris/25226139.html).

4 Ethnic Activity

From the 2000s, Iran's ethnic minority groups have demonstrated significant political organizational ability. They have been able to organize demonstrations, orchestrate letter-writing campaigns, and sometimes compel the central government to reverse policies. Accordingly, the regime needs to take their potential response into consideration on many issues, such as on water allocation plans, and foreign policy alliances like Tehran's support for Armenia in the war with Azerbaijan.

Since the regime does not allow explicit ethnic political organizations, parties, or activity in Iran, non-political arenas, such as sport and environmental activity, often serve as surrogates for political fora. At the same time, some of the minority groups engage in paramilitary activity.

The frequency and motivations of ethnic minority protests and other anti-regime activity is underreported, especially in mainstream Western media. In the 2000s, foreign journalists focus on reporting on political events in Tehran. When they do report on the protests or other anti-regime activity in the provinces, Western journalists often report in accordance with the official regime version of events and dismiss the ethnic factor. For instance, the summer 2021 wave of protests in Ahwaz was presented in most press reports as "water protests" with little mention of the Ahwazi Arab agenda. Western media coverage of Iran's ethnic minorities has regressed over time, despite the advent of social media which should have improved journalists' access to information beyond Tehran. The contrast between Western coverage on the provinces during the Iranian Revolution and first years of the Islamic Republic and the 2020s is stark. During the 1979 revolution, for instance, NBC had a team on the ground in Tabriz, was extremely knowledgeable of local politics, and accurately identified the main language and culture of the Azerbaijani inhabitants.[180]

Ties with co-ethnics abroad has helped facilitate political activity of ethnic groups in Iran. When Tehran closes down the internet in order to prevent reporting on developments in the provinces, activists often use the connection to neighboring states to gain access to media. For instance, the connection to the Republic of Azerbaijan and relatively easy border crossing allows Iranian Azerbaijanis in Iran to report about their protests even when Tehran restricts domestic access to the internet. For example, during the November 2019 wave of pro-

---

[180] Güney Azerbaycan, "NBC- Turkish people protest against Khomeini – 1980 – Tabriz, Iranian Azerbaijan," *YouTube*, June 4, 2018 (https://www.youtube.com/watch?v=IrciCoA7Gho&feature=youtu.be).

https://doi.org/10.1515/9783110796339-005

tests, Iranian Azerbaijanis were able to send films and news reports by crossing the border and using Azerbaijani Wi-Fi and cellular networks. Moreover, Azerbaijanis in Iran's border provinces can access television and radio broadcasts from the Republic of Azerbaijan without special satellites or other connections. Thus, Iranian jamming of foreign media does not disrupt them.

The existence of ethno-nationalist states next door to Iran's ethnically populated provinces provides access to cultural resources not found in Iran. In 2007, Mohammad Ali Qasemi, a researcher at the Presidential Institute for Strategic Studies, claimed that among Iran's ethnic movements, there is "no doubt that significant developments have taken place in the last 15 years." According to his report, the Republic of Azerbaijan's independence helped catalyze a "rise in ethnic awareness" among Iranian Azerbaijanis. Proximity to Azerbaijan yielded access to books, publications, films, and cultural figures.[181] At Iranian international book fairs, booths of publishers from the Republic of Azerbaijan selling books in the Azerbaijani language, for instance, are frequented by Iranian Azerbaijanis, and the meetings become informal cultural events. He also noted that several additional factors drove an increase in ethnic activity: wider literacy, activity of the ethnic groups in cyberspace, and minority activists' increased awareness of developments in other parts of the world due to the internet.

Identity trends among Iran's ethnic minorities have changed over time. Following the May 2006 riots by Iranian Azerbaijanis, official journals and government research centers conducted several studies analyzing their motivations and implications.[182] Qasemi wrote that protestors and other activists clearly had ethnically motivated demands, which included:

> recognition of the Turkish language as an official language, teaching it at different educational levels, allocation of television and radio channels to this language, modification of radio and television programs "to stop humiliating and offensive programs," local autonomy to the extent of federalism, some economic demands, [and] opposition to cultural assimilation.[183]

---

[181] Mohammad Ali Qasemi, "New Societal Movements: The Case of Azerbaijan," *Presidential Institute for Strategic Studies*, Tenth Year, Number 1, 2007.
[182] Mohammad Ali Qasemi, "New Societal Movements: The Case of Azerbaijan," *Presidential Institute for Strategic Studies*, Tenth Year, Number 1, 2007.
[183] Mohammad Ali Qasemi, "New Societal Movements: The Case of Azerbaijan," *Presidential Institute for Strategic Studies*, Tenth Year, Number 1, 2007.

In his study, Qasemi concluded:

> Analysts who regarded ethnic activists as a few illiterate and deceived foreign puppets were unable to predict and understand the incidents. The notion that ethnic issues are confined to a limited number of isolated and ineffective people in society was probably one of the causes of the continuation and escalation of the recent crisis... Although it is unlikely that the movement will find tendencies to be armed, it is possible to be radicalized, depending on the policies adopted.[184]

Despite Tehran's prohibition, the minorities often organize demonstrations against the regime's policies. In contrast to the messages in the revolutionary period and in the 1990s, which focused on attaining rights in Iran, in the late 2010s and early 2020s, many of the demonstrations have explicit messages calling for the end of the regime and also for their self-rule.

An annual event that often spurs demonstration and social media campaigns is the International Day of Mother Languages. On this day, ethnic minority members routinely call for the opening of schools in the minority languages.

Sports

Soccer games in Iran serve as a means of expressing ethnic identity and provide a venue for protests, including those with anti-regime messages. Intellectuals have poetry and literature; the wider public has soccer. Soccer stadiums are a logical venue for protests: Tens of thousands of people can gather without a permit or prior political organization. Thus, the soccer stadium becomes one of the only arenas where Iran's ethnic groups can express demands for rights and use their languages in a mass setting. Moreover, the regime is hesitant to break up protests at games due to the large crowds and the rowdy atmosphere, which could easily snowball into violence. It is for this reason the government built a new soccer stadium for Tabriz, outside the city, in a valley surrounded by mountains. The chief of security in East Azerbaijan Province, Colonel Mir Jomehri, reportedly described the motivation as follows: "Let them shout all they want in the stadium outside the city and return quiet."[185]

Indeed, the enthusiasm of Iran's main Azerbaijani soccer team, Tractor Azerbaijan, and its fans is well-known in Iran. The former head coach of Tractor,

---
[184] Mohammad Ali Qasemi, "New Societal Movements: The Case of Azerbaijan," *Presidential Institute for Strategic Studies*, Tenth Year, Number 1, 2007.
[185] Author's interview with a participant in the meeting, December 2020.

Faraz Kamalvand, likened the team to FC Barcelona and called Tractor "the Barcelona of Azerbaijan." In Spain, as well, ethnic politics notably play out on the soccer field.

The team's name was changed in 2019, reflecting ethnic motivations. For several decades, the Tabriz-based team was named Tractor Sazi Tabriz. In 2019, after the team's privatization, the team changed its name from association with a city to association with a land- Tractor Azerbaijan, a clear expression of ethno-nationalism. In official Iranian television, the team is referred to as Tractor, omitting the word Azerbaijan. In addition, Iranian national television stations have disrupted broadcasts of the Tractor games when the anti-regime messages were obvious, such as massive chants of "Death to Khamenei" in November 2017.[186]

Tractor fans frequently carry banners with political slogans, calling for independence of Azerbaijan from Iran. Examples include "South Azerbaijan is not Iran" and "Czechoslovakia or Yugoslavia? Choose one!" Fans frequently have called for the right to have schools in their native language.

Fans of Persian teams often chant racist slurs at Tractor Azerbaijan; they often call the players "*Tork-e khar*" ("donkey Turk").[187] On several occasions, the regime has arrested Tractor fans for pro-Azerbaijani chants during matches, such as the match between Tractor and Persepolis of Tehran in 2019. Tractor fans have protested the racism their team experiences at matches. In 2010, a group of academics and human rights activists wrote an open letter to then FIFA President Sepp Blatter, complaining about the racist treatment.[188]

Vahid Rashidi, who wrote his master's thesis at the University of Tabriz about the Tractor Football Club, noted:

> Tractor Sazi FC provides the Turkish community with an outlet to express their grievances and frustration through chanting nationalist slogans. They are demanding the recognition of their existence through guaranteeing their right to education in their mother tongue and broader recognition of minority rights, concerns, and experiences in the country. Hence, the Tractor Sazi FC is transformed into an outlet for activism by members of a marginalized ethnic group.[189]

---

[186] The author observed the game and the cutting off of the broadcast.
[187] See, for example, at a match with the Persepolis team: @TractorOfficial, *Twitter*, December 29, 2017 (https://twitter.com/TractorOfficial/status/946805728332873728).
[188] Vahid Rashidi, "Tractor Sazi FC and the Civil Rights Movement of Turks in Iranian Azerbaijan," *The International Journal of Sport and Society*, Volume 10 (2019), p. 61.
[189] Vahid Rashidi, "Tractor Sazi FC and the Civil Rights Movement of Turks in Iranian Azerbaijan," *The International Journal of Sport and Society*, Volume 10 (2019), p. 62.

Tractor fans run several social media accounts that regularly publish ethno-nationalist slogans and express solidarity with the Republic of Azerbaijan, including criticism of Tehran's support for Armenia during the 2020 war. Tractor fans have expressed sentiments against Armenia's occupation of lands of the Republic of Azerbaijan at matches in recent years. On March 1, 2019, following Armenian Prime Minister Nikol Pashinyan's visit to Iran, where he claimed the right to territories of the Republic of Azerbaijan, Tractor fans burned an Armenian flag during a match. In addition, they waved Azerbaijan's flag and chanted "Karabakh is and will be ours."[190] Iranian security forces subsequently arrested 29 Tractor fans.[191] Fans of teams from Persian-majority areas in Iran several times have hurled Armenian flags at matches with Tractor Azerbaijan[192] in attempt to incite the ethnic Azerbaijani players to break rules and thus incur fouls.

Ethnic politics has played out on sport social media as well. On October 11, 2019, Voria Ghafouri, an ethnic Kurd, while the captain of the team Esteghlal, posted a condemnation of Turkish soldiers stationed in Syria, and accused them of war crimes. In response, Tractor player Mehdi Babri, posted a pro-Turkish post, unleashing a round of ethnic slurs back and forth by their respective fans on social media. The government banned Babri from the soccer league for these exchanges.

Tractor fans frequently campaign to allow women, who the regime bars from soccer matches, to attend their games. At games, Tractor fans regularly sing together: "Oh my mother, sister and wife! You are ladies! Men and women are equal! Attending in community is your natural right! Azerbaijani Turk ladies rise and get your rights!" The stadium also chants, "Azerbaijan's girls are the stars of the skies!"[193] Organizations that promote gender equality among Iran's political opposition rarely give a platform to these calls or report on these activities which are not conducted in Persian.

Tractor fans have expressed ethnic solidarity with other minority groups on the soccer field. For instance, Tabriz has welcomed Ahwaz teams by singing pro-

---

[190] "Ethnic Azeris protest against Armenian premier's visit to Iran," *BBC Monitoring*, March 1, 2019.
[191] "Iran Detains 29 Azerbaijanis for Burning Armenian Flag," *Asbarez*, March 5, 2019 (https://asbarez.com/178135/iran-detains-29-azerbaijanis-for-burning-armenian-flag/).
[192] "Fans of Tehran football club attend match with Tabriz with Armenian flags," *News.Az*, March 12, 2013.
[193] Güney Azərbaycan Demokratik Türk Birliyi – GADTB, "Azərbaycan qızları-göylərin ulduzları şüarı [Azerbaijan's girls- are the stars of the sky chant]," *YouTube*, February 6, 2019 (https://www.youtube.com/watch?v=Ghtt4v3S8B4&feature=youtu.be).

Arab chants.[194] Moreover, Qashqai Turks often show support for Tractor at matches held in locations near where they live, such as Shiraz and Isfahan.

Fans of Ahwaz teams also often voice ethnic chants in Arabic at their soccer games.[195] Chants have included, "Listen Tehran, long live Ahwazis," and "Viva to Arabs, I am Arab, you are Arab, Ahwaz is Arab." When mainly Ahwaz teams, such as Esteghal Ahwaz and Foolad Khuzestan, play mainly Persian teams, such as Persepolis, the Persian speaking fans regularly shout derogatory slogans against Arabs and specifically the Ahwaz fans attending the match. Following long exchanges of ethnic slurs at a match between Persepolis and Foolad Khuzestan in August 2018, some Ahwaz fans reportedly burned an Iranian flag after the match and continued to voice pro-Arab chants.[196]

Soccer teams from Iran's northern provinces on the Caspian coast have also used matches to express ethnic identity and desires. For instance, in January 2022, Ramsar's (Mazandaran Province) soccer team and Rasht's (Gilan Province) team met for a match. The teams posed with a banner produced by the Damash team (Rasht) that stated that the teams represent "One culture, one history," expressing unity among the peoples bordering the Caspian Sea.[197]

Ethnic politics affects Iran's national team as well. In June 2018, Iran national team striker Sardar Azmoun, an ethnic Turkmen, announced his early retirement from Iran's national team due to frequent racist slurs from Persians.[198]

Minority athletes competing abroad sometimes express solidarity with their ethnic group when receiving awards. For instance, during the 2021 Olympics, Sajad Ganjzadeh, who won a gold medal in karate, stated on Iranian TV that he was dedicating his medal to the people of Khuzestan. The state TV live broadcast was abruptly cut off. During the time of the Olympics, in summer 2021, Ah-

---

194 @samireza42, *Twitter*, May 10, 2020 (https://twitter.com/samireza42/status/1259557666726326272?s=20&t=nwu7jh48cMi9ck6gHeGCzA).
195 "Ahwazi fans chant 'listen Tehran, we are Arabs' during football match," *Al-Arabiya*, November 7, 2019 (https://english.alarabiya.net/sports/2019/11/07/Ahwazi-fans-chant-listen-Tehran-we-are-Arabs-during-Foolad-football-match).
196 "Chants of 'Arabian Gulf,' 'Death to Dictator' ring out in Iran football stadia," *Al-Arabiya*, August 11, 2018 (https://english.alarabiya.net/News/middle-east/2018/08/11/Iran-Social-Media-Uproar-over-Arabian-Gulf-Death-to-Dictator-).
197 @ProfBShaffer, *Twitter*, January 16, 2022 (https://twitter.com/ProfBShaffer/status/1482744579459895296?s=20).
198 "Iran's Sardar Azmoun announces international retirement after World Cup abuse," *ESPN*, June 28, 2018 (https://www.espn.com/soccer/fifa-world-cup/story/3548973/irans-sardar-azmoun-announces-international-retirement-after-world-cup-abuse).

wazi residents of Khuzestan were conducting a wave of anti-regime protests triggered by water shortages.[199]

Environmental Activity

Environmental challenges clearly overlap with other minority grievances and continue to increase, furthering ethnic discontent. Iran's environmental challenges are growing more severe, with extreme water shortages in many parts of the country, frequent dust and salt storms, and health-threatening pollution. The most foreboding threats, especially water shortages, particularly affect Iran's ethnic minority provinces. Tehran *de facto* employs different environmental standards in the center and the periphery, exposing minorities to more pollutants.

Environmental issues are easy issues for ethnic groups to mobilize around due to their widespread appeal and broad support among ethnic groups that may split on other issues more directly related to ethno-nationalism. Members of ethnic minority groups often believe that their regions are enduring environmental damage due to discriminatory policies of the ruling regime. Environmental education can also be used to promote ethnic sentiments. Love for the land and animosity toward the outside ruler, who is seen as responsible for ecological damage, easily come together. This message is very clear, for instance, in the environmental movements of the Gilak and Mazan peoples ("Northerners") that view the Persians in Iran as responsible for the damage to their exceptionally beautiful landscapes.[200]

Environmental movements can also serve as surrogates for ethno-nationalist agendas.[201] In political systems in which ethnically based politics is illegal, en-

---

199 @IranNW, *Twitter*, August 8, 2021 (https://twitter.com/IranNW/status/1424284781798436867?s=20&t=PD6TOF1ICEAmzcy_qnkHwg).
200 See for instance: graffiti campaign in April 22, @caspianshahram, *Twitter*, April 12, 2022 (https://twitter.com/caspianshahram/status/1513921062295285770?s=11&t=B9NjNyzRk_Fy6H_IF4qbCA).
201 During the Soviet period, ethnic nationalism movements often conducted environmental campaigns. See, for instance: Jane I. Dawson, "Anti-Nuclear Activism in the USSR and Its Successor States: A Surrogate for Nationalism," *Environmental Politics*, Volume 4, Number 3, autumn 1995, pp. 443–444 (https://www.tandfonline.com/doi/abs/10.1080/09644019508414215); Marshall I. Goldman, "Environmentalism and Ethnic Awakening," *Boston College Environmental Affairs Law Review*, Volume 19, Issue 3, 1992, pp. 511–513 (https://core.ac.uk/outputs/71459370); Duncan Fisher, "The Emergence of the Environmental Movement in Eastern Europe and Its Role in the Revolutions of 1989," *Environmental Action in Eastern Europe: Response to Crisis*,

vironmental issues often provide a safe topic usually tolerated by non-democratic regimes. In Iran, the regime tolerates the activity of some environmental organizations and clubs. However, the regime has arrested and jailed several environmental activists as well, rendering this sphere of activity as potentially hazardous as well. These arrests serve to deter people from joining the environmental groups.

In addition, some government representatives and elected officials, such as members of Iran's parliament, often voice opposition to Tehran's policies in the environmental sphere, which affect specific provinces. Thus, the environmental issue is not just the privy of activists and opposition members.

Ahwazis

The residents of Khuzestan bear the brunt of health and environmental damage from Iran's oil production, which is centered in Khuzestan, but receive little economic benefit from this industry. The Ahwazis frequently protest environmental degradation in Khuzestan Province and the resulting public health dangers. Recognizing the link between environmental and ethnic political activity, the regime has arrested many Arab environmental activists.

One of Khuzestan's main challenges is a shortage of water for agriculture and safe drinking. Ahwazi activists contend that Tehran purposely diverts water from Khuzestan to the Persian-populated areas of Iran. Khuzestan Ahwazis claim that the regime intentionally creates water shortages in the province to force farmers to leave their lands, thus diluting the Arab presence there. Even Iranian government officials have criticized the central government's regional water-management policies.[202]

Ed. Barbara Jancar-Webster (Armonk, NY: M. E. Sharpe, 1993). In one example of an ethno-national protest, Azerbaijanis in 1988 protested against removing forest land and building in its place a facility for an Armenia-based aluminum enterprise in the Topkhana Forest, located in the Azerbaijani region of Karabakh. See: Brenda Shaffer, *Borders and Brethren: Iran and the Challenge of Azerbaijani Identity* (Cambridge, MA: MIT Press, 2002), p. 128.

202 Maasouma Ibtikar, director of the Iranian Environmental Protection Agency, spoke out against the water diversion. She said she opposed running the vital river dry and depriving the residents of drinking water. See: "Iran: Ahwaz residents protest against Karun River diversion," *Al-Arabiya*, October 26, 2013 (https://english.alarabiya.net/en/News/middle-east/2013/10/26/Iran-Ahwaz-residents-protest-against-Karun-River-diversion).

In October 2013, thousands of Ahwazis formed a five-kilometer human chain on the banks of the Karun River in Ahwaz to protest the river's diversion.[203] Ahwazis also frequently protest the drying up of Khuzestan's wetlands, which they believe stems from intentional policies.

Ahwazis regularly mount protests about environmental issues and water shortages. Most of the protests also voice anti-regime goals. In February 2017, demonstrators in Khuzestan Province chanted "Death to tyranny... We, the people of Ahwaz, won't accept oppression" and "Clean air is our right, Ahwaz is our city."[204] The demonstrators also called for the provincial governor to resign.

Caspian Groups' Activities

The peoples who inhabit the Caspian Sea coast in Iran's Mazandaran, Gilan and Golestan Provinces often engage in environmental protests. During this activity, some groups also express ethnic-based messages.

One focus of the protests is opposition to Tehran's plan to divert water from the Caspian Sea to Iran's central provinces, which threatens the marine environment. In March 2019, protests were held against the planned diversion of waters from the Caspian Sea to Semnan Province. In late 2021 and early 2022, activists organized large protests against the diversion of Caspian Sea waters to Iran's central provinces.[205] *Tasnim* reported in late 2021 that the Iranian budget for March 2022–March 2023 included a line for diversion of water from the Caspian Sea to the central Iranian plateau.[206]

In late 2019, 40 members of the Majles from Mazandaran, Golestan and Gilan sent a letter objecting to the plan to transfer Caspian Sea water to Semnan Province in the center of the country. In addition, on October 14, 2019 the lawmakers

---

203 Iran: Ahwaz residents protest against Karun River diversion," *Al-Arabiya*, October 26, 2013 (https://english.alarabiya.net/en/News/middle-east/2013/10/26/Iran-Ahwaz-residents-protest-against-Karun-River-diversion).
204 Alex MacDonald, "Protests over pollution in Iran's Khuzestan Province 'a national threat,'" *Middle East Eye* February 18, 2017 (https://www.middleeasteye.net/news/protests-over-pollution-irans-khuzestan-province-national-threat).
205 @CaspianShahram, *Twitter*, December 14, 2021 (https://twitter.com/CaspianShahram/status/1470718269535494145?s=20).
206 "Allocating the budget for 'transferring water to the central plateau of Iran' despite the opposition of the environmental organization," *Tasnim News Agency*, December 23, 2021 (https://www.tasnimnews.com/fa/news/1400/09/22/2624762/).

protested the plan during a session of the parliament.[207] Qassem Ahmad Lashki, representative from Mazandaran, criticized President Rouhani for promising the people of Semnan to transfer water from the Caspian Sea.[208]

Iranian experts have warned that the level of the Caspian Sea is expected to fall between nine and 18 meters in the current century, which could be exacerbated if the plan to transfer water from the Caspian Sea to the central plateau of Iran is implemented.[209]

Kurdish Activities

Iran's Kurds have several environmental organizations that, according to Kurdish representatives in the West, work to promote ethnic awareness through "green activities."[210] More than 20 Kurdish environmentally focused non-governmental organizations (NGOs) operate in Iran. Chya is one of the most prominent Kurdish environmental organizations.[211] It was founded in the late 1990s in the city of Marivan in Kurdistan Province. For more than a decade, the organization was denied a permit to operate. The organization is actively preserving Lake Zribar, wildlife and forests in the Kurdish-inhabited regions.

Some of the Kurdish environmental organizations organize nature walks and activities by young people to protect natural areas of Kurdistan. Local residents also self-organize for firefighting to protect forests and wildlife in the Zagros Mountains. Kurds have conducted campaigns against hunting in the mountains and environmental activists have released birds and other animals captured in traps in those regions. Kurdish NGOs often film the bird releases and disseminate the films on social media. For the Kurds, the bird releases symbolize their desire to be released from Tehran's control. Kurds also campaign against the environmental damage from the gold mining activity in Kurdistan Province.

---

207 "40 MPs protest against the plan to transfer Caspian water to the Central Desert," *Radio Farda*, October 14, 2019 (https://www.radiofarda.com/a/30215343/.html).
208 "The protest against the plan to transfer Caspian water to Semnan," *Deutsche Welle*, March 3, 2019 (https://www.dw.com/fa-ir/environment/a-47758987).
209 "Allocation of the budget for 'water transfer to the central plateau of Iran' despite the opposition of the Environment Organization," *Tasnim News Agency*, December 23, 2021 (https://www.tasnimnews.com/fa/news/1400/09/22/2624762/).
210 Author's interview with Rahim Rashidi, September 2020.
211 See Chya's website (https://en.chya.ir/?cat=39).

Figure 8: An Abandoned Ship Stuck in Lake Urmia
Source: Photo by Maximilian Mann

Azerbaijani Environmental Activity: Focus on Lake Urmia

Azerbaijanis in Iran also have multiple environmentally focused organizations, which promote the love of Azerbaijan land as part of their activities. A major focus of the Azerbaijani environmental organizations is prevention of further drying up of Lake Urmia.

Lake Urmia is the largest lake in the Middle East and the third-largest saltwater lake in the world. The lake straddles the Iranian provinces of East Azerbaijan and West Azerbaijan. By the 2000s, the lake's surface had receded significantly. The retreat of the lake affects mainly Azerbaijani and Kurdish communities who inhabit the shores of the lake.

Activists believe that government damming and causeway construction caused the lake's retreat. They have denounced the Iranian parliament's failure to allocate funds to combat this retreat. Instead, the parliament proposed relocating residents from around Lake Urmia due to emerging uninhabitable conditions, such as salt storms.

During multiple demonstrations in 2011–2012, protesters complained that Tehran's policies were causing Lake Urmia to dry up. In August and September 2011, thousands of protestors took to the streets of Urmia and Tabriz to protest the lack of government action to save the lake.[212]

In one Azerbaijani protest, demonstrators waved the flag of the Republic of Azerbaijan. Fans of Tabriz's soccer team, Tractor Azerbaijan, also took up the Lake Urmia issue, blaming government policies for its retreat.[213] While the formal demands of the 2011 protests were ecological in nature, the intensity of the struggle and the regime's fierce reaction to it suggest that the Lake Urmia protests were part of Iran's increasingly severe ethnic troubles. One Iranian government representative acknowledged that the protest motivations were beyond the ecological state of Lake Urmia. Mohammad-Javad Mohammadi-Zadeh, Iran's vice president for environmental affairs and head of its Environmental Protection Organization, accused activists of attempt to "politicize" the Lake Urmia issue: "The issue of Lake Orumieh is an environmental challenge [but] some want to exploit the situation, politicize it, and mount a social campaign."[214]

Many of the protests ended in violent confrontations with Iranian security forces, who arrested more than 30 people. Demonstrators that participated in the 2011 protests received hefty fines, prison sentences, and judicially ordered floggings.

In May 2012, a round of demonstrations took place in Tabriz and Urmia to protest regime policies that have led to Lake Urmia drying up. Hours before the planned demonstrations, Tehran arrested hundreds of Azerbaijani activists, including Hossein Ahmadian in Maragheh, Afsaneh Toghir, Secretary of the Azerbaijan Studies Center at University of Tabriz, and Mohammad Eskandarzadeh in Tabriz. The police used violent means to break up the demonstrations.

---

212 "The drying of Iran's Lake Urmia and its environmental consequences," *UNEP Global Environmental Alert Service*, February 2012.
213 "Azeri Activists Detained In Iran For Environmental Protests," *Radio Free Europe/Radio Liberty*, August 26, 2011 (https://www.rferl.org/a/azeri_activists_detained_in_iran/24309313.html).
214 Quoted in Robert Tait, "Fears Of Ethnic Tensions Rise In Iran Amid Azeri Clashes, Kurd Offensive," *Radio Free Europe/Radio Liberty*, September 5, 2011 (https://www.rferl.org/a/iran_fears_ethnic_tensions_in_northwest/24318682.html).

Militias and Violent Ethnic Organizations

The Islamic Republic has faced armed opposition from ethnic groups from the early days of the Iranian Revolution. As discussed in the previous chapter, as the Islamic Republic consolidated its rule in late 1979 and early 1980, it faced full-scale insurgencies and rebellions in most of the regions inhabited by Iran's ethnic minorities—especially Kurds, Azerbaijanis, Turkmen and Arabs.[215] The new regime used lethal force, executions, and mass arrests to quell the unrest, including an all-out war in the Islamic Republic's first decade to quash the Kurds. Yet, Tehran never achieved full control over the Kurdish-populated regions nor Baluchistan.

The major exception among Iran's ethnic groups in the approach to violent struggle are the Azerbaijanis. From the squashing of the Azerbaijani rebellion in Tabriz in December 1979, Iran's Azerbaijanis have adopted an approach of non-violent opposition and have not conducted violent attacks in Iran. Azerbaijanis that promote an ethno-linguistic agenda have determined that their movement should be non-violent. This non-violent strategy was tested in fall 2020, when some activists suggested blocking roads near the Iran-Armenia border crossing to disrupt supply convoys to Armenia during its war with the Republic of Azerbaijan. However, the movement leaders decided that maintaining their non-violent stance was more important for the movement's long-term success.[216]

For most of the 2000s–2020s, several of Iran's ethnic groups have conducted frequent strikes against Iranian military forces and IRGC. The insurgences were particularly active in 2005–2010. Since late 2017 there has been a new uptick in violent attacks on Iranian army, IRGC, and other government targets. Most of the attacks occur in regions where the groups predominate: Sistan-Baluchistan, Khuzestan, Kurdistan, and the southwest section of West Azerbaijan. Baluch, Arab, and Kurd groups frequently strike Iranian forces stationed on the country's borders. For instance, in October 2018, an ethnic Baluch group abduct-

---

[215] For details of the Azerbaijani rebellion, see: Güney Azerbaycan, "NBC- Turkish people protest against Khomeini – 1980 – Tabriz, Iranian Azerbaijan," *YouTube*, June 4, 2018 (https://www.youtube.com/watch?v=IrciCoA7Gho&feature=youtu.be) and Brenda Shaffer, *Borders and Brethren: Iran and the Challenge of Azerbaijani Identity* (Cambridge, MA: MIT Press, 2002), pp. 95–101. On the Kurdish rebellion, see: David McDowall, *A Modern History of the Kurds* (London: I.B. Tauris, 1997), pp. 270–272.

[216] Gunaz Television, "Iran rejimi işğalçı erməni dövlətinin arxasinda 1/3 [The Iranian regime is behind the occupier Armenian government]," *YouTube*, September 30, 2020 (https://www.youtube.com/watch?v=je1yjUGsQ9s).

ed 12 IRGC and security personnel in Iran's Sistan-Baluchistan Province,[217] which borders Pakistan. Kurdish insurgents regularly conduct attacks on Iranian soldiers and IRGC members in provinces with a large Kurdish presence, often in cooperation with Kurds in neighboring countries, such as Iraq. Consequently, Tehran attacks Kurdish targets in Iraq, too. In addition, both Iranian and Turkish officials have publicly acknowledged the Kurdish insurgency and at times their cooperation against it, including through coordinated attacks against Kurdish targets.[218]

Most of the violent anti-regime activity in Iran takes place in locations where the minorities are the main inhabitants. Thus, for Tehran, the situation is tolerable, because it doesn't regularly affect the lives of the governing elite. However, if the violent activity were to take place in Tehran and other locations in the Iranian heartland, this would be a much bigger challenge and likely met by severe crackdowns.

The Ahwaz have carried out audacious attacks on Iranian military and IRGC forces. The most daring attack in recent years occurred on September 22, 2018. Arab perpetrators attacked a military parade in Ahwaz city and killed more than 30 members of Iranian security forces as well as attendees. Following the attack, the regime executed more than 20 Ahwazis and arrested hundreds more in Khuzestan Province.[219]

Ahwaz militants have also succeeded in carrying out targeted assassinations against Iranian security officers that led operations against Ahwazis. For instance, on November 20, 2021, Ahwazi militants killed IRGC Colonel Hadi Kanani in Karun City (Kut Abdullah), which is located near Ahvaz city.[220] Kanani had been one of the main perpetrators of the deadly crackdowns against Ahwaz demonstrators in November 2019 and July 2021. In addition, Kanani had been personally involved in the investigations and torture of Ahwaz political prisoners. The official Iranian press reported that he was killed by "armed miscreants and rob-

---

217 "Iranian security staff unconscious when kidnapped to Pakistan—Guards chief," *Reuters*, October 17, 2018. (https://www.reuters.com/article/us-iran-security-kidnapping/iranian-se curity-staff-unconscious-when-kidnapped-to-pakistan-guards-chief-idUSKCN1MR1Q7).
218 "Turkey and Iran Unite to Attack Kurdish Rebels," *Associated Press*, June 6, 2008 (https://www.nytimes.com/2008/06/06/world/europe/06kurdish.html).
219 United Nations Human Rights Council, "Situation of human rights in the Islamic Republic of Iran," July 18, 2019 (https://digitallibrary.un.org/record/3823681?ln=en).
220 "The security defender, Hadi Kanaani, who was martyred will be buried in Karun tomorrow," *Fars News*, November 20, 2021 (https://www.farsnews.ir/khuzestan/news/14000829000 555/); (https://www.borna.news/fa/tiny/news-1263681).

bers in Karun city," and did not refer to an armed Ahwaz movement.[221] The regime often portrays attacks on officials targeted by ethnic militias as victims of crime, such as robbers or "villains."

Baluch militias have regularly threatened senior Iranian officials visiting the Sistan-Baluchistan Province, the governor of the province and his representatives as well as IRGC, military units and police operating in the province. In December 2005, armed Baluch groups carried out an attack on President Ahmadinejad's motorcade on the Zabol-Saravan highway, killing a driver and security guard.

Tehran portrays the violent activities of the Baluch, Kurds, and Arabs as Sunni extremism, since most Baluch and large percentages of Iran's Ahwazi Arabs and Kurds are Sunni. Tehran often describes the groups as allies of al-Qaeda and ISIS and tries to portray the regime as a victim of Sunni Islamic extremism. This effort resembles China's claims that Uyghur anti-regime activity is connected to ISIS.[222] Western journalistic reporting on these violent acts often fails to examine their actual motivations and instead simply echoes the regime's erroneous claims that the attacks are connected to transnational Sunni extremist movements.[223] In most cases, the activity is motivated by ethnic and economic factors, not transnational Sunni activity.

A Kurdish activist pointed out that as the Kurds have also developed non-violent ethnic-based activity in recent years, this has facilitated wider participation of Kurds in the movement. When the main vector of activity was violent activity, many were deterred from participation due to the high risk.

Threat to Iranian Oil and Natural Gas Production

Multiple parts of Iran's main strategic infrastructure are located in places inhabited mostly by ethnic minority groups, members of which are conducting armed struggles against Tehran's rule. Iran's oil and natural gas production, for exam-

---

[221] "The security defender, Hadi Kanaani, who was martyred will be buried in Karun tomorrow," *Fars News*, November 20, 2021 (https://www.farsnews.ir/khuzestan/news/14000829000555/); (https://www.borna.news/fa/tiny/news-1263681).
[222] See, for example: Charlie Campbell, "Uighur Extremists Joining ISIS Poses a Security and Economic Headache for China's Xi Jinping," *Time*, July 21, 2016 (https://time.com/4416585/isis-islamic-state-china-xinjiang-uighur-xi-jinping).
[223] See, for example: Thomas Erdbrink, "Iran Says Tehran Assailants Were Recruited Inside the Country," *New York Times*, June 8, 2017 (https://www.nytimes.com/2017/06/08/world/middleeast/iran-tehran-attack.html).

ple, is potentially vulnerable to disruption by the Ahwazi minority. Ahwazis inhabit two of the major centers of Iran's oil and gas production—Khuzestan Province and Bandar Abbas. Over 75 percent of Iran's oil production is located in Khuzestan Province, where over half of the population is Ahwazi. Attacks on Iran's oil production sites, export pipelines or oil ports would have significant impact on the global oil market. In addition, an attack on Iran's major Iranian oil refinery in Abadan would greatly disrupt Iran's domestic fuel supply. Routine study of the Ahwaz armed struggle is important for those making assessments of the global oil price, yet it seems to be regularly overlooked. This group has a proven ability to carry out attacks on strategic oil and natural gas infrastructure.

Iran's main ports in Bandar Abbas and Khuzestan Province are located in areas populated by Ahwazi Arabs. In addition, the strategic port of Chabahar on the Gulf of Oman is located in the Sistan-Baluchistan Province. Both provinces are frequently rocked by armed attacks on Iranian military and security forces and strategic infrastructure. Khuzestan and Bandar Abbas are also key nodes of major Iranian roads.

Local Council Elections

Since 1999, Iran has held elections for local councils. During his first election campaign, Khatami promised the establishment of local councils as a means to allow a greater degree of local government and potentially as a means to suffice demands of the minorities. In reality, these councils have little power, beyond modest impact on local planning and allocation of resources. Accordingly, the local council elections are of little interest in the Persian-majority areas. However, in several cities where a mix of ethnic minorities form the majority of the population, the local elections are viewed with interest and voter participation is greater. This is because the council seats are an arena of competition between the local ethnic groups, such as in the cities of Urmia (Azerbaijanis and Kurds) and Ahwaz (Arabs, Lurs, Kurds, and Persians). Turnout in the provinces is much higher for the elections to these local councils than in Tehran and other major Iranian cities.

University Student Groups

Several of Iran's ethnic minorities have established university student groups that conduct both cultural and political activities. Frequently the regime does not allow students that are active in political activity as undergraduates to graduate or pursue advanced professional degree programs. This sanction has been used frequently to punish Kurdish and Azerbaijani student activists and serves as a deterrent to other students.

Azerbaijani university student societies are active throughout Iran. As pointed out earlier, the Azerbaijani Academic Society (ABTAM) was established in 1995, when Azerbaijani students quit the general Iranian students organizations, when those failed to support their anti-racism protests in response to the 1995 IRIB survey on ethnic groups.

In addition, the Azerbaijan Studies Center (ATO: Azərbaycan Tanıtım Ocağı) was established in 2005 at the University of Tabriz. Thousands of students participated in the center's activities over the years. According to one of the founders of ATO, the goal of the center was to promote Azerbaijani identity among the students, through cultural, social, environmental and tourism activities exploring the Azerbaijani regions of Iran.[224] The Azerbaijani Studies Center also offered unofficial Azerbajiani language courses, held Azerbaijani book fairs and published a student magazine. Since its founding in 2005, the regime has attempted to shut it down several times, despite the fact that cultural associations are formally allowed to operate legally in Iran. For instance, in 2007, the cultural management of the University of Tabriz suspended publication of the center's student magazine, without providing any justification. In addition, university officials and Iran's security and intelligence forces have created difficulties for the center's activists, including suspension from the universities, banning the active members from continuing university studies, and even arresting of some of the core activists.[225]

Kurdish university students also have established student associations. Many were established during the Khatami presidency, when authorities were relatively lenient about the activity of non-government groups. Kurdish university student activities are active mostly in universities in Tehran and in Sanandaj, the capital of Kurdistan Province. The Kurdish students organizations in these two locations often coordinate their activities and conduct common campaigns and events. The regime has not allowed Kurds to open a student organization in Kermanshah, which Tehran views as more sensitive from a security perspective. Several of the students active in ethnic-based university associations have

---

[224] Author's interview with one of the founders of the Azerbaijan Studies Center at the University of Tabriz, October 2021.
[225] Author's interview with one of the founders of the Azerbaijan Studies Center at the University of Tabriz, October 2021.

been interrogated and arrested and some have been banned from completing their studies and finding employment.[226]

Iran's Ethnic Minorities Prefer Foreign Television

In light of Iranian state media's practice of mocking ethnic minorities, its lack of interesting programming, and the fact that it is predominantly in Persian, it is not surprising that large percentages of Iran's minorities watch foreign television broadcasts in their native languages instead. Each group tends to watch television broadcasts from different countries. Azerbaijanis in Iran watch television from Turkey, the Republic of Azerbaijan, and millions of Azerbaijani speakers watch the U.S.-based Gunaz TV, which is primarily broadcasted in the Azerbaijani language. Ahwazis watch television broadcasts in Arabic from Iraq and Saudi Arabia and some U.S. networks that broadcast in Arabic. Iranian Kurds tend to watch Kurdish-language television broadcasts, primarily from Europe and Iraqi Kurdistan.

Initiation of satellite television broadcasts reaching Iran in the ethnic minority languages has had a major impact on ethnic self-identification in Iran. Iranian Kurds point to the establishment of Med-TV in 1986 as a turning point in self-identity among Kurds in Iran. In addition, Iranian Kurds stated that these broadcasts also had a significant impact in creating a common language among Kurds. Up until then, many Kurds could not understand other Kurdish dialects. But the broadcasts helped create a standardized form of the language and to expose Kurds to differing pronunciations and thus to understanding them.[227] The most widely viewed broadcasts among Iranian Kurds are the Rudaw and Kurdistan-24 TV stations.

The TV viewing trends of Iran's Azerbaijanis changed dramatically in the early 1990s. The independence of the Republic of Azerbaijan following the Soviet breakup and the establishment of extensive broadcasts by Turkey on satellite TV greatly influenced broadcast options in Iran and had a significant influence on viewing trends. The broadcasts have had meaningful impact on ethnic self-identification. Iranian government researchers recognized the impact of these foreign broadcasts on the behavior of Iranian Azerbaijanis: According to the study by Qasemi, "Additional factors that are influencing the emergence of ethnic-

---

226 Report of the Special Rapporteur on the situation of human rights in the Islamic Republic of Iran, UNHRC statement (A/HRC/22/56), February 28, 2013, p. 33.
227 Author's interview with Salah Bayiziddi, March 2022.

based activity in Iran is the activity of ethnic TV stations from abroad and satellite TV broadcasts from Turkey and the Republic of Azerbaijan."[228] The popularity of Turkish TV broadcasting has influenced the development of the language spoken among Iran's Azerbaijanis, who have adopted many Anatolian Turkish words and phrases.

The foreign language TV broadcasts play a role in political activity in Iran. Through these broadcasts, activists abroad call for protests and provide information on planned activity. Some of these TV broadcasts, such as those from Iraqi Kurdistan or the Republic of Azerbaijan, are not dependent on satellite connection or internet, so can be viewed when Tehran shuts down internet access and jams satellite broadcasts. Many Azerbaijanis in the border provinces can access television and radio broadcasts from the Republic of Azerbaijan without special satellites or other connections.

Watching foreign television reinforces the native languages among Iran's minorities and surely increases ethnic self-identity and the potential for political mobilization. Iranian Azerbaijanis, deeply concerned by the 2020 war between Azerbaijan and Armenia, got most of their information from foreign broadcasts (as well as direct observation of the battles at the border) and this affected their political response.

The content of the foreign broadcasts has often been an issue of contention in Tehran's bilateral ties with its neighbors. For instance, Iran has requested that Turkey to refrain from hosting broadcasts beamed to Iran's Azerbaijanis.

U.S.-based Gunaz TV has been very effective in mobilizing demonstrations among Iran's Azerbaijanis. Azerbaijanis have responded to its calls to protest, even at times when hundreds of Azerbaijani activists were arrested for their role in planned protests. This was the case in July 2021, when Azerbaijanis demonstrated in solidarity with Ahwazi Arabs. The demonstrations took place despite the fact that on the eve of the demonstrations the regime had arrested over 200 people, which included organizers and planned participants.

Gunaz TV is influential among Iranian Azerbaijanis. Many of its shows are interactive, and Azerbaijanis in Iran participate in the shows despite the possible repercussions. These broadcasts serve as windows into the attitudes and developments in Iran's minority provinces.

---

[228] Mohammad Ali Qasemi. "New Societal Movements: The Case of Azerbaijan," Presidential Institute for Strategic Studies, Tenth Year, Number 1, 2007.

Many studies are conducted in the U.S. and Europe on TV viewing and social media trends in Iran.[229] These studies have several goals. Some of these studies aim to assess the impact of various foreign government-funded TV broadcasts, such as VOA in Persian and BBC Persian, and are thus used for evaluating funding priorities. In addition, the studies aim to understand the political orientation and attitudes of people in Iran. Studies that analyze social media trends in Iran aim to identify further details about the population's political orientation, social preferences, and habits. However, almost all of these studies analyze only TV broadcast viewing and social media trends in Persian, and based on this, draw conclusions about Iran. Consequently, they miss analysis of the attitudes, behavior, and developments related to half of the population of Iran that tend to watch TV broadcasts and conduct social media activity in their native languages, and not in Persian. The Group for Analyzing and Measuring Attitudes (GAMAAN) study[230] on TV viewing trends is especially misleading, since it did not ask open-ended questions on which TV broadcasts the surveyed watched, but rather asked which Persian language network they watched. If the surveyors had added networks like TV stations from Turkey, or the Gunaz TV station, the answers would have been fundamentally different. The fact that the survey was conducted exclusively in Persian already determines that the results will reflect high viewership of Persian-language broadcasts. This survey asked eight demographic questions (sex, age group, level of education, province, urban/rural region, employment status, household income level, and voting behavior). However, the survey did not ask a very basic and relevant question to media behavior—primary language. Even surveys conducted in less multilingual countries, such as the United States, on TV and other media trends typically take into consideration viewers' primary language.

Cultural Activity

In the public cultural sphere, the regime does not impose formal prohibitions on the use of the minority languages or ethnic cultural activity. However, many cultural works in the minority languages and cultural activities are publicly shunned and some prohibited. An example is the wave of criticism in 2020[231] by of-

---

229 Examples of studies on social media and TV viewing trends in Iran which ignore trends in languages other than Persian, see Holly Dagres, *Iranians on #SocialMedia* (Atlantic Council, 2022); Ammar Maleki, *Iranians' attitudes toward media: A 2021 survey report* (Gamman, 2021).
230 Ammar Maleki, *Iranians' attitudes toward media: A 2021 survey report* (Gamman, 2021).
231 "Turkish film controversy as the Iranian 'Fajr' Film Festival," *Voice of America*, February 8, 2020 (https://www.amerikaninsesi.org/a/5279264.html).

ficial Iranian media of the Azerbaijani language film *Atabay*.[232] During a press conference at the Iranian Fajr Film Festival in February 2020, journalists attacked director and actress Niki Karimi and writer Hadi Hejazifar for producing the film in the Azerbaijani language. The film was shot in Khoy in West Azerbaijan Province, where most of the residents speak Azerbaijani. The film appeared with Persian subtitles. Karimi claimed in defense that "there were not enough films in different languages spoken in Iran."[233] The writer of the film, Hejazifar, responded to the criticism that non-Persian language films should not be produced in Iran:

> I speak to you as a Turk. I speak as a writer. Your thinking is a fascist thought … You and no one else have the right to humiliate the Turkish language. According to Iran's Constitution, Turkish literature should be taught at the university in Turkish. I feel sorry for you, and I say without hesitation that the look is a fascist view. I say it out loud. The separatist ideas that emerge are also the product of this vision.[234]

For many years, Iran's Azerbaijanis annually have held a cultural festival that was eventually shut down by the regime. Since 1998, Azerbaijanis in Iran have gathered each year in July at the Babak Fortress to commemorate the presumed birthday of Babak Khorramdin who led a fight against the Islamic Arab conquest of the ninth century. Professor Mohammad Tagi Zehtabi called for the first gathering in 1995 to the Babak Fortress, to which Zehtabi brought his university students. In the first years, the gatherings were cultural celebrations, marked with picnics, music, and dance, without explicit political activity. However, even in the early years, some of the poems and slogans voiced there had political content. Over the years, the political dimension of the gatherings grew.

The embrace of Babak as a major figure of the Azerbaijani movement in Iran is significant, since Babak led a revolt against foreign rule and refused to accept the culture of the conquerors. Azerbaijanis see him as a symbol of revolt against foreign rule, meaning Tehran. Many Iranian nationalists have also adopted Babak as a symbol against foreign rule and religious rule. Ironically, several Persian nationalists claim that the fact that the Azerbaijanis revere Babak Khorramdin as a national symbol means they identify as Iranians, not understanding that

---

[232] "A trailer of the Iranian film in Turkish has been made," *Mehr*, February 7, 2020 (https://tr.mehrnews.com/news/1884383/İran-yapımı-Türkçe-filmin-fragmanı-yayınlandı).
[233] "Turkish film controversy as the Iranian 'Fajr' Film Festival," *Voice of America*, February 8, 2020 (https://www.amerikaninsesi.org/a/5279264.html).
[234] "Turkish film controversy as the Iranian 'Fajr' Film Festival," *Voice of America*, February 8, 2020 (https://www.amerikaninsesi.org/a/5279264.html).

groups can attribute different meanings to the same symbols. However, the Azerbaijanis in Iran that conjure him as symbol see the Persians as the foreign rulers.

Over the years, following the first get together in 1995, the number of people attending the annual Babak gathering increased dramatically. The size of the gatherings made it impossible for the regime and the Iranian media to ignore their existence. In the early years, Iranian media tried to portray the event as environmentally oriented and often referred to the participants as "nature lovers." The media ignored the cultural and political motivations and significance of the gatherings.

While formally allowing minority cultural events, the regime at times cracks down and arrests participants, deterring future and wider participation. As part of the selective suppression of cultural events, the regime officially prohibited the festival from 2004. Azerbaijanis continued to gather despite the ban.

In 2018, to prevent the people from gathering, the authorities declared that the military was holding an exercise in the area and that civilians could not enter. The regime arrested more than 80 Azerbaijanis days before the planned event,[235] as well as those who tried to gather there on the planned date. The regime also succeeded in preventing the planned gathering in 2019. On the eve of the 2019 gathering, the regime's security services threatened organizers and some expected participants with arrest and made them sign statements that they would not attend. In 2020, the Babak Fortress gathering did not take place, due to Covid-19 policy limitations on public gatherings.

Professor Zehtabi, the festival founder, was probably the most important figure in the Azerbaijani national movement in Iran during the early Islamic Republic period. He engaged in cultural and academic activity. Zehtabi was likely assassinated by the regime in 1998.

Zehtabi taught Azerbaijani language at the University of Tabriz for a short period after the Islamic Revolution. He was expelled from the University of Tabriz and imprisoned for supporting Azerbaijani national rights. After his release from prison, he wrote his most famous book, *Ancient History of Iranian Turks*. He was not able to publish the book initially, but several years later during the period of relative social leniency under President Khatami, the book was published and had a significant influence on Iranian Azerbaijani consciousness.

Zehtabi wrote numerous books on the history, culture, language, and identity of the Azerbaijani Turks and voluntarily gave lectures at various Iranian universities where there were large numbers of Azerbaijani students. His activities

---

235 "Dozens Of Arrests Reported Ahead Of An Annual Gathering In Iran," *Radio Free Europe/ Radio Liberty*, July 8, 2018 (https://en.radiofarda.com/a/iran-arrests-babak-fortress-azerbaijan/29350557.html).

were instrumental in the establishment of Azerbaijani university student societies and he inspired many young Azerbaijani people and students in Iran. Zehtabi died in suspicious conditions at home alone in his native Shabester in December 1998, during a period when the regime assassinated a string of intellectuals. This series of murder of intellectuals in Iran in 1998 became known as the "Serial Killings."

The regime often tolerates holding certain cultural events of the ethnic minorities, but puts limitations on the symbols and flags that can be displayed. For instance, in spring 2022, Tehran informed the Iranian Kurds that they can hold their distinct Nowruz celebrations under several conditions. In the application form for holding Nowruz celebrations, Tehran stated the applicants' obligations are:

- Prevention of the interference and influence of ethnic activists and individuals affiliated with counter-revolutionary groups
- No norm-breaking and civil disobedience
- Do not use ethnic and [political] group symbols (flag, specific clothing, white scarf and red rose)
- Refrain from use of destructive slogans
- Avoiding anti-values, immoral, contrary to the common religion and common customs, including male and female dancing together and using vulgar songs
- Refraining from playing epic songs of counter-revolutionary groups
- Use of the symbols of the Islamic Republic (flag, etc.)
- Performers and artists should be warned to refrain from raising ethnic and [political] group issues
- Prevent thugs and problematic people[236] from entering the participants and disclose them to the police and judicial authorities
- Interaction and cooperation with the district governor, local police, and military forces

The content of Tehran's order to the Kurds is quite illuminating regarding Kurdish ethnically based activity. By making the effort to forbid this activity, the regime effectively confirms that the activity is taking place. Despite Tehran's prohibition, the Kurds displayed Kurdish symbols in the 2022 Nowruz celebrations.

---

236 Term often used by authorities to refer to ethnic activists in Iran.

Figure 9: Tehran's Order to Kurds Prior to the 2022 Nowruz Celebrations

5 The Mainstream Opposition's View on Ethnic Minority Rights

The ethnic question splits the opposition to the Islamic Republic in Iran and abroad. It also creates an obstacle to cooperation between the general anti-regime groups and the ethnic-based ones, thus weakening the anti-regime movement. Furthermore, the ethnic question also serves as a fundamental barrier to full democracy in Iran.

Iran faces a situation common to many multiethnic empires. This can be termed the *democracy conundrum of multiethnic states:* "in multi-ethnic states where one non-majority group prevails over others, democratization entails risk of loss of empire."[237] In the case of Iran, one non-majority group—the Persians—prevails over others, thus democratization in Iran would risk Tehran's loss of control over territories inhabited by some of Iran's ethnic minorities. And thus, the ethnic question serves as a major brake on Iran's democratization movement.

In general, the trends of democratization and loss of empire are connected. The threat of the loss of empire has often squashed reform programs of various multiethnic empires and states. For instance, each time the USSR initiated serious domestic reforms after World War II, powerful protest movements broke out in Eastern Europe hoping to take advantage of Moscow's new openness to regain their freedom. Moscow violently suppressed these challenges to its control of Eastern Europe, and subsequently ended the domestic reforms that had catalyzed the anti-Soviet activity. In contrast, in the late 1980s, Moscow did not suppress the challenge to its rule in Eastern Europe that emerged during the Gorbachev period and maintained its reforms; subsequently, Russia not only lost its Eastern European satellites but also its domestic empire, including territories where Russians had prevailed for hundreds of years.

The downfall of the Islamic Republic's rule in Iran would clearly result in at least temporary weakness of the central government in Tehran, and this would allow the ethnic minorities to part ways with Tehran. Both the ruling regime and the main opposition forces are aware of this fact. The ruling regime uses this common fear to hamper the opposition. There is almost no cooperation between the general anti-regime movements and the ethnic-based groups outside Iran

---

[237] For a wider discussion on Iran's ethnic democracy conundrum, see: Brenda Shaffer, "Iran's multiethnic society explains why Tehran fears democracy," *The National Interest*, August 31, 2020 (https://nationalinterest.org/feature/irans-multiethnic-society-explains-why-tehran-fears-democracy-168128).

https://doi.org/10.1515/9783110796339-006

due to the vast difference of opinions on the status of ethnic rights in a future government in Iran. This lack of cooperation deeply weakens the anti-Islamic Republic movement and its ability to succeed.

Not only would the process of regime change create opportunity for ethnic minorities to part ways with Tehran, democracy itself in Iran would pose a challenge to Iran's continued control of the ethnic groups. Indeed, it would be hard for a democratic government in Iran to explain why it allows various freedoms, such as gender freedom and religious freedom, but does not allow cultural and linguistic freedom for more than half of the population. If a new regime did not allow these freedoms, it would most likely need to violently suppress minorities, and effectively end democracy in Iran.

All mainstream Iranian opposition groups want to preserve Iran's current borders and Persian hegemony within the country, including the unquestioned dominance of the Persian language. In addition, almost all of the main opposition groups do not support granting any language or cultural rights to Iran's ethnic minorities. The Islamic Republic skillfully uses this fact to its advantage, fostering fear among these opposition groups that regime change would threaten Iran's territorial integrity. Representatives of the Islamic Republic tell opposition leaders that they need to work with the Islamic Republic and not threaten its stability in order to prevent loss of territory, which could ensue if the regime was brought down.[238]

While the fear of loss of empire constraints the anti-regime movement, Iran's minority groups are deterred from working for regime change, if it only meant sacrificing their lives in order to replace one racist regime with a new racist one. In this context, York University Professor Alireza Asgharzadeh eloquently explains this lack of support of the ethnic groups for the wider anti-regime struggles during the 2009 Green Movement protests:

> Is it any wonder then, that the major non-Persian nationalities of the country have accompanied the Greens with a deafening silence? And why shouldn't they? Why should an Azeri-Turk, a Kurd, a Turkmen, a Baluch or an Ahwazi Arab sacrifice his/her life so that one exclusionary and racist leadership, or regime for that matter, is replaced by another? If the Green Movement cannot transparently discuss such vital issues as federalism, multiculturalism and multilingualism now, what guarantees are there that they will do so after coming to power?[239]

---

[238] Author's interviews, summer 2020.
[239] Alireza Asgharzadeh, "Movements for Democracy and Recent Obstacles: The Case of Iran," Speech delivered at the parliament of the Republic of Italy at a session sponsored by UNPO, Rome, June 29, 2010.

Most of the general opposition groups outside Iran oppose even engaging in discussion about Iran's multiethnic composition and try to block publications and events that analyze the ethnic factor or the desire of the minorities for language and cultural rights. There is a perception among many of the opposition groups, especially the monarchist groups, that even discussions about the ethnic groups will give some credence to their claims and aspirations. The monarchist groups subsequently actively campaign against academic and policy examinations of the ethnic minorities, including reporting violations of their human rights. Illustrating the success of these efforts to silence discussions on Iran's ethnic minorities is the fact that in American policy discussions on the plight and views of Kurds in Iraq, Turkey, and Syria are frequently analyzed and aired, while almost never are the positions and activities of Kurds in Iran.

Iran's ethnic minorities are even banned from discussions on human rights abuses in Iran. Activists in groups based in the United States that are campaigning for ethnic minority rights in Iran report that conferences devoted to human rights abuses in Iran refuse to allow their representatives to participate and present evidence of human rights abuses of the ethnic groups.

This policy of blocking any discussions of the ethnic question is reflected in most of the Persian-language media broadcasting from outside Iran, such as Voice of America and BBC Persian. These media outlets rarely discuss protests and political prisoners with an ethnic agenda or grievances and demands of the ethnic groups.

The topic of Iran's ethnic groups in the politics of the Islamic Republic is a taboo topic among most Iran experts, and Western scholarship on Iran suffers as a result. Most Iran researchers refuse to participate in academic debates discussing the ethnic minorities.

One of their main claims as to why the ethnic minorities rights should not be addressed is that this divides the anti-regime movement and could lead to a civil war instead of a struggle focused to bring the Islamic Republic down. However, the mainstream opposition groups do not entertain the option that this scenario could also be prevented by addressing some of the demands of the ethnic groups.

It is interesting that both regime representatives and opposition figures use the same terminology in referring to the need to suppress Iran's ethnic minorities and prevent "Syrianization of Iran." Another theme common to both the Islamic Republic and its opposition is the idea of the unquestionable unity of the Iranian people. The word *unity* appears in every discussion of Iran's multiethnic makeup. Iran is described by the regime and the opposition as a country that is exceptional in its degree of unified internal cohesiveness.

In contrast to the mainstream anti-regime movement, ethnic minority activists claim that the Islamic Republic cannot be brought down without participation of members of ethnic groups from the provinces. Activists point out that Tehran-centered movements, like the 2009 Green Movement, were easily suppressed because the regime could subdue one city. However, an uprising that took place in multiple locations simultaneously would be much harder for the regime to subjugate.[240]

Not only does the mainstream opposition oppose discussions of the rights of Iran's ethnic minorities, the movement outside Iran often co-opts the struggles of Iranian ethnic groups and distorts their motivations, purposely neglecting the ethnic factor and portraying their activity as part of broader general anti-regime activity. Examples of this are the November 2019 protests in Khuzestan. The regime's crackdown was especially brutal in Khuzestan—forces tracked Ahwaz activists who had found refuge in the region's marshlands and killed 130 of them one-by-one. Iranian human rights organizations and subsequent media reports rarely mentioned that these victims were Ahwazis, or that their protests were ethnically motivated. Similarly, Iranian human rights organizations and media portrayed the July 2021 protests in Khuzestan as water shortage protests, and ignored the ethnic motivations, slogans, and symbols of the Ahwazi protestors.

Mainstream opposition groups rarely advocate for political prisoners in Iran that have an ethnic rights agenda. For example, when discussing the kidnapping or attempted kidnapping of Iranian citizens from abroad, Iranian activist groups abroad rarely mention the Ahwazi activist and citizen of Sweden, Habib Chaab, who was kidnapped in October 2020 from Istanbul and brought to Iran.

Most of Iran's opposition parties and organizations claim to support the establishment of a democratic and secular government in the event of regime collapse. However, these parties want Iran to remain a unitary state with a strong central government rather than becoming a federation or confederation. Some opposition parties have expressed concern that in the transition to democracy, a weakened central government would give minorities an opportunity to win autonomy or split off. For this reason, some Iranian opposition figures seem to prefer a transitional period of military or strongman rule to preserve firm control over Iran's provinces.

The political programs of Iran's opposition parties focus on individual rights, such as freedom of religion and speech, but few mention communal

---

[240] Karim Abdian, "The future movement of ethnic and religious minorities in Iran in the light of regional and international changes," *Journal for Iranian Studies* Year 1, Issue 2, March 2017, pp. 47–49.

rights for groups in Iran, with the exception of labor rights. A former Green Movement activist stated: "[T]here is no such thing as ethnic rights. There will only be universal citizenship rights in the future democratic Iran. We are all on this ship together. Either there is a democracy, and we all flourish under such a system or nobody can make it to prosperity and freedom."[241]

Almost all general opposition figures want Persian to remain Iran's only national language and do not support a policy of multiculturalism or multilingual government. Some opposition parties support the right to teach minority languages in high schools, like a foreign language or foreign literature or culture class, but all parties want Persian to be the primary language of instruction. Most of the mainstream opposition groups oppose teaching minority languages alongside Persian. Moreover, most of the mainstream Persian-language opposition media outside Iran frequently mock and portray Iran's ethnic minorities in a negative light, like the official regime media in Iran.[242]

The most ardent opponents of granting language and culture rights to Iran's ethnic minorities are the monarchist organizations. Most of these organizations do not even recognize Iran as ethnically diverse, claiming that Iranian identity is supranational and applies to all groups. The monarchists' opposition to granting any collective rights to Iran's ethnic minorities goes beyond a practical approach to ensuring Iran's continued control over the current borders of the Islamic Republic. Rather, they possess an ideological element, according to which there is no conception of separate ethnic groups in Iran.[243]

In contrast to the monarchists and majority of the Iranian opposition groups, left-wing political organizations are less averse to limited language rights for minorities, so long as they do not jeopardize the unitary state in Iran. For instance, Esmail Nooriala, head of the Iranian Secular Democracy Movement (Mahestan), stated that his party believes that education in a student's mother tongue is acceptable and that individuals should be able to establish, fund, and run private schools in their mother tongue. The California-based Constitutionalist Party of Iran stated that Persian will continue as the official language, while it supports the options of mother-tongue instruction for non-Persian pupils. The Iran Tran-

---

241 Interview conducted by Ahmad Hashemi, December 2020.
242 See, for example: @et_eci, Twitter, February 2, 2022 (https://twitter.com/et_aci/status/1488917913457377285?s=20&t=gidYADpye9Nl80 V8GKK3Pg); (https://twitter.com/et_aci/status/1488918005564071937?s=20&t=gidYADpye9Nl80 V8GKK3Pg); (https://twitter.com/et_aci/status/1488918143758127111?s=20&t=gidYADpye9Nl80 V8GKK3Pg).
243 An excellent book that discusses the monarchists' ideological approach to the Iran's ethnic minorities is Alireza Asgharzadeh, *Iran and the Challenge of Diversity: Islamic Fundamentalism, Aryanist Racism, and Democratic Struggles*, (New York City: Palgrave Macmillan, 2007).

sition Council is the only organization that has addressed the potential for a future ethno-federal system and the importance of education in mother tongues.

In addition, the Mujahedin-e-Khalq (MEK) organization supports limited rights for the Kurds in Iran, probably based on the movement's cooperation with some Kurdish groups in the 1980s against the Islamic Republic regime.

Nobel Peace Prize Laureate Shirin Ebadi is an exception to the mainstream opposition, having come out in favor of the rights of ethnic minorities to teach their children their native languages.[244] Ebadi attributes the secessionist views of some Iranian ethnic groups to long-term discrimination, not only from the Islamic Republic, but also the Pahlavi monarchial regime. In an interview in late 2021, Ebadi claimed that "Ethnic discrimination in Iran is as severe as possible." She continued:

> Given this kind of discrimination, as well as the fact that they are deprived of teaching their mother tongue, and no one cared about their demands and all their efforts were in vain over the years, some, I repeat, not all of the, some have come to the conclusion that perhaps separating from Iran should be the cure. If this happens one day, it is the fault of the government that has not been ready to listen to the demands of the people for years.

In this interview, the interviewer, Mohsen Rasouli, asked Ebadi if opposition pro-centrists cooperate with the regime regarding policy toward Iran's ethnic minorities. She answered: "Fundamentalism is not specific to religion. Fundamentalism can be seen elsewhere, including among nationalists. Some of our nationalists are fundamentalists. There is no doubt that the minorities are oppressed." She claimed that:

> People who believe in secession from Iran should be allowed to act, they should be able to form an official party, and they should explicitly declare that they want to secede, and for the reasons they want to secede. They should engage in political activity. There is a right to self-determination, not in Iranian law. It is clear that the right to self-determination must be granted. This right cannot be denied anyone. But, I would also like to point out that this should be done with the establishment of parties, through civil means, peacefully and without bloodshed.

---

244 Interview with Shirin Ebadi, Ant TV, May 14, 2020. Partial video of interview found at @endofmonoling, *Twitter,* November 6, 2021 (https://twitter.com/endofmonoling/status/1457000462121537541?s=20).

However, Ebadi assesses that if ethnic groups are allowed to air their grievances in the political arena, they are not likely to pursue secession:

> Through the existence of parties that believe in secession and their civic activity, without violence, the issue of independence, spontaneously, will be like snow melting in the sun, as we have seen in Scotland and Quebec. We can live together in friendship, provided that we accept each other. Not everyone has equal rights in Iran... My ethnic friends and compatriots should blame the government instead of blaming the Persian speakers.[245]

Ethnic activist groups located outside Iran tend to view the refusal of the mainstream opposition groups to recognize the rights of the ethnic groups as a racist policy. Those living in the West observe how most Western countries, such as Canada, Belgium, and Switzerland, are comfortable with granting language rights to minorities, and many see this as a basic human right. Thus, the ethnic awareness and self-definition of many Iranian émigrés to the West increases when living abroad.

Among Iran's political opposition, the ethnic groups are particularly hostile to the pro-monarchist groups, due to their current policies of non-recognition of Iran as a multiethnic society and the policies of the Pahlavi monarchy, which systematically instituted racist policies toward Iran's minority groups and promoted Persian supremacy. Western policymakers mostly do not adequately grasp the opposition of the ethnic groups to the Pahlavi legacy and their lack of support for the return of the monarchy.

Little interaction and no cooperation takes place between the general opposition groups and the ethnic-based ones abroad. The groups have not held serious discussions to forge a compromise vision of a future Iran that would grant some rights to the ethnic groups. Representatives of the ethnic groups abroad occasionally meet with representatives of mainstream opposition groups to discuss potential models of government in post-Islamic Republic Iran. However, the ethnic group representatives do not meet with the pro-monarchy groups.

Few representatives of ethnic-based groups are willing to join the general opposition movement in efforts to topple the Islamic Republic, since they believe that the post-regime government would similarly deny rights to their groups and thus it is not worth risking their lives to merely change oppressors. Accordingly, lack of agreement on the ethnic issue divides the country's opposition movements and prevents cooperation.

---

[245] Interview with Shirin Ebadi, Ant TV, May 14, 2020. Partial video of interview found at @endofmonoling, *Twitter*, November 6, 2021 (https://twitter.com/endofmonoling/status/145700 0462121537541?s=20).

Increased Persian Nationalism Increases Minority Distinct Identification

If Iranian identity were a supra-identity akin to American or Canadian identity, which is not based on a specific ethnic group, there would conceivably be a place for Iran's ethnic groups under the Iranian identity umbrella. However, as pointed out in this study, in the twentieth century, both main ruling regimes— the Pahlavi dynasty and the Islamic Republic, have placed Persian language and Persians in a preferred position.

In the twenty-first century, Persian-based nationalism is getting a further boost in Iran and the Iranian diaspora, including opposition groups. As the ruling regime has become weaker and as its Islamicist and Shia ideology has lost appeal, the regime has increasingly promoted Persian nationalist messages. This has led to an additional common element uniting the mainstream opposition and the regime in suppressing Iran's ethnic minorities and preventing Tehran's loss of control over all of Iran's territories. Subsequently, the increase in Persian-based nationalism further isolates the non-Persian speakers in Iran and increases their perception that their cultures cannot be accommodated under Tehran's control.

Many elements in the regime and the opposition are united in the Persian nationalist Iranshahr ideology.[246] Iranshahr refers to the land of Iran. The Iranshahr ideology has gained traction since 2010 among intellectuals in Iran and in the Iranian diaspora. The Iranshahr ideology connects and unites in common activity elements in the regime with elements in the opposition. Due to this ideology, even many monarchists, fiercely opposed to the Islamic Republic, revered Qassem Soleimani, due to his role in expanding Iran's influence and power in the Middle East over the Arabs.

This ideology promotes the return to an imagined Persian world, where Iran would have ties and influence among speakers of Persian and other Iranian languages and to peoples that were once ruled by various Iranian empires. It seeks to revive Greater Persia, at least in the cultural sphere, but potentially governmentally as well. The ideology promotes the establishment of institutions to strengthen ties between Iran and speakers of Iranian languages (such as Tajiks, Dari speakers in Afghanistan, Ossetians, and Kurds).

---

[246] This discussion on Iranshahr draws upon Ahmad Hashemi's excellent research on the topic. See, Ahmad Hashemi, "The common link between Qasem Soleimani and Cyrus the Great." (unpublished paper).

Intellectual figures in the Iranian diaspora, such as University of California, Irvine Professor Touraj Daryaee[247] and Islamic Republic academics close to the ruling regime such as Tehran University Professor Javad Tabatabai promote the Iranshahr ideology. The head of Iran's Academy of Persian Language and Literature, Gholam-Ali Haddad-Adel, who is a close confidant of Supreme Leader Ali Khamenei, is one of the main proponents of Iranshahr ideology in Iran.

The ideology excludes non-Persians in Iran and outside, and promotes "re-Persianization" of Iran's ethnic minorities. Most of the Iranshahr ideologists see Persian language and culture as supreme to that of Iran's ethnic minorities. Javad Tabatabai contended that Azerbaijani Turkish and the other minority languages in Iran are weak, devoid of culture, and literary heritage: "what sources of human culture exist in the Azeri language that they [Azerbaijanis] want to establish Azeri language schools? All available Azeri literary resources can be taught to the Pan-Turkists in two semesters at the university."[248]

This theme of Iran's ties with Persian speakers abroad has even emerged as part of Iran's foreign policy, and not just in academic and intellectual circles. For instance, following the establishment of a Twitter hashtag in 2022 in which Iranian citizens and expatriates described instances of ethnic discrimination and racism in Iran, Iran's foreign ministry spokesman officially condemned the campaign and claimed that it "aims to threaten the two hundred million Persian speakers in the world."[249]

In addition, Iranshahr holds that Iran's cultural leadership should be expanded beyond Iran's current borders to regions which are viewed by the Iranshahr supporters as the traditional lands of Iran. The regions Iran should encompass are defined as those which speak Persian and other Iranian languages (such as Dari, Urdu, Ossetian, and Kurdish), to regions that observe Iranian cultural traditions, such as the Novruz holiday (thus, Afghanistan, Caucasus, Central Asia, and parts of Pakistan), and any regions that were ruled in the past by Iran (includes Afghanistan and the Caucasus). Per Iranshahri ideology, the historical borders of Iran extend to all places that Arash the Archer's (Arash Kamangir) golden arrows landed. Arash the Archer is a figure of ancient Iranian mythology.

---

247 Touraj Daryaee, "Iranshahr as an Idea and Ideology," *Persianate World* blog (https://tourajdaryaee-blog.tumblr.com/post/97064454181/iranshahr-as-an-idea-and-ideology/amp).
248 Javad Tabatabai quoted in Ahmad Hashemi, "The common link between Qasem Soleimani and Cyrus the Great," (unpublished paper).
249 @MRAhmadHahemi, *Twitter*, February 8, 2022 (https://twitter.com/MrAhmadHashemi/status/1490981454901563395?s=20&t=N4-WoUrLmEHIPP_EcWprZg).

Touraj Daryaee believes that the entire Caucasus, Central Asia, and part of Eurasia are parts of Iranshahr: "This term should not automatically be associated with the political boundaries of modern Iran. It is a term that included a much larger landmass... The Nowruz, an all-important Iranian celebration of the changing of the seasons, is one of the core cultural values of Iranshahr. It is today celebrated in such countries as Turkey, the Republic of Azerbaijan, Uzbekistan in addition to Afghanistan, Iran, and Tajikistan. Even in part of Iraq and Syria, there is celebration of Nowruz."[250]

Shia zealotism and Persian nationalism can co-exist well. Since Shiism is found most in Iran and places where Iranian empires ruled in the past (such as Azerbaijan), many Persian nationalists see Shia as a Persian branch of Islam and a way to move away from a faith with predominant Arabic leadership and where knowledge of Quranic Arabic is essential, to an Iran-led religion. In addition, Shia is a good tool to mobilize control of groups outside of Iran's border, such as in Lebanon and Syria. Javad Tabatabai expresses the easy co-existence of Shiite Islamism and Persian nationalism, defining Iranshahr as "the continuation of Iranian thought in the Islamic period."[251]

The Iranshahr ideology and Persian nationalism explain the admiration and support of many secular Iranians in Iran and abroad for Qassim Soleimani and the activity of the Islamic Revolutionary Guard Corps (IRGC) Quds Force throughout the Middle East. This is not about support for the spread of Islam or Islamic government, but support for Iranian dominance over Middle Eastern countries. Qassim Soleimani's activities led to the rule of Persians over Arabs in the Middle East, which appealed to the Persian nationalism of many Iranians. Many non-religious Iranians support Iran's presence and power in neighboring Arab countries. The Persian nationalist appeal was evident in the descriptions of his activities, for example, by *New York Times* journalist Farnaz Fassihi: "Young and old. Rich and poor. Hard-liner and reformer, General Suleimani, Iran's most powerful military leader, was almost universally admired and had near cult figure status."[252]

In her reporting on Soleimani's death, Fassihi quoted analysts that praised him. She turned to Ariane Tabatabai, an advisor to the U.S. government on Iran during the Biden administration: "Every major political actor within Iran, from

---

[250] Touraj Daryaee, "Iranshahr as an idea and ideology," Persianate World blog, (https://tourajdaryaee-blog.tumblr.com/post/97064454181/iranshahr-as-an-idea-and-ideology).
[251] Ahmad Hashemi, "The common link between Qasem Soleimani and Cyrus the Great," (unpublished paper).
[252] Farnaz Fassihi, "Iranians close ranks behind leaders after U.S. kills popular general," *New York Times*, January 4, 2020.

reformist to hard-liner, is saying this is a great loss."[253] Following Soleimani's death, Fassihi distributed films of Soleimani reciting Persian poetry on social media, bolstering his image as a figure that promoted the Persian nation and not just an Islamic-motivated figure.

Many Iranians, in praising the work of Soleimani conquering and controlling foreign countries, framed it in Iranian nationalist terms. Saeed Laylaz, a prominent Iranian economist who was an advisor to Iran President Mohammad Khatami, referred to Soleimani and the Quds Force as akin to the activities of the mythological Arash Kamangir:

> Soleimani was like Arash Kamangir for Iran...What made Mr. Soleimani look like Arash to me was that fact that Arash, in myths, and legends, brought the borders of Iran to the Jeyhun river, but Soleimani expanded Iran's spiritual borders to the Mediterranean Sea, not in the realm of myth and legend, but in reality.[254]

Iran specialist Ahmad Hashemi claims that "the fear of Iran's disintegration and the hope for the revival of Iranshahr pushes, increasingly, the Persian opposition forces to reconsider their struggle for the prospect of a regime change."[255]

The ascent of the Iranshahr ideology alienates members of Iran's ethnic minorities. For instance, ethnic minorities by and large view its main symbols and figures negatively. Cyrus the Great, the founder of the Achaemenid Empire, is revered by Iranshahr proponents and other Persian nationalists, since he greatly expanded Iran's borders. In contrast, many of the minorities view Cyrus the Great as a conqueror that subjugated non-Persians. When Westerners praise Cyrus the Great to compliment Persians, or call for the establishment of "Cyrus Accords" they are not aware that this inadvertently alienates many among Iran's ethnic minorities.

---

[253] Farnaz Fassihi, "Iranians close ranks behind leaders after U.S. kills popular general," *New York Times*, January 4, 2020.
[254] Ahmad Hashemi, "The common link between Qasem Soleimani and Cyrus the Great," (unpublished paper).
[255] Ahmad Hashemi, "The common link between Qasem Soleimani and Cyrus the Great," (unpublished paper).

6 Iran's Foreign Policy: The Domestic Ethnic Factor

Iran's domestic ethnic composition affects Tehran's foreign policy with almost every bordering state, since all of Iran's major ethnic minorities share ties with groups in neighboring Turkey, Iraq, Azerbaijan, Turkmenistan, Pakistan, and Afghanistan.

Three of Iran's border regions—with Iraq, Turkey, and Pakistan—are security hotspots with the shared ethnic factor playing a major role. In these areas, the presence of shared ethnic groups that straddle the frontiers—the Kurds along Iran's borders with Iraq and Turkey and the Baluch on the border with Pakistan—has created transnational conflicts. Tehran's internal strife with its Kurdish and Baluch minorities sometimes spills over Iran's borders, often requiring coordination with its neighbors. The insurgencies led by these two groups frequently receive support from co-ethnics in other countries. Sometimes these insurgencies even receive direct support from neighboring governments.

Illustrating the cross-border element of these conflicts, the involved states have built border walls between each other. For example, to mitigate Baluch incursions and support for co-ethnics, Iran built a wall in 2011 on its border with Pakistan. In March 2019, Pakistan also began building a fence on part of its side of the border with Iran. In 2020, Turkey built a wall on its border with Iran to thwart attacks from Iranian Kurds and to reduce direct cooperation between Turkish and Iranian Kurds.

Iranian official media frequently claim that terrorist groups cross the country's borders with Pakistan, Afghanistan, and Iraq to conduct attacks, indicating that Tehran sees the connections between Iran's ethnic minority groups and their co-ethnics in neighboring countries as a threat. Iranian media and government representatives have drawn a connection between Iran's border security and the actions of its neighbors. In November 2020, for example, *Iran Daily* reported, "Tehran has frequently advised its neighbors to step up security at the common borders to prevent terrorist attacks on Iranian forces."[256] Accordingly, the activity of these shared ethnic groups affects Iran's bilateral relations with most of its neighbors: Pakistan, Afghanistan, Iraq, Turkey, and Azerbaijan.

Iran and many of its neighbors treat each other's ethnic minorities as tools of foreign policy, despite the fact that each state is vulnerable to similar external

---

[256] "Three border guards killed in clashes with terrorists in NW Iran," *Iran Daily*, November 14, 2020 (http://www.irandaily.ir/News/276766.html).

https://doi.org/10.1515/9783110796339-007

intervention. For instance, Iran regularly tries to incite Azerbaijan's Talysh minority[257] against the government of Azerbaijan and runs programs to encourage separatism. Iran even ran a Talysh-language radio station directed at Azerbaijan's Talysh minority, which resides primarily in the south of the Republic of Azerbaijan. The Iranian station was based in Shusha, while Armenia occupied the city, indicating Tehran worked together with Yerevan to try to undermine Azerbaijan's stability though the Talysh minority. At times, Iran, Iraq, and Turkey have supported Kurdish movements active in neighboring states, while in parallel suppressing their own Kurds. Islamabad also at times lends support or, at a minimum, does not intervene when the Pakistani Baluch provide aid and refuge to Baluch movements and militias in Iran. Concurrently, Islamabad condemns Tehran's incitement of Pakistan's Shiites and may see support for Iran's Baluch as a deterrent against Tehran's outreach to Pakistani Shiites.

In parallel to government policies, members of Iran's ethnic minority communities interact directly with co-ethnics in neighboring states on a regular basis, engaging in trade and cultural exchanges, and holding family gatherings. Several universities in Iran in the minority regions have partnerships and exchanges with universities in bordering countries, providing faculty and students the opportunity to conduct research in minority languages. For instance, the University of Tabriz in Iran's East Azerbaijan Province has for decades partnered with several universities in Baku.

The ethnic factor affects Iran's bilateral relations with all of its neighbors. Turkey and Iran generally do not openly discuss their lack of concord on ethnic policies. However, the ethnic factor from time to time emerges into the public view, especially at times of strained relations. In December 2020, during the victory celebration in Baku following the 2020 Azerbaijan-Armenia War, Turkey's President Erdogan read the poem "Lachin," which is famous in both Azerbaijan and Turkey and speaks of the Araz River, which runs along the Iran-Azerbaijan border, as separating two parts of the Azerbaijani nation.[258] Tehran viewed President Erdogan's recitation as an attempt to incite Iran's Azerbaijani Turkish population against Tehran's rule.[259] Senior Iranian officials, including then-Foreign Minister Mohammad Javad Zarif, condemned Erdogan.

---

[257] The Talysh minority in Azerbaijan speak an Iranian language and are relatively observant Muslims. Iran had hoped this group would thus be more susceptible to Iranian influence, though this did not develop.
[258] "Erdogan: Azerbaijan has assured territorial integrity," *Report.Az*, December 10, 2020 (https://report.az/qarabag/erdogan-azerbaycan-erazi-butovluyunu-temin-edib).
[259] "Zarif responds to Erdogan's 'wrong' poem on Iranian Azerbaijan," *Tehran Times*, December 11, 2020 (https://www.tehrantimes.com/news/455619/Zarif-responds-to-Erdogan-s-wrong-

Both before and after the speech, the Turkish media increased its coverage of Iranian human rights abuses against its Azerbaijani minority. While relations between Ankara and Tehran formally returned to normal after the clash over the poem reading, Tehran sees Turkey as a provocateur of Iran's Azerbaijanis, and Ankara understands that it can touch an Iranian pressure point if needed. Indeed, Azerbaijanis in Iran received Erdogan's poem-reading gesture enthusiastically.[260] Erdogan was likely spurred to do so because Tehran in the 2020s has increased its support for Kurdish groups conducting terrorist attacks in Turkey.

In October 2021, President Erdogan referred again to the ethnic Azerbaijani issue in Iran, at a point of renewed tensions between Iran and Azerbaijan. President Erdogan remarked that Tehran will not continue its threats to Azerbaijan, "out of concern about its own Azeri speaking population." Iran's National Security Chief Ali Shamkhani responded that Turkey should worry about its treatment of its own minorities.

Case Study: Iran's Relations with the Republic of Azerbaijan and Policy Toward the Armenia-Azerbaijan Conflict

Iran borders both protagonists in the Armenia-Azerbaijan conflict. This is not some faraway conflict like those in the Gaza Strip or Lebanon. Many of the battles in the countries' two major wars took place close to Iran's borders and during the first war there was a major refugee flow into Iran of Azerbaijanis escaping Armenia's troops. Thus, the results of the conflict have high-stakes national security implications for Tehran, including those that impact Iran's domestic security and potentially the stability of the ruling regime.

Iran's northern neighbors—Azerbaijan and Armenia—have warred since their post-Soviet independence in 1991. The Iranian provinces bordering those countries are inhabited primarily by ethnic Azerbaijanis. From the beginning of the Armenia-Azerbaijan conflict, domestic security concerns related to Iran's Azerbaijani minority drove Tehran's policies toward both countries.

Iran did not welcome Azerbaijan's independence in 1991. It viewed an Azerbaijani state as a potential magnet for ethno-nationalism among its own Azerbaijani minority. Most Azerbaijanis in Iran have relatives in the Republic of Azerbaijan. Many visit the Republic of Azerbaijan, and some feel inspired by a place

---

poem-on-Iranian-Azerbaijan); "Her sözün bir yeri var," *Tehran Times*, December 13, 2020 (https://www.tehrantimes.com/news/455697/Her-sözün-bir-yeri-var).
260 Author's observation based on the surge in Azerbaijani-language social media activity in Iran discussing the event.

that uses their national language and culture. Tehran wanted Azerbaijan engaged in war, so the republic would not be attractive to its own Azerbaijani minority and hoped the conflict would hamper Baku's ability to resist its policy demands.

Tehran acknowledges that its stance toward the conflict is forged by its national security interests and especially its domestic security concerns. Following the Soviet breakup, Tehran did not express enthusiasm to "export the revolution" to the new Muslim-majority states, but rather was on the defensive. Several days following the official fall of the USSR, the *Tehran Times* expressed the Iranian government fear that nationalism in the new post-Soviet states would project onto co-ethnics in Iran:

> The first ground for concern from the point of view in Tehran is the lack of political stability in the newly independent republics. The unstable conditions in those republics could be serious causes of insecurity along the lengthy borders (over 2,000 kilometers) Iran shares with those countries. Already foreign hands can be felt at work in those republics, [e]specially in Azerbaijan and Turkmenistan republics, with the ultimate objective of brewing discord among the Iranian Azeris and Turkmen by instigating ethnic and nationalistic sentiments.[261]

Mahmoud Va'ezi, who served as deputy foreign minister of Iran responsible for the former Soviet region in the early 1990s during the first war, pointed to internal considerations as one of Iran's major factors in its policy toward the Karabakh conflict:[262]

> Iran was in the neighborhood of the environment of the conflict. Karabakh is situated only 40 km distance from its borders. At that time, this possibility raised that the boundaries of conflict extended ... beyond ... Karabakh. Since the[n], Iran's consideration was based on security perceptions... Iran could not be indifferent to the developments occurring along its borders, security changes of the borders and their impact on Iran's internal developments.[263]

---

[261] "Gorbachev's Downfall, and New Concerns in Tehran," *Tehran Times*, December 30, 1991, p. 2.
[262] Mahmud Va'ezi in *Interfax*, March 25, 1992 (FBIS-SOV-92-059). See also: *Tehran Times*, March 10, 1992, p. 2 for reference to the internal Azerbaijan and Armenian factor as affecting Iran's suitability to mediate in the conflict.
[263] Mahmoud Va'ezi, "Mediation in the Karabakh Dispute," *Center for Strategic Research*, January 2008 (https://web.archive.org/web/20110722014529/http://www.csr.ir/departments.aspx?lng=en&abtid=07&depid=74&semid=989); see also: "Iranian Official on Solution to Conflict," *Interfax*, March 25, 1992.

Va'ezi stated further that during the first war with Armenia, Azerbaijan's governing Popular Front of Azerbaijan support for unity with Iran's Azerbaijanis affected Tehran's policy toward the conflict:

> One of the main slogans of the government of People Front was "Unity of Two Azerbaijans." The People Front tried to establish a united front consisting of Azerbaijan and Turkey to confront with Iran, Armenia and Russia. Extremist policies taken by the People Front reduced the level of support of Azerbaijan and paved the way for Armenians to capture major parts of Azerbaijan's territory.[264]

While the regime in Iran formally declares that its foreign policy is based on Islamic solidarity, Tehran almost always puts pragmatic concerns above religious fraternity.[265] In the case of the war between Iran's two northern neighbors, the clash between ideology and pragmatic considerations was unmistakable: Christian Armenia had invaded Shiite Azerbaijan, captured close to 20 percent of its territory, and turned almost a million Azerbaijani Shiites into refugees. Tehran hoped that the devastation and poverty created by the war and occupation in Azerbaijan in the early years of the conflict would serve the Iranian regime's goal of limiting ties between its Azerbaijani minority and the new Republic of Azerbaijan. As part of this policy, Tehran supported Yerevan in its war with Azerbaijan and has continued close cooperation with Armenia.

Throughout the three-decade conflict, Iran sought to preserve a large *de facto* northern border under Armenian control. Despite formal declarations that it supported Azerbaijan's territorial integrity, Tehran actively opposed Azerbaijan regaining control of its territories that were under Armenian occupation. Accordingly, Iran had no qualms with economic cooperation and investments in the occupied territories or with the exploitation of resources and the refugees' homes and other property. Following the 2020 war, a barrage of articles appeared in the Iranian state media warning that Iran could face commercial losses from the change of control over the territories.[266] This is an indication that Iran's

---

[264] Mahmoud Va'ezi, "Mediation in the Karabakh Dispute," *Center for Strategic Research*, January 2008 (https://web.archive.org/web/20110722014529/http://www.csr.ir/departments.aspx?lng=en&abtid=07&depid=74&semid=989).
[265] For more on this topic, see: Brenda Shaffer, "The Islamic Republic of Iran: Is it really?" in Ed. Brenda Shaffer, *Limits of Culture: Islam and Foreign Policy* (Cambridge, MA: MIT Press, 2006).
[266] "Economic Consequences of Azerbaijan-Armenia Agreement for Iran—Loss of Iran-Armenia border belt," November 13, 2020 *Fars News* (https://www.farsnews.ir/news/13990823000074/); "Developments in the northern borders and Iran's involvement in traditional approaches to foreign policy," *Tasnim News Agency*, November 22, 2020 (https://www.tasnimnews.com/fa/news/1399/09/02/2394551/); Brenda Shaffer, "The Armenia-Azerbaijan War: Downgrading Iran's regional role," *Central Asia and Caucasus Analyst* November 25, 2020 (https://www.cacianalyst.

economic activity in the occupied territories was extensive and significant to Tehran.

During the period of Armenia's occupation, Iran engaged in direct trade and cooperation with Armenian occupation authorities. The most ostentatious Iranian commercial project in the occupied territories was inaugurated in 2010. Iran and Armenia established a hydropower plant complex and dams on the Araz river near the Khudafarin Bridge, which is on the border between Iran and the previously occupied territories.[267] In addition, more than 40 Iranian companies operated in Azerbaijan's territories during the three decades of Armenian occupation.[268] An Iranian company conducted restorations of the Govhar Agha mosque in Shusha. Moreover, Iran and Armenia attempted to portray this mosque as "Persian" in order to undermine Azerbaijani claims to the city.

For several years, the Armenian occupation authorities allowed Iranian citizens to enter the occupied territories and pillage Azerbaijani homes, including stripping the doors and windows and metal frames from the refugees' homes for a small fee.[269]

Several times during the period of occupation, videos were circulated of Iranian trucks bringing supplies to the Armenian occupation authorities. Such videos tended to set off public spats between Baku and Tehran on Iran's involvement in the occupied territories. On the eve of the war in April 2020, an open row emerged between Azerbaijan and Iran.[270] The clear view of the Iranian trucks in the occupied territories also triggered protests by Iranian Azerbaijanis.

Moreover, during the period of Armenia's occupation of Azerbaijan's territories, Iran built its main land transportation route to Armenia through the occu-

---

org/publications/analytical-articles/item/13650-the-armenia-azerbaijan-war-downgrading-iran's-regional-role.html).

267 In 2016, Iran and Azerbaijan signed an agreement formally allowing Iran to use the occupied territories, thus Iran formally recognized Azerbaijan's sovereignty over the territory.

268 "İşğal zamanı Qarabağda fəaliyyət göstərən İran şirkətləri – Siyahı," *Qavqazinfo.az*, October 11, 2021 (https://qafqazinfo.az/news/detail/isgal-zamani-qarabagda-fealiyyet-gosteren-iran-sirketleri-siyahi-339271).

269 In winter 2003, the author witnessed dozens of Iranian cars and trucks in Ağdam, engaging in the pillage. The local occupation authorities explained to the author that they allow the Iranians in to collect scrap metal and other building materials from the homes of the Azerbaijani refugees.

270 "Состоялся телефонный разговор между МИД Азербайджана и Ирана," *Trend*, April 15, 2020.

pied territories. Tehran protested when Azerbaijan retook control of the road.[271] For example, Fada-Hossein Maleki, a member of the Iranian Parliament's National Security and Foreign Policy Committee, threatened Azerbaijan after it retook control of its territories on the road between Iran and Armenia:

> Underlining that blocking Iran's trade with Armenia was not the right thing to do... Armenia is an independent country and the Islamic Republic has trade with the region, and Baku should reconsider its recent actions so that no excuses be provided for countries seeking to create problems which will impinge on Baku more.[272]

According to Va'ezi, Iran preferred to preserve a large de facto border with Armenia.[273] Va'ezi further stated Iran's desire for continued use of the conflict as a lever over Azerbaijan:

> Iran expressed its opposition to the change of political geography of the region. If this plan could have been somehow implemented it would have had wide political, economic and security effects on the region. Linking Nakhchevan to Azerbaijan would have reduced the importance of Iran's unique and distinctive position in the Caucasus and interrupted Iran's linkage with Armenia.[274]

Some analysts have explained Iran's hostility toward the Republic of Azerbaijan as a response to Baku's close ties with Israel. The timeline of this claim is simply not correct. Strategic cooperation between Azerbaijan and Israel commenced in 1995/1996. In contrast, Tehran has acted against Azerbaijan from the reestablishment of independence in 1991, long before Baku formed close links with Israel. Tehran's strategic disposition toward Azerbaijan is primarily rooted in its concern that a strong and prosperous Azerbaijan could be a source of attraction to its own Azerbaijani minority and it thus preferred Baku embroiled in war with Armenia.

Frequently, perceiving that some Azerbaijanis in Iran identify strongly with the Republic of Azerbaijan and that Baku has made overtures toward Iran's eth-

---

[271] "Iran warns of third-parties malign influence over Tehran-Baku ties," *Tehran Times*, September 24, 2021 (https://www.tehrantimes.com/news/465406/Iran-warns-of-third-parties-malign-influence-over-Tehran-Baku).

[272] "Iran warns of third-parties malign influence over Tehran-Baku ties," *Tehran Times*, September 24, 2021 (https://www.tehrantimes.com/news/465406/Iran-warns-of-third-parties-malign-influence-over-Tehran-Baku).

[273] Author's interview with a former senior Armenian official, winter 2000.

[274] Mahmoud Va'ezi, "Mediation in the Karabakh Dispute," *Center for Strategic Research*, January 2008 (https://web.archive.org/web/20110722014529/http://www.csr.ir/departments.aspx?lng=en&abtid=07&depid=74&semid=989).

nic Azerbaijanis, Tehran warns that it might recapture the territory that makes up the Republic of Azerbaijan. This territory was a part of the Iranian empire up until the 1828 Turkmenchai Treaty with the Russian Empire that passed it to Russia's control following several wars. For example, remarks of the Tabriz Prayer leader, Ayatollah Mohsen Shabestari:

> The Azarbaijan Republic once was ours. So, if there is any talk of unification of the two Azarbaijans, it is they who should come back to Iran... Some agents of world arrogance are trying to damage our national unity by spreading secessionist sentiments in our region. Unfortunately some of their mercenaries in Tabriz repeat these words, and talk of Pan-Turkism. The policy of the Islamic Republic is to avoid such polemics. We do not want to create a hue and cry. But if we are faced with these satanic plots, we should remind everyone, including the people of the Azarbaijan Republic, that we have lost some Azari cities, and we could one day claim them back.[275]

Iran's Direct Involvement in the Armenia-Azerbaijan Wars

Iran was directly involved in both the First Armenia-Azerbaijan War (1992–1994) and the Second Armenia-Azerbaijan War (2020). This involvement included serving as the main conduit of supplies to Armenia during both wars, sharing military knowhow and intelligence with Armenia, and direct involvement of its troops in the 2020 war. In contrast with Tehran's regular pattern of using proxies to conduct its wars in foreign countries, Tehran directly placed Islamic Revolutionary Guard Corps (IRGC) forces in the battle zone.

During the two wars, Iran served as the main conduit of supplies—military and otherwise—to Armenia. Russia—Armenia's main strategic backer—does not share a border with Armenia and thus depends on transit through Iran. During the first Armenia-Azerbaijan War, Armenia was only able to continue the war effort and conquer Azerbaijan's territories because of critical fuel and food supplies that reached it via Iran. Armenia's Prime Minister Pashinyan later said that Armenia would never join efforts against Iran, since Iran had served as "Armenia's lifeline" during the first war.[276]

In 1992 and 1993, supply routes from all of Armenia's neighbors except for Iran were closed or unreliable; the civil war in neighboring Georgia prevented

---

[275] "Ayatollah Shabestary addresses religious students in Tabriz," *Sobh*, May 28, 1996, quoted in "Iran," Human Rights Watch, 1997, pp. 4–5.
[276] *Armenpress*, October 3, 2021; "PM Pashinyan: Armenia will never be involved in any anti-Iran conspiracy," *PressTV*, October 4, 2021 (https://www.presstv.ir/Detail/2021/10/04/667821/Armenia-never-engaged-anti-Iran-plots-Armenian-PM).

Russia from providing supplies by land to Yerevan. For example, in April 1992, at one of the most crucial points in the escalation of the conflict between Azerbaijan and Armenia, Iran agreed to supply fuel and to improve transportation links with Armenia.[277] Moreover, fuel from Russia during the war was often delivered to Armenia by way of Iran, thus further contributing to Yerevan's war effort.[278] Iranian fuel supplies critical for the war effort included oil for heavy vehicles and coal for heat and cooking.

Armenian officials thanked Iran several times for the supplies and for serving as a supply route during the first war. For instance, in a May 1992 ceremony commemorating the opening of a bridge over the Araz River, Armenian Prime Minister and Vice President Gagik Arutyunyan declared that the bridge would contribute to stabilizing Armenia's economic situation by providing alternatives to transport routes hindered by the war.[279] The bridge was opened just after Armenian forces had captured the pivotal city of Shusha. Despite the embarrassing timing of the fall of Shusha, Tehran offered no condemnation of Yerevan, and its reaction did not go beyond an expression of "concern over the recent developments in Karabakh."[280] Hrant Melik-Shahnazaryan, an Armenian specialist on Iran's policies in the South Caucasus, wrote in May 2011 that "Iran [had] provided Armenia's food safety during the war."[281]

Again in the 2020 war, Iran was the major conduit of Moscow's supplies to Armenia. Russian ships arrived at Iran's Caspian port of Anzali and brought Russian arms and other supplies by truck into Armenia and into the battle zone. Russian supply flights to Armenia also transited Iran's airspace. During the wars, Azerbaijanis in Iran called on Tehran to halt this transit to Armenia, which, adding insult to injury, passes through Azerbaijani-populated regions in Iran and is directly visible to this community.

In the 2020 war, Tehran increased its involvement to actual military intervention. Iran intervened directly in the battlefield during the 2020 war in an attempt to prevent or at least slow down Baku's advance. When Azerbaijan's forces reached the province of Zangilan, which borders Iran, and were engaged in serious battles with Armenia, Iranian forces crossed the border into the newly liberated territories of Azerbaijan on October 17, 2020 and placed large concrete

---

277 *Interfax*, April 15,1992.
278 *SNARK*, January 29, 1993.
279 *Interfax*, May 7, 1992.
280 *IRNA*, May 13, 1992.
281 Hrant Melik-Shahnazaryan quoted in "Ayatollah Ameli played up to Azeris, Armenian expert says," *PanArmenian*, May 11, 2011 (https://www.panarmenian.net/eng/politics/news/69470/Ayatollah_Ameli_played_up_to_Azeris_Armenian_expert_says).

blocks on the road in a section in Jabrayil region, close to Zangilan, cutting off the Azerbaijani forces in Zangilan from supplies and reinforcements, aiming to halt Azerbaijan's return of control of the territories bordering Iran.[282] Iranian forces stayed in the Azerbaijani territory for three days, claiming they were protecting the Khudafarin hydropower plant, which Iran had built in cooperation with the Armenian occupation forces.

Azerbaijani commanders attempted to convince the Iranian forces to leave and they refused. Subsequently, the Azerbaijani government brought the Iranian military attaché in from Baku to Jabrayil where the Iranian troops were located and sought his aid in their withdrawal. The Iranian forces only agreed to leave and permit the withdrawal of the concrete blocks when Baku threatened to publicize the Iranian intervention. Likely Tehran feared publicity about their intervention, since this knowledge would further incense ethnic Azerbaijanis against the regime. The Iranian roadblock succeeded in cutting the Azerbaijani forces off from each other and delayed the arrival of reinforcements and supplies to the forces in battle in Zangilan. Accordingly, six Azerbaijani soldiers were killed due to the Iranian intervention. Azerbaijani forces were forced to use a different, longer route to join their troops in Zangilan. The delay in the arrival of the Azerbaijani forces to Zangilan also allowed the Armenians to regroup and resupply and thus indirectly led to additional Azerbaijani casualties.

In addition to the intervention of troops in Jabrayil, during the 2020 war, Iranian forces also crossed several times into Nakhchivan, Azerbaijan's exclave that borders Iran.[283] Tehran actively supported Armenia in the 2020 war through blocking of communications of Azerbaijani military units. In addition, Iran provided Armenia with information on Azerbaijani troop movements during the war.[284]

Iran has provided military knowhow and intelligence to Armenia during the three decades of the conflict. Yerevan maintains strong security cooperation with Iran and has not complied with U.S. and UN sanctions and other policies aimed at isolating Iran.

Iran was also likely involved in the development of Armenia's tunnel warfare capacity, which Armenia used in the 2020 war. In 2018, Armenia adopted a new

---

[282] "How Iran invaded Azerbaijan during 44-Day War in 2020," Contreras Report, *YouTube*, October 10, 2021 (https://www.youtube.com/watch?v=iuzJbnl12xw).
[283] Author's interviews, October 2020.
[284] Author's interviews, September 2021; Contreras Report, *YouTube*, "How Iran invaded Azerbaijan during 44-Day War in 2020," October 11, 2021 (https://www.youtube.com/watch?v=iuzJbnl12xw); "Иран вторгся в Азербайджан: сенсационные подробности 44-дневной войны," *Caliber*, October 9, 2021 (https://caliber.az/ru/post/28990/).

strategic doctrine of "new wars for new territories," under which Armenia would open new fronts with Azerbaijan in order to deter Baku from attempting to retake its occupied territories. The new doctrine also involved adopting a more dynamic military strategy: using offensive actions as part of its defense, and not remaining in static positions, such as trenches, but moving troops and conducting surprise attacks on Azerbaijani forces.

As part of the new Armenian doctrine, Yerevan employed tunnel warfare, and built tunnels in the occupied territories, including in Zangilan at the border with Iran, and near Tovuz. There are indications that Armenia gained tunnel expertise from Iran's IRGC. Tunnel warfare is used extensively by Iranian proxies Hizballah and Hamas. The tunnels in the Tovuz region contributed greatly to Armenia's ability to launch a surprise attack on Azerbaijan on July 12, 2020, and thus to inflict a large number of Azerbaijani causalities.

In the post-2020 war period, Tehran has provided intelligence information to the Armenians living in Karabakh, in the area under control of Russian peacekeepers. There are also indications that Iran has delivered weapons and surveillance equipment to Armenians in Karabakh, in areas under the control of Russian peacekeepers. Tehran's goal was to prevent a full regional peace agreement, which would have allowed opening of trade and transportation between Armenia and Turkey, and the access of Russian and Turkish forces to roads in Armenia close to the border with Iran. To undermine the changes of a regional peace agreement, in addition to fuel and consumer goods, Iran delivered surveillance equipment and heavy military equipment. This was the main trigger to the fall 2021 tensions between Iran and Azerbaijan. Several of the Iranian trucks that entered the Armenian-populated areas under Russian peacekeeper control did not depart from the region, instead served as platforms for intelligence and military equipment delivered to the region:

> From August 11 through September 10, 58 trucks with materials for various purposes, in particular with fuel and lubricants, entered Khankendi, 55 of them later left... It should be noted that illegal transportation from Iran to Karabakh was carried out despite repeated warnings from official Baku about the availability of modern video surveillance systems.[285]

Iran tried to deceive the Azerbaijani authorities by placing Armenian license plates on their trucks. Azerbaijan President Ilham Aliyev claimed that Tehran is supplying military equipment to the Armenians living in Karabakh in the areas under control of Russian peacekeepers:

---

[285] "Illegal cargo transport to Karabakh – reason to talk about Iran's insincerity, says MP," *Trend*, September 13, 2021 (https://en.trend.az/azerbaijan/politics/3482712.html).

> [O]f course, we began to monitor the situation and by the beginning of each month we collected information on how many trucks have entered and how many have left, what they brought in and took out. We have all the information, including their license plates, and they have been published in the media. But what happened after that? They tried to attach Armenian license plates to Iranian trucks. They committed this falsification in an attempt to deceive us. An extremely incompetent step was taken – a tank truck with a Persian sign but Armenian license plate. I should also note that they attached the same license plates to different cars. So what does such sloppy work testify to? They wanted to continue this business and just disguise themselves. This took place in mid-August. We hoped this would be stopped. However, from 11 August to 11 September, about 60 trucks from Iran illegally entered Karabakh again. Today, only 25,000 people live there, in the Karabakh region under the responsibility of the Russian peacekeeping forces. Is this market really so important?[286]

In fall 2021, President Aliyev noted that Iranian trucks regularly entered the occupied territories prior to and after the 2020 war:

> This is not the first time that Iranian trucks have entered the Karabakh region. It has happened several times during the occupation. These trucks went there on a regular basis. We saw that trucks keep traveling there even after the war.[287]

Iran displayed a lack of respect for the Republic of Azerbaijan's territorial integrity: Iranian trucks' travel documents stated that their destination was "Stepanakert, Armenia."[288] Stepanakert is the Armenian name for the city Khankendi, which is in the legal territory of Azerbaijan, and in 2021, was under supervision of Russian peacekeepers. Iranian trucks entered the areas of Karabakh under the control of Russian peacekeepers, violating Azerbaijani sovereignty by not asking for permission to pass in the area. The Iranian trucks attempted to deceive the Azerbaijani troops when they passed into the area, by replacing their Iranian license plates with Armenian ones, but they were easily discovered.

Iranian-Azerbaijani Mobilization in the Armenia-Azerbaijan Conflict

As Iranian officials have stated openly, Tehran views with concern its Azerbaijanis' identification with the Republic of Azerbaijan and the situation of conflict

---

[286] "Ilham Aliyev's interview with Turkish Anadolu Agency," *president.az*, September 28, 2021 (https://en.president.az/articles/53249).
[287] "Ilham Aliyev's interview with Turkish Anadolu Agency," *president.az*, September 28, 2021 (https://en.president.az/articles/53249).
[288] "DIN Gorus-Qafan yolunda iki iranlı sürücünün saxlanıldığını" *Modern.Az*, September 15, 2021.

has served Tehran's interests by keeping Baku bogged down in a conflict. However, it seems that Tehran went too far with this policy and its open support for Yerevan's occupation and in the war with Azerbaijan incensed many Azerbaijanis in Iran and has created a major rupture between large numbers of Azerbaijanis in Iran and Tehran.

Throughout the conflict period, Iranian Azerbaijanis have frequently mobilized to support Baku. The 2020 war was a turning point in this community's relationship with Tehran and the results of the war have led to heightened ethnolinguistic pride that has political implications. In addition, Iran's support for Armenia in the war incensed large swathes of the ethnic Azerbaijani community in Iran, increasing their opposition to the ruling regime.

Social media has enabled Iran's Azerbaijani community to obtain a better picture of Iranian-Armenian cooperation, including Tehran's direct aid to Armenia's forces in the war. Flare-ups in the conflict that resulted in significant Azerbaijani casualties, and the all-out war in 2020, have also galvanized opposition to Tehran among Iran's Azerbaijanis.

During the initial war period (1992–1994), Iranian ethnic Azerbaijani activists publicly criticized Tehran's policy toward the conflict. The activists distributed petitions, held demonstrations, and ethnic Azerbaijani members of the Iranian parliament condemned Armenia's occupation of Azerbaijan's lands and Tehran's support for Armenia. In May 1992, over 200 students demonstrating at Tabriz University chanted "Death to Armenia" and, alluding to Tehran, described the "silence of the Muslims" in the face of the Armenian "criminal activities" as "treason to the Quran."[289] According to the Iranian newspaper *Salam*, the Azerbaijani demonstrators in Tabriz urged Tehran to support the Republic of Azerbaijan in this struggle during a march that was marked by "nationalist fervor and slogans." *Salam* reported that the demonstration was held "despite the opposition of the authorities."[290] The next year, Tehran University students held a demonstration in front of the Armenian Embassy to show their support for Azerbaijan in the conflict.[291] During the demonstration, the embassy was stoned, and subsequently the Iranian ambassador in Yerevan was summoned by the Armenian foreign minister to present an explanation of the incident.[292]

Iranian Majles deputies from the Azerbaijani provinces led campaigns aimed at compelling Tehran to end its support for Armenia in the conflict and demon-

---

289 *Salam*, quoted by *Reuters*, May 25, 1992.
290 *Salam*, as quoted by *Agence France Presse*, May 25, 1992.
291 *IRNA*, April 13, 1993.
292 Armenia's Radio First Program, April 14, 1993 (FBIS-SOV- 93–071).

strated against Yerevan's behavior.²⁹³ They distributed petitions and succeeded in attaining the signatures of the majority of the Majles members in a call for a change in Tehran's stance on the conflict.

Armenian Prime Minister Pashinyan's visit to Iran in February 2019 was a trigger for anti-regime activity by Iranian Azerbaijanis. During his visit, in meetings with Pashinyan, Iranian Armenians openly displayed banners stating that "Karabakh is Armenia." The prime minister posted pictures on his social media accounts with these banners, which appeared widely in the Iranian media without protest from Pashinyan's Iranian hosts. Azerbaijanis in Iran responded with protests in front of the Armenian embassy in Tehran and stuck posters on the embassy walls stating, "Karabakh is part of Azerbaijan."²⁹⁴

Azerbaijanis in Iran reacted to an April 2020 publication of information indicating that Iran was supplying Armenians in the occupied territories of Azerbaijan. In response, some Iranian Azerbaijanis suggested blowing up Iran's natural gas pipeline to Armenia or sabotaging the bridges between Armenia and Iran, all of which run through areas of Iran inhabited by ethnic Azerbaijanis.²⁹⁵

In July 2020, an Armenian attack in Azerbaijan near the East-West energy and transit corridor from Azerbaijan to Europe led to more than a dozen Azerbaijani casualties. In response, Iranian Azerbaijanis called for protests against Armenia in front of the Armenian Embassy in Tehran and many Azerbaijani cities in Iran.²⁹⁶ Iranian security forces arrested dozens of Azerbaijani Iranian activists on the eve of the planned demonstrations to preempt them. Consequently, only a small number of protestors managed to demonstrate against the Armenian attacks of July 2020. In early 2021, the regime put several Azerbaijani activists on trial for attempting to organize the demonstrations and sentenced them to prison terms.

During the 2020 war, several rounds of demonstrations took place in Iranian cities with large Azerbaijani populations.²⁹⁷ In addition, Azerbaijani groups pro-

---

293 *IRNA*, April 13, 1993.
294 "Ethnic Azeris protest against Armenian premier's visit to Iran," *BBC Monitoring*, March 2, 2019.
295 Author's interviews, summer 2020.
296 Brenda Shaffer, "Armenia-Azerbaijan Conflict poses threat to European energy security," *FDD Policy Brief*, July 17, 2020 (https://www.fdd.org/analysis/2020/07/17/armenia-azerbaijan-conflict-energy-security/).
297 Brenda Shaffer, "Armenia-Azerbaijan Conflict poses threat to European energy security," *FDD Policy Brief*, July 17, 2020 (https://www.fdd.org/analysis/2020/07/17/armenia-azerbaijan-conflict-energy-security/); "Pro-Azerbaijan Protestors in Tabriz Demand Closure of Iran-Armenia Border," *Daily Sabah*, October 1, 2020 (https://www.dailysabah.com/politics/pro-azerbaijan-protestors-in-tabriz-demand-closure-of-iran-armenia-border/news); "Iran Arrests 11 Pro-Azerbai-

tested Tehran's help with arms and supplies to Armenia. Hundreds of Azerbaijanis were arrested for participation in the demonstrations, receiving long prison sentences and lashes.[298]

Azerbaijani student groups in Iran were active during the 2020 war, expressing their opposition to Tehran's support for Armenia. A coalition of several groups, collectively called the "Azerbaijani Student Movement," issued a statement:

> The resumption of Azerbaijan's advance to take its occupied territories back from the occupying Armenian regime was accompanied by the joy of the Azerbaijani people on this side of Araz [South of Araz River]...
>
> In recent days, a large number of different Iranian political actors have either remained silent regarding Iran's actions, regardless of their political orientation; or have openly supported Armenia in accordance with their political as well as ideological interests.
>
> We believe that there is no greater interest than respecting the values of the people living within a political geography. It is clear to everyone that the Turks of Iran, including the Turks of Azerbaijan, compose a relative majority of the population in Iran; so, this should provide sufficient reason for national expediency. Nevertheless, we are witnessing that the Iranian political actors are taking a stand against the values of the Turkic and Azerbaijani peoples. Activists, who in their struggles expect any action from Azerbaijan, by raising the issue of Iranian nationality, should take another look at this concept. Nationality makes sense by mutually respecting the values of different peoples within a single political geography, not by attacking the values, under the pretext of political expediency. An expediency that ignores the existence as well as identity of a large part of the people within a political geography and attacks their values with the elimination literature, based on this expediency, no political or economic rights will be granted to these people and they will always be discriminated against; The behaviors that we Azerbaijanis have seen over and over again in the last century and have had a profound effect on our historical and collective memory.
>
> Meanwhile, allowing the Russian military trucks to be transported from Iran to Armenia, as well as supplying energy to Armenia in wartime is not what the Azerbaijani people expect; and it is contrary to Article 11 of the Constitution, which introduces all Muslims as the same nation. In the last two days several compatriots as well as sympathizers of Azerbaijan have been detained by security forces for sympathizing with their brothers in the

---

jan Protestors," *Anadolu Agency*, September 30, 2010 (https://www.aa.com.tr/en/asia-pacific/iran-arrests-11-pro-azerbaijan-protesters/1991314).

298 "Urmiyədə Qarabağa dəstək mitinqləri ilə bağlı həbs edilənlər məhkəməyə çağırılıb," *Voice of America*, November 24, 2020 (https://www.amerikaninsesi.org/a/urmiyədə-qarabağa-dəstək-mitinqləri-ilə-bağlı-həbs-edilənlər-məhkəməyə-çağırılıb/5674662.html); "Ərdəbildə Qarabağa dəstək aksiyası ilə əlaqədar 12 vətəndaşa ümumilikdə 15 il həbs və 888 şallaq cəzası kəsilib," *Voice of America*, October 11, 2021 (https://www.amerikaninsesi.org/a/ərdəbildə-qarabağa-dəstək-aksiyası-ilə-əlaqədar-12-vətəndaşa-ümumilikdə-15-il-həbs-və-888-şallaq-cəzası-kəsilib/6266344.html).

northern side of Araz, in contrary to the Article 27 of the Constitution as well as despite the fact that the Friday Imams of several Azerbaijani cities issued a statement in support of the Republic of Azerbaijan. While the value of a statement is in coordinating the behaviors with the content of that statement, otherwise it is considered a contradictory action. However, the position of the Azerbaijani student movement against such behavior is nothing but a phrase: We are Azerbaijan itself. This phrase well defines our expectations and values. So, we condemn such behaviors that are contrary to our values and call on such groups to think more deeply on the concept of nation.

The list of signatories of this letter is extensive and indicates that multiple Azerbaijani cultural societies and publications are active in the major Azerbaijani population centers in Iran: Center for Azerbaijani Studies, University of Tabriz, Poetry and Literature Center of Shahid Madani University of Azerbaijan, Culture and Thought Center of Shahid Madani at the University of Azerbaijan, Sahand Center at the Tabriz University of Medical Sciences, Zanjan University Eshraq Center, Khatayi Center of Mohaghegh Ardabili University, Azerbaijan Cultural Circle, Urmia University Shams Social Cultural Center, Urmia University of Technology, Islamic Culture and Civilization Center, Payame Noor University of Tabriz, Ostad Shahriyar Assembly, University of Hamadan, Assembly of Turkic Speakers of the Ethnics Center at the Shahid Beheshti University of Medical Sciences, Heyat Center at the Zanjan University of Medical Sciences, *Barish Magazine* at the Shahid Madani University of Azerbaijan, *Farhang Magazine* at Shahid Madani University of Azerbaijan, *Ulduz Magazine* at Shahid Madani University of Azerbaijan, *Tanish Magazine*, University of Tabriz, *Gelejek Magazine* at the University of Tabriz, *Soz Magazine*, Tabriz University of Medical Sciences, *Identity Seeking Magazine* at Zanjan University, *Savalan Magazine*, Mohaghegh Ardabili University, *Araz Magazine*, Mohaghegh Ardabili University, *Anlam Magazine* at the Urmia University of Technology, *Gunesh Magazine* at the Urmia University of Technology, *Guzgu Magazine*, Payame Noor University of Tabriz, *Guzel Vatan Magazine*, Payame Noor University of Tabriz, *Yaghish Magazine* at Gilan University, and *Araz Magazine* at Zanjan University of Medical Sciences.

In addition, the Azerbaijani university students group based at the University of Tabriz, Azərbaycan Tanıtım Ocağı, issued a statement during the war declaring its support for Azerbaijan liberating its territories and condemnation of Tehran's military transfers to Armenia.[299]

The 2020 war was a watershed moment for Iranian Azerbaijanis and spurred ethnic solidarity with the Republic of Azerbaijan among Iranian Azerbaijanis.

---

[299] @Behzad, *Twitter*, October 6, 2020 (https://twitter.com/Behzad_Jeddi_B/status/1313541154328244225?s=20).

They could personally witness Tehran's support for Armenia in the battlefield, observing in real time Iranian trucks transiting Russian arms and supplies to Armenia. Hundreds went to the border area with Azerbaijan, observed the battles, and cheered on the Republic of Azerbaijan's soldiers as they regained control of their lands bordering Iran. Azerbaijani soldiers communicated several times with ethnic Azerbaijanis on the other side of the border.[300] Iranian Azerbaijanis openly expressed encouragement to the Azerbaijani soldiers despite the regime's best efforts to prevent them from going to the border area.

The Republic of Azerbaijan's subsequent success on the battlefield inspired ethnic pride among Iranian Azerbaijanis. During the war, several rounds of demonstrations took place in Iranian cities with large Azerbaijani populations.[301] Even some elected officials in Iran of Azerbaijani origin expressed their criticism of Tehran's support for Armenia in the war. For instance, Pouya Mojarad, the representative of Ardabil Province in the Supreme Council of Provinces, strongly criticized Iran's stance.[302]

These expressions of solidarity worried Tehran. In an attempt to limit this jubilance, Tehran arrested hundreds of protestors and activists who had criticized Iran's support for Armenia.[303] For example, Azerbaijanis were arrested in the town of Tikantapa on November 13, 2020, for celebrating the liberation of the city of Shusha from Armenia's occupation.[304] Many Iranian Azerbaijanis received long prison sentences and lashes for their part in the demonstrations against Tehran.[305] Among them, an Iranian court sentenced 12 Azerbaijani acti-

---

300 @Behzad_Jeddi, *Twitter*, October 18, 2020; (https://twitter.com/Behzad_Jeddib/status/1317892041456668673); @metalbash, *Twitter*, September 11, 2021 (https://twitter.com/metalbash/status/1436669102161121282?s=11).
301 "Pro-Azerbaijan protestors in Tabriz demand closure of Iran-Armenia border," *Daily Sabah*, October 10, 2020 (https://www.dailysabah.com/politics/pro-azerbaijan-protestors-in-tabriz-demand-closure-of-iran-armenia-border/news); "Iran arrests 11 pro-Azerbaijan protesters," *Anadolu Agency* September 9, 2020 (https://www.aa.com.tr/en/asia-pacific/iran-arrests-11-pro-azerbaijan-protesters/1991314).
302 Azerbaycan, *YouTube*, January 13, 2021 (https://www.youtube.com/watch?v=6bnjk1OKFB8&t=2s).
303 "Hundreds of Protesters Arrested for Opposing Iran's Support of Armenia," *IranWire*, October 4, 2020 (https://iranwire.com/en/features/7720).
304 Author's interview, October 2021.
305 "Urmiyədə Qarabağa dəstək mitinqləri ilə bağlı həbs edilənlər məhkəməyə çağırılıb," *Voice of America*, November 24, 2020 (https://www.amerikaninsesi.org/a/urmiyədə-qarabağa-dəstək-mitinqləri-ilə-bağlı-həbs-edilənlər-məhkəməyə-çağırılıb/5674662.html); "Ərdəbildə Qarabağa dəstək aksiyası ilə əlaqədar 12 vətəndaşa ümumilikdə 15 il həbs və 888 şallaq cəzası kəsilib," *Voice of America*, October 11, 2021 (https://www.amerikaninsesi.org/a/ərdəbildə-qarabağa-

vists who were arrested during protests in Ardabil in October 2020 to 14 months in prison and 74 lashes.[306]

Following the war, Azerbaijan made several gestures of solidarity with the Azerbaijanis in Iran. For instance, in November 2021, Baku issued a new currency note (500 Manat) that depicted the Khudafarin Bridge. The bridge is a symbol of unity between the Azerbaijanis in Iran and those in the Republic of Azerbaijan. Like the Berlin Wall, prior to the fall, it is a symbol of separation of the divided Azerbaijani nation. In addition, Azerbaijan placed a large slogan on a mountain facing Iran in the liberated territories, stating in the Azerbaijani language "Motherland comes first," attempting to appeal to ethno-linguistic sentiments among Azerbaijanis in Iran.

Azerbaijan President Ilham Aliyev's first trip to the liberated territories in the regions bordering Iran following the war included a visit to the Khudafarin Bridge. The Khudafarin Bridge straddles the Araz River which forms the border between Azerbaijan and Iran. Aliyev personally hoisted an Azerbaijani flag on the bridge, which generated enthusiasm among Iranian Azerbaijanis. Azerbaijani soldiers had previously placed a flag on Azerbaijan's side of the bridge, but this was removed by the Iranians. Aliyev thus made a point of himself hoisting the flag. During the visit, an Iranian sniper published pictures of Aliyev and his wife taken through his gun's scope, suggesting the ability of Iran to assassinate him.[307]

During the war, Iranian Azerbaijanis observed that Israel gave Azerbaijan extensive support as part of their strategic partnership. In addition, Azerbaijanis in Iran observed that Israeli doctors granted extensive medical aid to Azerbaijan's injured soldiers. This increased positive feelings toward Israel among the group, creating another reason for anti-regime sentiment.[308]

In November 2021, Baku marked the one-year anniversary of the 2020 Second Armenia-Azerbaijan War and its subsequent liberation of its territories. Many Azerbaijanis in Iran openly celebrated the victory as well. For instance,

---

dəstək-aksiyası-ilə-əlaqədar-12-vətəndaşa-ümumilikdə-15-il-həbs-və-888-şallaq-cəzası-kəsilib/6266344.html).
306 United Nations Human Rights Council, "Situation of human rights in the Islamic Republic of Iran," January 13, 2022 (https://www.ohchr.org/en/documents/country-reports/ahrc4975-situation-human-rights-islamic-republic-iran-report-special).
307 "Iranian sniper posts provocative photo taking aim at Azerbaijani President Aliyev," *Daily Sabah*, November 19, 2020 (https://www.dailysabah.com/politics/diplomacy/iranian-sniper-posts-provocative-photo-taking-aim-at-azerbaijani-president-aliyev).
308 @AhmadObali, *Twitter*, March 5, 2021 (https://twitter.com/AhmadObali/status/1367848470556667911?s=20); Itamar Eichner, "Most Iranian people are pro-Israel, expatriate says," *Ynet*, March 23, 2021 (https://www.ynetnews.com/magazine/article/r10h00SUEd).

Figure 10: "Öncə Vətən" (Motherland First), Jabrayil Province, Azerbaijan in close proximilty to the Khudafarin Bridge.
Source: Photo by Brenda Shaffer

shopkeepers in bazaars in Azerbaijani-populated areas distributed sweets and posted pictures of themselves on social media with signs celebrating the victory.

Case Study: The Kurds and Iran, Turkey, and Iraq

Iran's border regions with Iraq and Turkey are a significant security challenge for Tehran. Kurds inhabit areas on both sides of these borders. Iranian media reported, for instance, in 2020 five to 10 Iranian soldiers and IRGC members died every month in these border regions.[309]

Kurds in Iran, and in general, are divided into very different political orientations toward Iran and other bordering states. Some cooperate with Iran, while other oppose cooperation and sometimes their stances change on the issue.

---

[309] Author's calculations based on Iranian state media reporting on numbers of casualties.

The policies of Iraq, Turkey, and Iran toward their domestic Kurdish communities are intertwined with the wider transnational conflicts. As there are many divisions and animosities among the Kurds, the three states often exploit these fissures and at times maintain good ties with a Kurdish group in a neighboring country while suppressing Kurds at home.

Over time, the nature of cooperation between Iran, Iraq, and Turkey in combatting their Kurdish populations has changed multiple times. At times, each of the states has supported Kurdish movements active in a neighboring state, while in parallel suppressing their domestic Kurds. This was typical of Iran and Iraq in the 1960s and 1970s. At times, some of the states conduct joint operations against Kurds. At other times, one of the states has attacked Kurds in a neighboring state. Iranian senior officials have acknowledged conducting cross-border raids into Turkey as well to battle Kurdish militias.[310]

The shared Kurdish communities also affect these states' foreign policies toward one another. At times, they conduct joint operations against Kurds.[311] This interstate cooperation against the Kurds is transitory and can vanish quickly. For instance, in fighting against domestic Kurdish militants, Tehran sometimes shells Kurdish villages in Iraq, eliciting criticism from Baghdad.[312] In late September 2018, Iran fired ballistic missiles at a Kurdistan Democratic Party-Iran (KDP-I) base in northern Iraq, killing 17 and wounding more than 50, possibly in retaliation for an earlier Kurdish attack that killed 10 Iranian border guards.[313] Days later, Iran shelled targets in Erbil. In addition, in October 2020, IRGC units shelled Kurdish villages in Iraq.[314]

In the 2020s, Turkish officials have openly complained about Iran allowing refuge and support for PKK members based in Iran, which operate against Turkey. In 2020, Turkish Minister of Interior Suleyman Soylu, while visiting the bor-

---

310 "Iran continues operations against terrorist organization," *Zaman*, October 22, 2010.
311 See, for instance: "Turkey, Iran carried out joint operation against Kurdish militants: minister," *Reuters*, March 18, 2019 (https://www.reuters.com/article/us-mideast-crisis-turkey-iran/turkey-iran-carried-out-joint-operation-against-kurdish-militants-minister-idUSKCN1QZ1CI); "Turkey and Iran Unite to Attack Kurdish Rebels," *Associated Press*, June 6, 2008.
312 "Iraq condemns Iranian shelling of Kurd villages," *Reuters*, May 5, 2009.
313 Bilal Wahab, "Iran's Missile Attack in Iraqi Kurdistan Could backfire," *Washington Institute for Near East Policy*, September 11, 2018 (https://www.washingtoninstitute.org/policy-analysis/view/irans-missile-attack-in-iraqi-kurdistan-could-backfire); "Iran Guard claims missile attack on separatist Kurds in Iraq," *Associated Press*, September 9, 2018 (https://apnews.com/article/39a6e79233574b0fb8ef2a794625ed33).
314 "Iran's Revolutionary Guards 'Shell Border Villages' In Iraqi Kurdistan," *Iran International*, October 30, 2020 (https://old.iranintl.com/en/iran-in-brief/iran's-revolutionary-guards-'shell-border-villages'-iraqi-kurdistan).

der town of Dogubayazid in the Turkish province of Agri to inspect the construction of the border wall with Iran stated, "Currently, about 100 terrorists [PKK] are present in the Dambat area of Maku in northwestern Iran. It is Iran's responsibility to clear there." Soylu threatened that Turkish security forces would enter Iran if Tehran did not eliminate this threat: "This is important for us... If we enter the Dambat area of Maku, we will not leave a terrorist there alive. This is the responsibility of our neighbor Iran, and they are aware of this responsibility. We hope this happens soon."[315]

In parallel, Kurds in Turkey and Iraq provide critical support to the Iranian Kurdish insurgency against Tehran. At times, this support brings Tehran into conflict with Ankara and the Iraqi Kurdistan authorities, which Tehran criticizes for failing to rein in their Kurdish populations. In parallel, Kurdish groups are at times active against Turkey, and receive support from Tehran. In the last decades, attacks by the PKK and other Kurdish groups on the natural gas pipeline from Iran to Turkey frequently disrupted Iranian gas exports.

Tehran has significant influence in Iraqi Kurdistan. Tehran frequently coerces Erbil to hand over Iranian Kurds that are wanted by Tehran. For instance, the Iraqi Kurdish authorities returned a Kurdish activist to Iran that had busted out of an Iranian prison in 2020 and escaped to Iraqi Kurdistan. After the return of many of these Kurds to Iran, some have been subsequently executed.[316]

Events in Iraqi Kurdistan have significant impact on Kurds in Iran. For instance, Saddam Hussein's use of chemical weapons on Kurds in Iraq in 1988 awakened among many Iranian Kurds the belief in a need for self-government as necessary to protect themselves.

Tehran has also been willing to use foreign policy carrots in its attempt to encourage the loyalty of Kurds in Iran. During the swearing in ceremony of Iran's President Ebrahim Raisi, Iraqi Kurdistan Region's President Nerchirvan Barzani was treated as a head of state. The flag of Kurdistan was flown at official ceremonies, alongside the flag of Iran, and not the flag of Iraq.[317] Tehran's gesture in welcoming Barzani was received well among Kurds in Iran and likely one of the regime's motivations in this exceptional act was to appeal to them. In parallel, Tehran continued to air complaints against Iraqi Kurdistan, claiming that

---

315 "Currently, about 100 terrorists (PKK) are present in the Dambat area of Maku in northwestern Iran," *Anadolu Agency*, June 6, 2020.
316 "Political Prisoner Extradited From Iraqi Kurdistan, Executed in Iran," *Iran Human Rights*, April 11, 2020 (https://iranhr.net/en/articles/4191/).
317 "Kurdistan Region president in Iran for Raisi's swearing-in," *Kurdistan24*, August 5, 2021 (https://www.kurdistan24.net/en/story/25180-Kurdistan-Region-president-in-Iran-for-Raisi's-swearing-in).

Figure 11: Iraqi Kurdistan Region's President Nerchirvan Barzani in Iran
Source: Official Website of The Presidency of the Kurdistan Region – Iraq

the region harbored anti-Iranian Kurdish elements, as well as Israelis and Americans, signaling that there was no intent to show special respect for Barzani, but more aimed at appealing to its domestic Kurds.[318]

Case Study: The Baluch in Iran and Pakistan

For most of the period of the Islamic Republic, Iran's Baluch have waged an anti-regime insurgency in Sistan-Baluchistan Province. This insurgency intensified beginning in 2005. As part of their string of attacks on Iranian military, IRGC, and government representatives in December 2005, insurgents attacked the motorcade of the newly elected President Mahmoud Ahmadinejad in Sistan-Baluchistan, killing three in his security detail. In October 2009, Baluch fighters attacked an IRGC delegation, killing 42 people, including the deputy commander of the IRGC ground forces and five other senior IRGC commanders. In October

---

318 "Iraqi Kurdistan's inaction over Kurdish militants angers Iran," *Tehran Times*, September 7, 2021 (https://www.tehrantimes.com/news/464824/Iraqi-Kurdistan-s-inaction-over-Kurdish-militants-angers-Iran); "Tehran vows tough response against U.S., Israeli bases in Iraqi Kurdistan," *Tehran Times*, September 25, 2021 (https://www.tehrantimes.com/news/465453/Tehran-vows-tough-response-against-U-S-Israeli-bases-in-Iraqi).

Figure 12: Iran Treats Iraqi Kurdistan Region's President Nerchirvan Barzani as a Head of State
Source: Official Website of The Presidency of the Kurdistan Region – Iraq

2018, Baluch groups abducted more than a dozen Iranian IRGC members.[319] The next year, Baluch paramilitary forces attacked an IRGC convoy transiting the region, killing nearly 30.[320]

Two main Baluch groups that have engaged in anti-regime attacks on Iranian military and IRGC members are Jundullah and Jaish ul-Adl. Jundullah was especially active from 2005 to 2010, conducting more than a dozen major attacks in Sistan-Baluchistan, including a December 2010 bombing that killed 38 at a mosque in Chahbahar.[321] Tehran captured Jundullah's leaders, the brothers Abd al-Malik Rigi and Abdolhamid Rigi, and executed them in 2010.[322]

---

[319] "Militants seize 14 Iranian security forces near Pakistan," *Associated Press*, October 16, 2018 (https://apnews.com/article/a2cc578c430245289372210833f56bdf).
[320] "Nearly 2 Dozen Iranian Revolutionary Guards Reportedly Killed In Bomb Attack," *NPR*, February 13, 2019 (https://www.npr.org/2019/02/13/694352657/nearly-two-dozen-iranian-revolutionary-guards-reportedly-killed-in-bomb-attack).
[321] "Iran: Internal Politics and U.S. Policy and Options," *Congressional Research Service*, December 9, 2020 (https://crsreports.congress.gov/product/pdf/RL/RL32048).
[322] Nazila Fathi, "Iran Executes Sunni Rebel Leader," *New York Times*, June 20, 2010.

Cross-border ties with Baluch in Pakistan affect Iran's Baluch capacity to wage an insurgency against Tehran. Iranian Baluch share significant ties with Baluch in Pakistan and Afghanistan. The porous Iran-Pakistan border facilitates illicit cross-border economic activity, and Baluch from each side often cross the border to visit relatives and attend family events. Iranian Baluch militias and groups frequently receive support from Baluch in Pakistan. Militants often escape to Pakistan after conducting armed attacks in Iran. Iranian forces have crossed into Pakistan seeking to subdue and capture Iranian Baluch militants. Baluch insurgents have captured Iranian border guards in Pakistan and held them captive there.[323]

The Baluch insurgency directly affects bilateral relations between Pakistan and Iran. At times, Iran also has claimed that the Jundullah organization has links to the Pakistani security services.

Following Baluch attacks, Iran's leaders often directly call on Pakistan's leadership to take action against Iranian Baluch militants that they claim are operating from Pakistan.[324] Iranian official media has claimed that Pakistan is a "safe haven" for Baluch terrorists.[325] The IRGC has periodically threatened to cross the border unilaterally or attack Pakistani Baluch with missiles if Islamabad does not curtail support for the insurgency.[326]

Iran's Baluch insurrection especially strained Iran's relations with Pakistan in 2014. On February 14, 2014, the Baluch militia Jaish al-Adl abducted five Iranian border guards and brought them to Pakistan. It took months of diplomacy before Islamabad facilitated their release.

Iranian-Pakistani tensions over the cross-border Baluch revolt reached new heights in October 2014, when 30 Iranian security forces crossed the border in pursuit of Baluch insurgents, leading to clashes with the Pakistani military and the death of a Pakistani soldier. Following these clashes, Iran and Pakistan agreed to increase counterterrorism cooperation and attempted to defuse the crisis. However, the Baluch insurgency and Islamabad's perceived complacency or even support continue to trouble Iranian-Pakistani relations. Moreover, Iranian forces and agents likely continue to cross into Pakistan's territory to pursue Ba-

---

[323] Alex Vatanka, *Iran and Pakistan: Security, Diplomacy and American Influence*, (London: I.B. Tauris, 2017), p. 230.
[324] Amir Taheri, "Suicide bombing comes home to Iran," *New York Post*, December 18, 2010; "Iran hangs 11 Sunni rebels, urges Pakistan to act," *Reuters*, December 20, 2010.
[325] For example, "Security in Sistan-Balouchestan to be handed over to locals: IRGC chief," *Tehran Times*, January 2, 2011.
[326] Alex Vatanka, *Iran and Pakistan: Security, Diplomacy and American Influence* (London: I.B. Tauris, 2017), pp. 235–236.

luch leaders they view as terrorists. In November 2020, the leader of the Iranian Baluch organization Jaish-ul-Adl, Omar Shahoozi, and his sons were killed in Turbat, Pakistan. While Iran did not formally take credit for this assassination, media close to the IRGC celebrated the murders.[327]

The Iran-Pakistan border is also route for illicit smuggling, including of drugs and Iranian subsidized fuels. In February 2021, Baluch protestors attacked the district governor's office in Saravan in Sistan-Baluchistan Province after several smugglers had been killed at the Pakistan-Iran border.[328]

Pakistan's policy toward Iran's Baluch is probably affected to some extent by Iran's policy toward Pakistan's large Shiite community, which makes up about one-fifth of Pakistan's population. Tehran has attempted to appeal to Pakistan's Shiites and often releases statements in support of this community. Islamabad likely responds subsequently with leniency toward the Baluch support for co-ethnics in Iran.

Saudi Arabia's conflict with Iran also impacts Pakistan's policy toward Iran's Baluch. Riyadh shares close ties with Pakistan and reportedly occasionally encourages Islamabad to increase support for Baluch groups operating in Iran or along the Iran-Pakistan border.[329] Pakistan's policies toward Iran's Baluch is also affected by the state of Tehran's ties with New Delhi. The presence of an Indian consulate in the Iranian city of Zahedan, the capital of Sistan-Baluchistan, and India's investment in Sistan-Baluchistan's Chabahar Port, suggests New Delhi is interested in the Baluch region and may see it as a pressure point against Pakistan.

---

[327] "The leader of the Jaish al-Adl group was killed; Who was Mulla Omar Baluchi?," November 18, 2020 (https://fararu.com/fa/news/462703/) quoted by Fatemeh Aman, "A top Baluchi terrorist was killed—how will this impact insurgencies in Iran?," *IranSource* December 1, 2020, Atlantic Council.

[328] Isabel Debre, "Mob storms south Iran governor office after border violence," *Associated Press* February 23, 2021.

[329] Stephane A. Dudoignon, *The Baluch, Sunnism and the State in Iran* (Oxford: Oxford University Press, 2017), p. 2; Shay Shaul, "The tensions between Iran and Pakistan," *International Institute for Counter-Terrorism* May 18, 2020 (https://www.ict.org.il/Article/2548/The_Tensions_between_Iran_and_Pakistan#gsc.tab=0).

7 The Future: Impact on Regime Stability

The ruling regime in Iran and mainstream scholarship claims that Iran is an outlier among multiethnic states which is unified as one big happy mosaic where most of Iran's ethnic minorities strongly identify as Iranians. They point to the large numbers of ethnically mixed families and also to the fact that most of Iran's population is united under Shia identity.

To be sure, ethnic diversity does not necessarily translate into political opposition to the regime and its policies, nor to desire for self-rule. There is great variation in the level of identification and relationship with the regime and identification with Iran among members of Iran's ethnic minorities. Many minority citizens identify completely as Iranian, and their ethnic identity has little political significance for them. In fact, some of the regime's most important pillars hail from minority communities. For example, Iran's leader Ali Khamenei himself hails from an ethnically mixed family and speaks some Azerbaijani, while Iran's Secretary of the Supreme National Security Council Ali Shamkhani is an ethnic Arab, indicating that individual members of ethnic minorities can rise high in the regime.

Other factors working in Iran's favor in holding the country together is that the Islamic Republic is not a federation or confederation, nor are the ethnic groups concentrated in overseas territories of a country. The Islamic Republic's status as a unitary state rather than a federation or confederation favors continuation of Iran's control over its territories. Federative and confederative structures facilitate empire disintegration, thanks to their clear internal borders and the existence of local government officials who often benefit from the demise of central rule. As an additional protection, the regime has a track record of appointing governors and local security chiefs who are not native to the regions they govern and do not speak the local languages. Thus, in contrast to the Soviet model, there are few official local leaders with an interest in breaking away from the center. Nor do these appointees benefit from local support, as did many Soviet-era leaders and security services heads in the republics.

In addition, many of Iran's ethnic groups do not inhabit contiguous territories. For instance, millions of Azerbaijanis in Iran live in Tehran and other regions outside of the provinces where Azerbaijanis are the clear majority. On this, however, a similar assessment was made by those who judged that the USSR would not break up into separate states. Proponents of this view pointed to the large numbers of ethnic Russians that were living in the Soviet republics, while Russia itself hosted large numbers of ethnic minorities. Before the Soviet collapse, many purported that this mixing of peoples throughout the territory of the USSR would prevent its breakup. Despite this, the Soviet Union did collapse into 15 new states, and the sorting out of peoples took place relatively peacefully, with most choosing to stay in their state of residence and embrace civic identity over ethnic, and not join co-ethnics in other states.

In addition, most of Iran's neighbors do not support a change in its borders. Furthermore, many of the minority groups infight over control of land and other resources in shared regions, such as Kurds and Azerbaijanis in Iran's West Azerbaijan Province, and Lurs and Arabs in Khuzestan, and are unlikely to cooperate against the regime. Tehran is quite skilled in exploiting these conflicts.

In addition, in contrast to Iranian regime propaganda, few outside powers conduct active policies in support of Iran's ethnic minorities. Certainly not Tehran's "usual suspects"—the U.S., United Kingdom, and Israel. The U.S. government doesn't even take a serious interest in the issue, as illustrated by the lack of Congressional hearings that examine the activities of ethnic minorities in Iran. Mainstream human rights organizations, like Amnesty International and Human Rights Watch, from about 2007 have stopped serious reporting on the human rights violations of Iran's ethnic minorities. However, it is not clear if lack of outside support actually hinders or helps the struggle of Iran's ethnic minorities. Perhaps because their movement is rooted on the ground in Iran, and people don't have illusions about external help, the activists make better and more realistic decisions on how to further their rights and goals.

Furthermore, the regime's violent suppression of ethnic political activity still serves as a potent deterrent. As noted in this study, Iran's ethnic minorities have the highest incarceration and execution rates. Cultural leaders are periodically incarcerated, deterring others from engaging in even non-political ethnically based activity. The regime's proven reach to kill and kidnap ethnic leaders abroad, as with the November 2020 abduction of a Sweden-based Arab leader visiting Istanbul, Habib Chaab,[330] likely also deters some ethnic activism both in and outside of Iran. The regime's consistent violent measures against Iran's ethnic minorities, likely indicates, however, that Tehran has a formindable challenge from these groups.

---

[330] "Iran Intelligence Ministry Nabs Ringleader of Saudi, Israeli-Sponsored Terror Group," *Tasnim News Agency*, November 12, 2020 (https://www.tasnimnews.com/en/news/2020/11/12/2388122/iran-intelligence-ministry-nabs-ringleader-of-saudi-israeli-sponsored-terror-group); Kareem Fahim and Erin Cunningham, "Turkey says Iranian intelligence was behind elaborate plot to kidnap opponent in Istanbul," *Washington Post*, December 13, 2020 (https://www.washingtonpost.com/world/middle_east/iran-intelligence-turkey-kidnap-plot/2020/12/12/818e0c30-3b2c-11eb-8328-a36a109900c2_story.html).

The Islamic Republic's policies have a mixed impact on the activities and attitudes of Iran's ethnic minorities. Some of the Islamic Republic's policies are unintentionally strengthening the political relevance of the ethnic identity of many of the minorities. First, Iran does not allow any legitimate arena of activity or ability to advocate for language rights as Iranian citizens, often forcing citizens into illegal activity just to ask for rights supposedly guaranteed by the Islamic Republic's Constitution. The regime brands all requests for ethnic rights as "separatist." Expressions of ethnic identity of Azerbaijanis and their calls for rights are always branded as "Pan-Turkist" even though this ideology has little traction among Iran's Azerbaijanis.

Tehran's policies and the views of the Iranian opposition abroad push people to "separatism" who are not separatist. They have no rights in Iran, and endure racism and mockery. Tehran actually pushes them to undertake exactly what the regime is trying to avoid. As Shirin Ebadi explained:

> the main cause of separatism is the unjust discrimination that has been committed against Iran's ethnic minorities... Given this kind of discrimination, as well as the fact that they are deprived of teaching their mother tongue and whatever they shouted has not come to fruition over the years, some, I repeat, not all of them, some have come to the conclusion that perhaps separating from Iran should be the cure.[331]

In addition, Tehran faces armed militias and groups that seek to promote the independence of some of Iran's ethnic groups. Ethnic-based movements are carrying out regular violent attacks on the regime and its institutions. In addition, economic disparities among ethnic groups can also pull Iran apart. The ethnic minority-populated provinces are poorer, have lower levels of government services and lower quality infrastructure than the Persian center. Even water supplies are unstable mostly in the areas populated by Arabs, Kurds, and Baluch. Also, while ethnically mixed families in Iran may be common in the central cities, this is not the case in the provinces, where local languages and cultures prevail. As pointed out in this study, 40 percent of Iranians are not fluent in Persian. Tehran is not representative of the culture, language, and attitudes of the inhabitants of most of Iran's border provinces.

In parallel, social and other mass media are fostering the revival of ethnic-linguistic identities. Most of the minority populations in Iran watch television and receive their news in their native languages by satellite TV or internet,

---

[331] Interview with Shirin Ebadi, Ant TV, May 14, 2020. Partial video of interview found at @endofmonoling, *Twitter*, November 6, 2021 (https://twitter.com/endofmonoling/status/1457000462121537541?s=20).

and not from Tehran's government-controlled or foreign Persian media. Through the foreign media, traveling to neighboring countries, and interactions on social media, many are gaining ethnic awareness and pride. Iranian official media and Persian broadcasts from abroad, in contrast, routinely present very negative images of members of the ethnic groups, based on widely held stereotypes. The regime policy of mocking ethnic minorities in official media and claiming in school curricula that the ethnic identities of Iran's minorities are not genuine is backfiring, provoking mass demonstrations and increasing resentment toward the regime.

Technological changes have had a large impact on ethnic identity trends in Iran. Ties to states and entities abroad have strengthened ethnic identity in Iran especially since the 1990s, when technology has helped reinforce those ties. In addition, from the early 1990s, Iranian citizens gained regular access to television broadcasts from abroad via satellite transmission. The establishment of Kurdish autonomy in Iraq in 1992 created a cultural, economic, and logistical center for Kurds in Iran. TV and other media broadcasts from Iraqi Kurdistan and Europe have become the major TV source for Kurds in Iran. In addition, Iran's Azerbaijanis overwhelmingly watch Turkish and Azerbaijani television and the U.S.-based Gunaz TV, all of which became available beginning in the 1990s.

Access to TV broadcasts from abroad since the 1990s has increased ethnic minorities' knowledge of their native languages and boosted their ethnic pride: They suddenly saw positive images of their co-ethnics that differ strongly from Iranian official media, which often ridicule the ethnic minorities and reflect ethnic stereotypes. Access to foreign media has raised the self-identification of many members of the ethnic minorities. For instance, viewing of Turkish TV broadcasts and films erased the sense of Persian superiority that many Azerbaijanis in Iran had internalized.[332] In fact, Iran's media policies that frequently portray the ethnic minorities in a derogatory fashion is counter-productive and creates significant animosity among the minority population. In their protests, including at soccer games, for instance, indignation at the policy of humiliation in Iran's media is frequently voiced. Aware of the impact of the foreign TV broadcasts, the regime has sought to prevent access to foreign television broadcasts, and frequently has confiscated home satellite receivers in the provinces.

Social media has been a huge driver of increased ethnic identity in Iran. It has encouraged many of the members of the ethnic minorities in Iran to develop

---

[332] Brenda Shaffer, *Borders and Brethren: Iran and the Challenge of Azerbaijani Identity* (Cambridge, MA: MIT Press, 2002), p. 174.

written ability in their mother tongues. Through social media, members of groups that are split over state borders are interacting regularly, forging a shared identity with co-ethnics outside Iran, which reinforces their specific ethnic identity.

Ethnic groups in Iran are also exposed via social media and TV to the global wave of identity politics currently popular around the globe, and this may be contributing to a desire for action, particularly among Iran's youth. Previous generations in Iran had, by and large, internalized the messages of the Pahlavi regime that the ethnic minorities are inferior to the great Persian nation that rules them. This ideology does not seem to have the same hold over Iran's younger generations that grew up in cyberspace and with satellite television.

In addition, the fall of the USSR and the subsequent independence of the Republics of Azerbaijan and Turkmenistan created important cultural and media sources for co-ethnics in Iran. Family ties were renewed after the fall of the Soviet Union between Azerbaijanis and Turkmen on both sides of the border and commercial, academic, and cultural cooperation was established between the communities.

Many that dismiss the ethnic factor in Iran state that Iranians are united by love for the Persian language. The statement contradicts that fact that 40 percent of Iran's citizens report that they are not fluent in Persian. In addition, the government aggressively suppresses the attempt to use minority languages, especially in Iran's schools. As pointed out in this study, Tehran uses the police to enforce use of Persian and criminalizes in some circumstances non-use of the language. If the love and use of the Persian language were widespread in Iran, these measures would not be necessary.

In the 2020s, faced with growing opposition, some of it violent, the ruling regime in Iran has turned to fostering Persian nationalist messages as a way to bolster support among Iran's core ethnic group. This is reminiscent of Stalin's use of the Russian Orthodox Church and Russian nationalism to galvanize Soviet subjects to fight during World War II. While this may be a useful tool to galvanize the Persians to stick with the ruling Islamic Republic, it is further isolating and inciting Iran's ethnic minorities against Tehran's rule.

The regime's future hold over Iran's ethnic minorities is far from guaranteed. In the case of the Soviet Union, once Moscow's grip on the republics weakened, nationalist groups organized and hastened Soviet collapse. Throughout modern Iranian history, when central control over the provinces has weakened significantly, Iran's ethnic minorities have risen up and attempted to achieve self-rule. Notable examples include the 1920 Khiyabani Rebellion at the end of Qajar Rule, the Azerbaijani and Kurdish short-lived autonomies during the allied occupation after World War II, and autonomy attempts of Kurds and Azerbaijanis in the immediate aftermath of Iran's 1979 Islamic Revolution.

In an acute regime crisis, the ethnic factor could play a role in toppling the government, as it did with the collapse of the Shah's regime and the Islamic Republic's ascent to power in 1979. As shown in this study, Iran's ethnic minority groups have demonstrated substantial organizational ability.

Yet rebellions by ethnic minorities are not likely to trigger an all-out anti-regime uprising, since the Persian opposition is unlikely to cooperate with ethnically based movements. Most of the mainstream opposition does not support granting rights to Iran's ethnic minorities or any activity that could threaten Persian control over Iran's current territory.

Moreover, some of Iran's ethnic minority groups themselves are unlikely to cooperate with each other. Tehran has successfully exacerbated inter-group conflicts by pitting minority groups against each other, such as by organizing police forces along ethnic lines to police rival groups and appointing governors from competing groups to rule over others. Many groups now have a history of competing for resources in multiethnic provinces, such as in West Azerbaijan, which is populated by both Kurds and Azerbaijanis. It is likely that if the Islamic Republic regime collapsed, violent conflict would emerge between ethnic groups as they staked control over territories and resources.

Identity trends are dynamic. A major development may have taken place among Iran's largest ethnic minority, the Azerbaijanis. For many decades, Western scholarship has assumed that Azerbaijanis are "the most well-integrated minority in Iran,"[333] sharing common Shiite faith with Persians. But that may be a misreading of this ethnic group, especially after Iran's support for Armenia in the 2020 war with Azerbaijan. The war was a watershed moment for Iranian Azerbaijanis, who observed in real time Iranian trucks transiting Russian arms and supplies to Armenia. Hundreds went to the border area with Azerbaijan, observed the battles, and openly expressed encouragement to the Azerbaijani soldiers despite the regime's best efforts to prevent this. The Republic of Azerbaijan's subsequent success on the battlefield inspired ethnic pride among Iranian Azerbaijanis. The Iranian government's arrests of dozens of Azerbaijanis during and following the war did little to curb that.

---

[333] Many published works have claimed that Azerbaijanis are a "well-integrated minority." See, for instance: Patricia J. Higgins, "Minority–State Relations in Contemporary Iran," *Iranian Studies*, Volume 17, Number 1, Winter 1984, p. 59; Bijan DaBell, "Iran Minorities 2: Ethnic Diversity," *United States Institute of Peace*, September 3, 2013 (https://iranprimer.usip.org/blog/2013/sep/03/iran-minorities-2-ethnic-diversity).

For most of its history, the Islamic Republic has faced insurgencies and security threats in Iran's Kurdish, Baluch, and Arab provinces. The Islamic Republic had to violently impose its rule on most of Iran's minority-populated provinces. Tehran has rarely enjoyed satisfactory security in the Kurdish, Baluch and Arab-populated areas. However, these insurgencies have proven manageable for Tehran, since those ethnic groups are relatively small and the attacks were confined to their home regions. Their armed attacks have rarely affected Iran's Persians and the power centers of the regime, since they take place in minority-inhabited provinces. However, the Azerbaijani Turks are a different story. If a large percentage of this group were to break with the regime, it would pose a formidable threat. Losing Azerbaijani support would be akin to the Soviet Union's loss of support of Ukraine during the Gorbachev era, on the eve of the Soviet demise.

In addition, a major alliance has emerged between Iran's Ahwaz Arabs and the Azerbaijanis. Iran's ethnic minorities have begun to band together against Tehran. In July 2021, a critical development emerged with Iran's Azerbaijanis expressing solidarity with the Ahwaz minority. After several days of demonstrations in the Khuzestan Province of Iran's Ahwaz, resulting in several deaths and mass arrests of Ahwazi activists, Azerbaijanis successfully held solidarity demonstrations in several Azerbaijani-populated cities in Iran. On the eve of and during the Azerbaijani protests, hundreds of Azerbaijani activists were arrested. Among them, an Iranian court sentenced Azerbaijani activist, Parviz Siabi, to 16 years imprisonment for his role in the July 2021 protests.[334] The main slogan of the Azerbaijani demonstrations was: "Azadlıq, Ədalət, Milli Hökümət!" (Freedom, Justice, National government). Through this statement, the Azerbaijanis called for independence from Tehran, and not just for specific rights within Iran.

This seems to have cemented a new strategic bond between Iran's Azerbaijanis and Ahwazis and this creates a new formidable challenge to Tehran's rule. Activists from both groups have continued to cooperate. It seems that in the future, Tehran will face simultaneous and coordinated challenges in both the Ahwaz-populated areas, such as Khuzestan and Bandar Abbas and the Azerbaijani-populated provinces in northwest Iran. The Azerbaijanis also have forged over decades cooperation with Iran's Turkmen population, adding to the geographic spread of a potential challenge to Tehran's control.

---

[334] United Nations Human Rights Council, "Situation of human rights in the Islamic Republic of Iran," January 13, 2022 (documents/country-reports/ahrc4975-situation-human-rights-islamic-republic-iran-report-special).

Another challenge to regime stability is the environment. Iran's environmental challenges are growing more severe, with extreme water shortages in many parts of the country, frequent dust and salt storms, and toxic pollution. The most worrisome threats, especially the water shortages, are largely located in Iran's ethnic minority provinces. Thus, environmental challenges reinforce ethnic grievances. As Iran's environmental threats mount, they will fuel additional ethnic unrest.

A major potential weakness of the regime in facing rebellions of the ethnic minorities is the prospective unreliability of some of the members of the security forces. Police units in Iran are locally based and units serve mostly in the communities they live in and generally share ethnic ties with these communities. Army recruits in mandatory service are not reliable to use violence against their co-ethnics. While IRGC units are much more reliable than the police and army units, even here there is a weakness. Ethnic minorities have conducted dozens of targeted assassinations against IRGC commanders living in the minority provinces. Commanders that have participated in crackdowns against ethnic minorities have been targeted for retribution, often at their homes. The IRGC commanders are clearly aware of this policy and during a serious uprising that has prospects of success, some IRGC commanders may not reliably use arms.

Ethnic activists in the provinces frequently appeal to police, army, and even some IRGC commanders living in the communities, offering them amnesty from punishment for serving the Islamic Republic if they refrain from violent action against the local population. Ethnic activists appeal to police commanders in the provinces and offer that they could continue to serve as police officers following the demise of the Islamic Republic if they do not use violence against the local population. The behavior of the security services in the face of large-scale rebellions in the provinces will be a major factor determining the success of these uprisings in contributing to the end of the rule of the Islamic Republic. This policy of appealing to local commanders and offering them to switch sides and amnesty for their previous affiliation with the regime was implemented by Boris Yeltsin in Russia during the seize of Moscow's White House and by Mikhail Saakashvili in Georgia during the Rose Revolution. This policy contributed significantly to the success of both of these uprisings.

The first step to understanding the impact of Iran's ethnic minorities on politics in Iran and regime stability is to analyze information in languages in use in Iran other than just Persian. As pointed out in this study, studies of social media patterns in Iran, TV broadcast viewing, and more, examine trends in the Persian language. That only covers half the population in Iran and focuses on urban dwellers. The other half needs to be researched to understand the anticipated developments in Iran.

This book shows that clearly substantial percentages of Iran's ethnic minorities are actively campaigning for language and cultural rights and many for self-rule and even independence. In Iran, the ethnic factor clearly overlaps with higher rates of poverty, water shortages, and environmental issues, and thus public health challenges. This is a potential volatile combination. While self-identity and desire for minority rights does not imply desire for independence and thus to secede from Iran, since the regime and its opposition offer not an inkling of accommodation of the demands of the ethnic minorities, those that actually aspire most to Tehran's continued control of all the provinces may be themselves creating the biggest obstacle to continued unity of Iran. What is clear is that the ethnic factor is worth watching in Iran and will be an important element in any revolution or major political change in Iran, as it has throughout the twentieth century.

Appendix: Notes on Transliteration and Terms

The names and spelling of place names in multilingual and multiethnic locations is very complicated and designations are often viewed as having political meaning. Different ethnic groups in Iran refer to the same cities and geographic locations with different names. In this book, most place names appear as commonly referred to by the central government in Iran. Others were transliterated from the names in use by the ethnic group that forms the majority in the specific geography. For instance, Mount Savalan, which is located in Ardabil Province, where the overwhelming majority of the population is ethnic Azerbaijani is written in the Azerbaijani pronunciation and not the Persian Mount Sabalan. The Araz River, which forms the border between the Republic of Azerbaijan and the Azerbaijani-populated provinces of Iran, is referred to in the Azerbaijani pronunciation versus the Persian Aras, or Araxes River, which is the term often used in English-language publications. The city of Urmia, which is predominately populated by both Azerbaijanis and Kurds, is referred to in the book transliterated from the Persian pronunciation, and not "Wermiye" or "Werme" as the city name is pronounced by some Kurds, or "Urmu" or "Urmiye," as pronounced by the Azerbaijanis.

Many regions were referred to in the book by both the official Iranian government designation and the reference of the local population. Thus, Khuzestan Province is referred to in the book also as a part of al-Ahwaz.

Within groups there is often diversity of the terms used to self-reference. Persians refer to the Azerbaijani Turks in Iran as Azeris and their language as Azeri. In the Azerbaijani language, members of this group self-refer as Turks or as Azerbaijanis and their language as Azerbaijani. In scholarly publications, authors often use both terms—Azerbaijani Turks—to refer to the groups. In this book, the group is referred to both as Azerbaijanis and Azerbaijani Turks, except for a direct quote, where for instance, Persian speakers referred to the group as Azeris.